AF605875

MUSÉE NATIONAL DES ARTS ASIATIQUES – GUIMET, PARIS

ILLUSTRATIONS OF MYANMAR

Manuscript Treasures of the Musée Guimet

Edited by

WILLIAM PRUITT

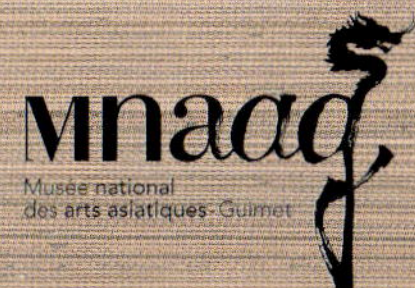

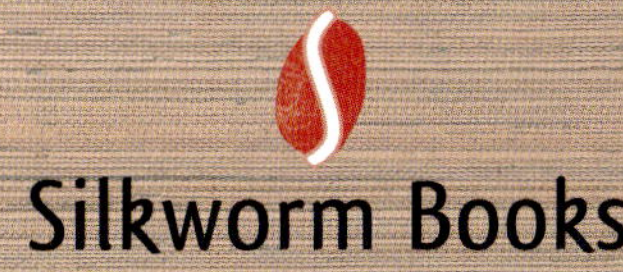

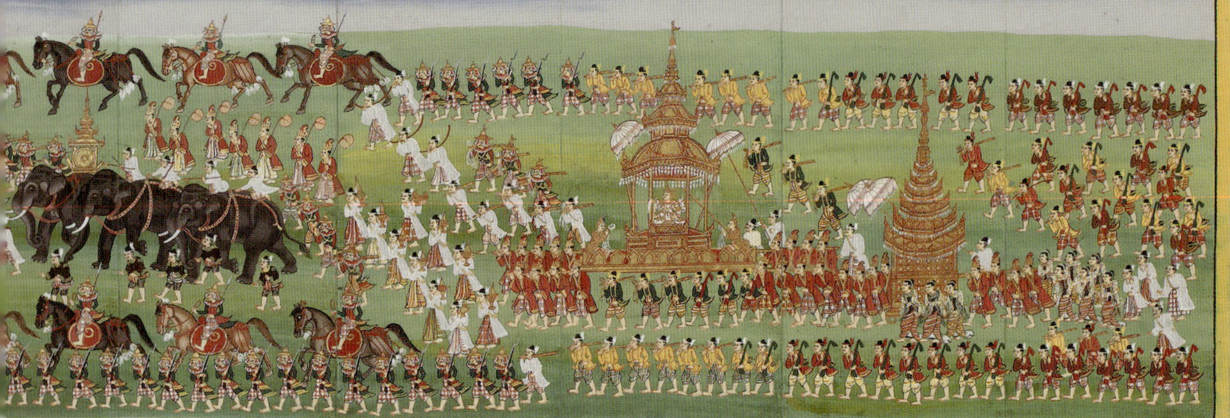

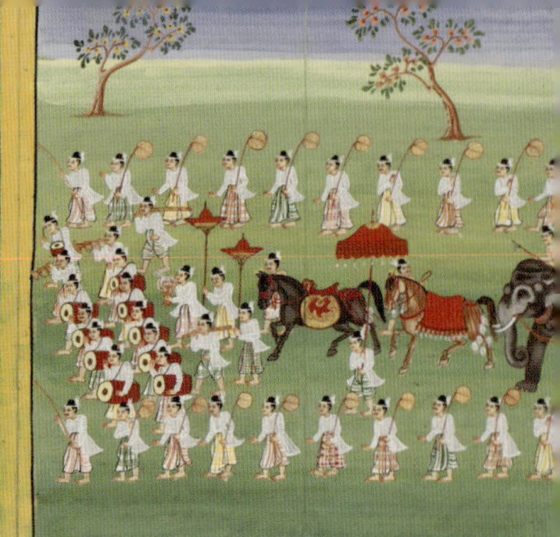

Musée national des arts asiatiques – Guimet, Paris
Sophie Makariou, *President*

Curating Exhibition
Francis Macouin, *former General Curator Librarian, Guimet Museum*

Authors
Pierre Baptiste, *General Curator, South-East Asia collections of the Guimet Museum*
Dr. Cao Thi Liễu, *Librarian in charge of the Library's Southeast-Asia collections*

Editorial Work and Translation
Anne Leclercq, *Head of Publishing in the Guimet Museum*
Dr. William Pruitt, *Publications Administrator for the Pali Text Society and Specialist of Myanmar*

Silkworm Books
Ms. Trasvin Jittidecharak, *Director*

ISBN: 978-616-215-148-4

First edition published in 2019 by
Silkworm Books
430/58 Soi Ratchaphruek, M. 7, T. Mae Hia, A. Mueang Chiang Mai, Thailand 50100
info@silkwormbooks.com
http://www.silkwormbooks.com.

Typeset in Gentium Basic 11 pt. by Silk Type

Printed and bound in China

5 4 3 2 1

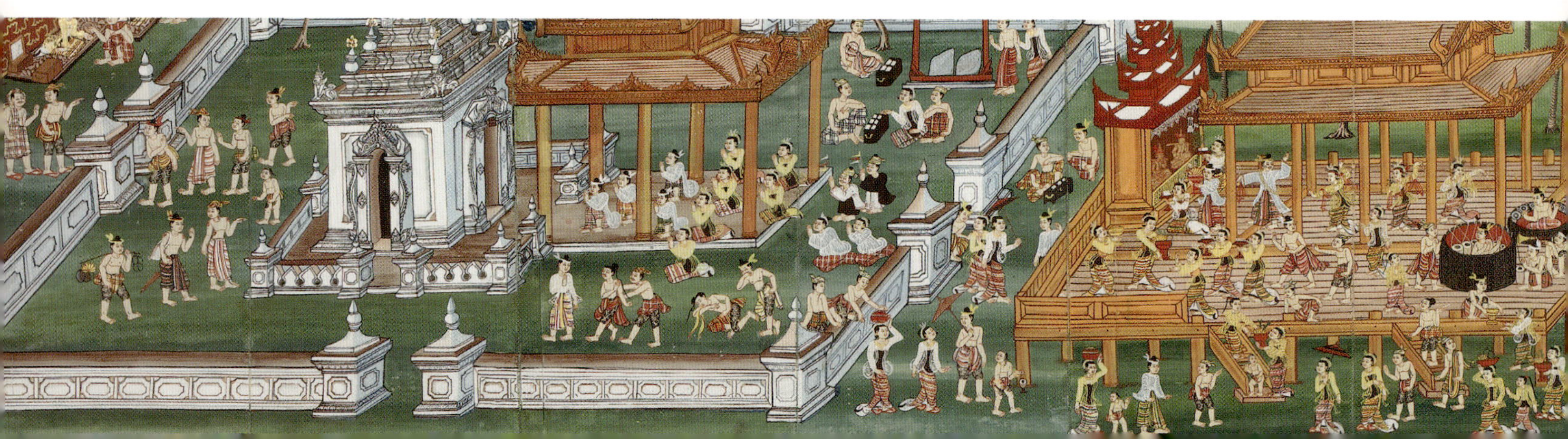

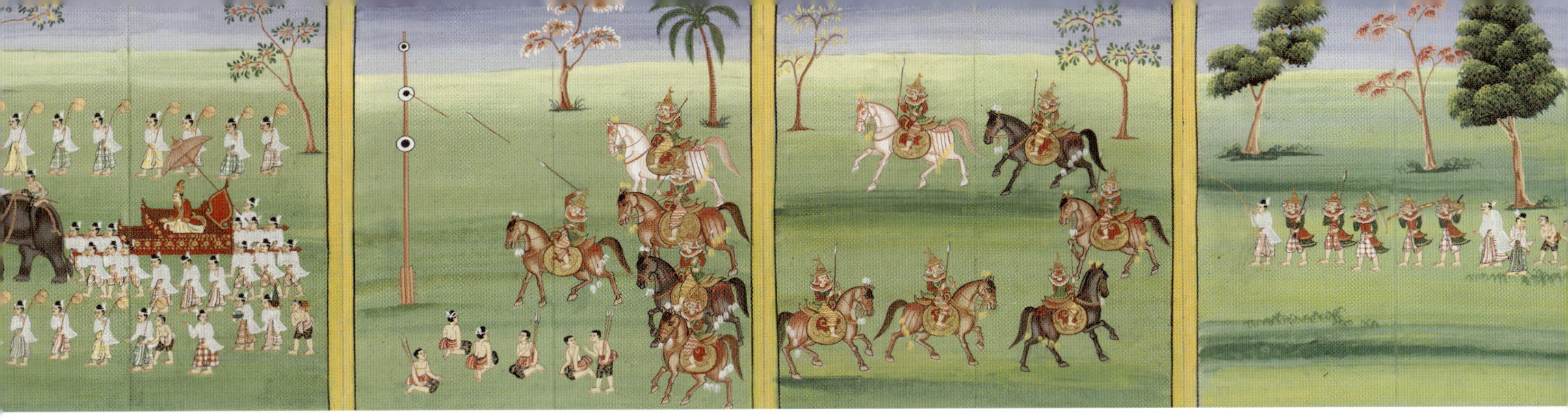

CONTENTS

Acknowledgments v

INTRODUCTION 1
William Pruitt

AN EIGHTEENTH-CENTURY ACCOUNT 2

LANGUAGES AND SCRIPTS IN MYANMAR (BURMA) 9
Cao Thi Liêu

BURMESE BOOKS: FORMS AND MATERIALS 28
Francis Macouin

THE PAGEANTRY OF A VANISHED KINGDOM 35
Pierre Baptiste

BURMESE MONASTERIES 118
Francis Macouin

THE BURMESE MODEL OF A MONASTERY BUILDING 120
Pierre Baptiste

A MAP OF AVA 126
Cao Thi Liêu

Catalog Numbers and Illustration Credits 130

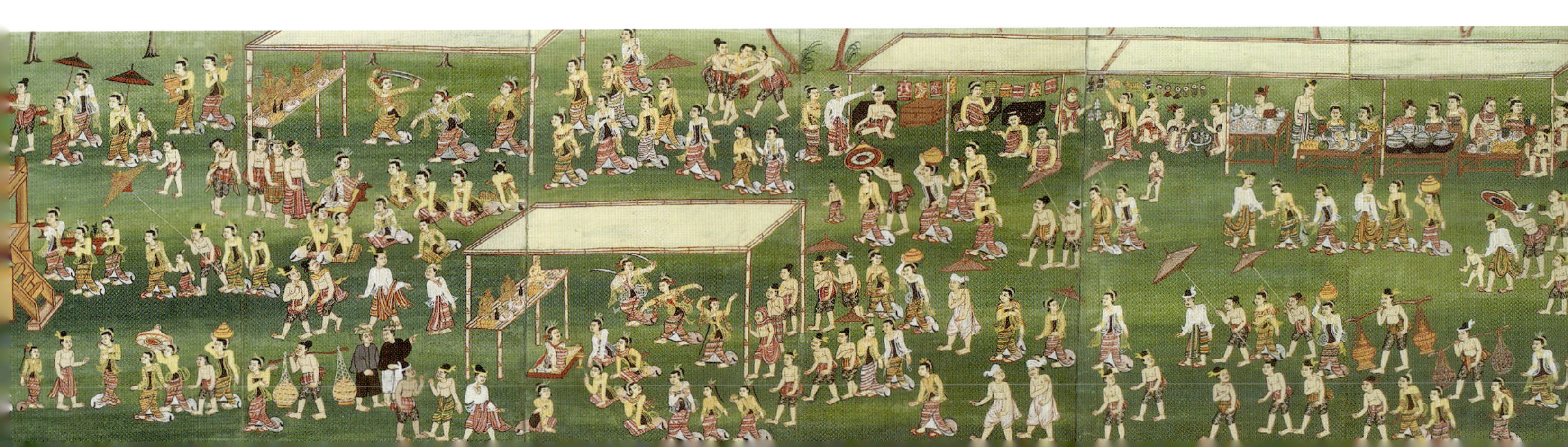

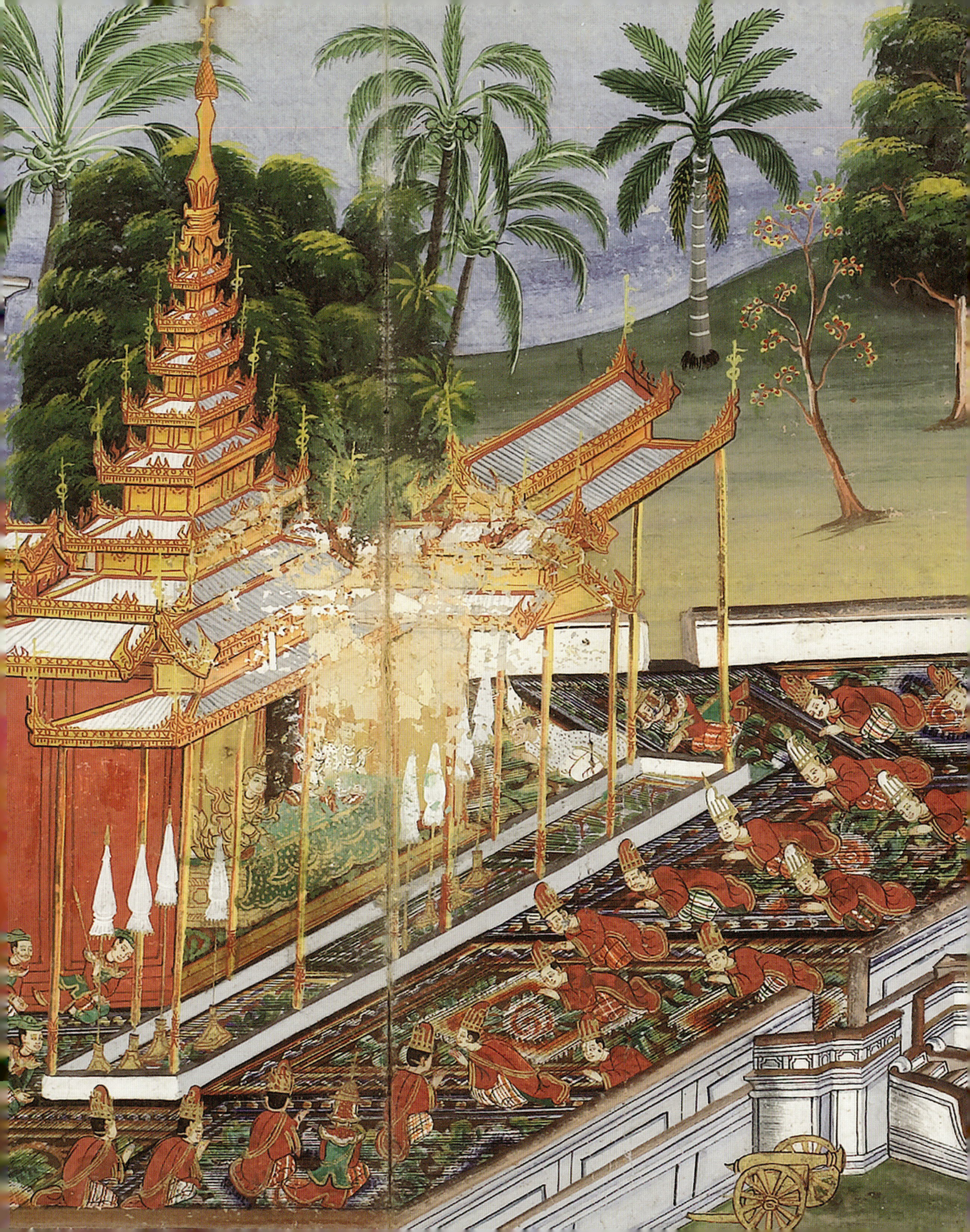

Acknowledgments

IN 2011 there was an exhibition of Myanmar art in Paris at the Guimet Museum entitled *De laque et d'or, manuscrits de Birmanie*. This was the first time the museum had shown its collection of Burmese manuscripts. A great deal of interest was expressed in the treasures of Myanmar shown in the exhibition, and so the museum decided to publish a book in English based on the French booklet published in connection with the exhibition. The book is in a larger format than the booklet and has illustrations large enough to communicate the beauty of the images in the *parabaik*s.

Ms. Sophie Makariou, president of the Guimet Museum, and her staff were delighted by this project, even with the arduous task of translating the articles in the booklet and finding a publisher. Dr. William Pruitt, a Pāli and Burmese scholar, was very helpful with his advice and assistance, patiently correcting the texts and helping find the publisher, Silkworm Books in Chiang Mai, Thailand.

All the *parabaik*s that were in the exhibition catalogue are found here in high-quality reproductions, depicting details of life at the royal court in Myanmar—the joy and the mischievousness found there. Everyone interested in Myanmar can be grateful to the museum for the excellent booklet that is the basis of the present book.

We are very grateful to President Sophie Makariou, who has always supported the project, even with the long delay in finalizing the book since the exhibition. Thanks are due to Mrs. Anne Leclercq, who has been very efficient in expediting matters. And again, we thank Dr. Pruitt for his input and productive collaboration.

We hope this book will serve to show the splendor and importance of Burmese art, which in many ways has been underappreciated.

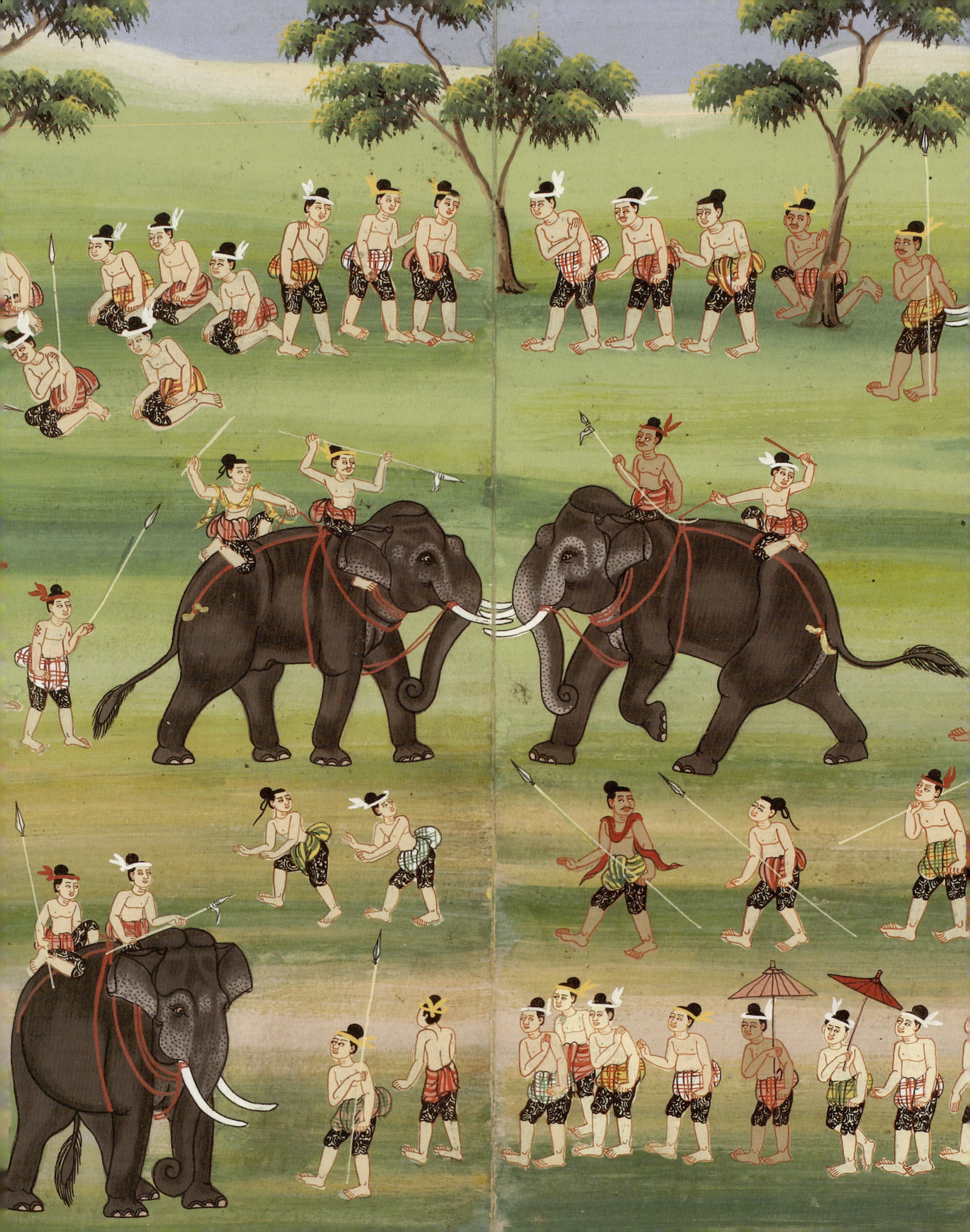

INTRODUCTION

William Pruitt

MUSEUMS, libraries, and private collections around the world possess a vast quantity of Burmese manuscripts, sculpture, lacquerware, and other arts and crafts. They came out of Burma in a number of different ways. Some were purchased, some were given to missionaries and diplomats, some were looted as the spoils of war, some were stolen.

A number of the Burmese treasures in the collection of the Musée national des Arts asiatiques–Guimet in Paris were given to French people working in Burma. For example, Philibert Bonvillain, an engineer who worked in Mandalay from 1875 to 1885, was given illustrated manuscripts by King Thibaw. The French diplomat Frédéric Haas was in Mandalay for eight months in 1885. He collected a number of items which he offered to the museum.

The essays here are from a booklet in French that was published in connection with the exhibition *De lacque et de d'or, manuscrits de Birmanie* held in the Guimet Museum between October 19, 2011, and January 23, 2012. This exhibition was the first time many of the manuscripts had been on display in the museum, as they are stored in the French Bibliothèque nationale.

Dr. Cao Thi Liêu translated her articles, and I am responsible for translating the rest of the booklet. In editing the book, I have made a number of corrections in the texts. I am responsible for the final version. Thanks are due to Mr. Peter Nyunt for his help with the original booklet.

AN EIGHTEENTH-CENTURY ACCOUNT

Figure 1. Papañcasūdanī (Majjhima-nikāya-aṭṭhakathā, Mūlapaṇṇasā-aṭṭhakathā) by Buddhaghosa. Bamboo manuscript, 9.5 × 53.5 cm, between AD 1763 and 1776. The text is a commentary by Buddhaghosa (fourth or fifth century AD) on a section of one of the texts in the second section of the Pāli canon, the *Sutta-piṭaka*. The manuscript was given to the museum by Philibert Bonvillain in 1891.

IN 1795, the governor-general of the English in Bengal sent an ambassador to the Burmese king, who had conquered the kingdom of Arakan ten years earlier. One of the members of the delegation was Michael Symes (1753?–1809). He wrote an account of the mission, *An Account of an Embassy to the Kingdom of Ava, Sent by the Governor-general of India, in the Year 1795*, which was published in London in 1800. It was immediately translated into French by J. Castéra and was published in the same year in Paris under the title *Relation de l'ambassade anglaise, envoyée en 1795 dans le royaume d'Ava, ou l'empire des Birmans*. The visit to the library mentioned in the extracts given here took place in Amarapura, which was the capital city of King Bodawpaya (r. 1782–1819).

○ ○ ○ ○ ○

"The Birmans write from left to right, and though they leave no distinguishing space between their words, they mark the pauses of a sentence and the full stops. Their letters are distinct, and their manuscripts are in general very beautiful.

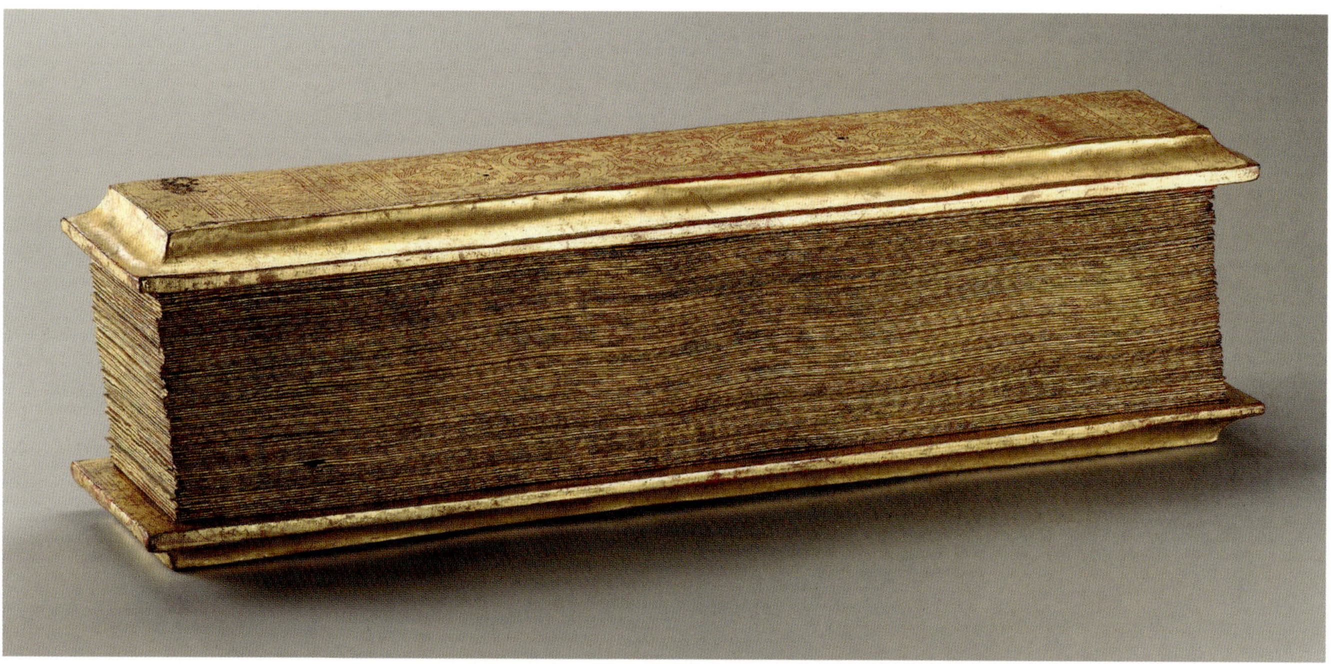

The common books of the Birmans, like those of the Hindoos, particularly of such as inhabit the southern parts of India, are composed of the palmyra leaf, on which the letters are engraved with a stylus; but the Birmans far excel the Braminical Hindoos in the neatness of the execution, and in the ornamental part of their volumes. In every Kioum, or monastery, there is a library or repository of books, usually kept in lacquered chests. Books in the Pali text, are sometimes composed of thin stripes of bamboo, delicately plaited, and varnished over in such a manner, as to form a smooth and hard surface upon a leaf of any dimensions; this surface is afterwards gilded, and the sacred letters are traced upon it in black and shining japan. The margin is illumined by wreaths and figures of gold, on a red, green, or black ground.

In the recitation of poetry, the language is exceedingly melodious; even the prose of common conversation appears to be measured, and the concluding word of each sentence is lengthened by a musical cadence, that marks the period, to the ear of a person wholly unacquainted with the meaning. . . .

From the kioum we proceeded to visit the adjacent library; it is a large brick building, raised on a terrace, and covered by a roof of very compound structure. It consists of one square room, with an enclosed virando, or gallery, surrounding it: this room was locked, and as we had not brought a special order for seeing it, the person who had the care of the library said that he was not at liberty to open the doors, but assured us that there was nothing in the inside different from what we might see in the virando, where a number of large chests, curiously ornamented with gilding and japan, were ranged in regular order, against the wall. I counted fifty, but there were many more, probably not less than a hundred. The books were regularly classed, and the contents of each chest, were written in gold letters on the lid. The librarian opened two, and shewed me some very beautiful writing on thin leaves of ivory, the margins of which were ornamented with flowers of gold, neatly executed. I saw also some books written in the ancient Pali, the religious text. Every tiling seemed to be arranged with perfect regularity, and I was informed that there were books upon divers subjects; more on divinity than on any other; but history, music, medicine, painting, and romance, had their separate treatises. The volumes were disposed under distinct heads, regularly numbered; and if all the other chests were as well filled, as those that were submitted to our inspection, it is not improbable, that his Birman Majesty may possess a more numerous library, than any potentate from the banks, of the Danube, to the borders of China."

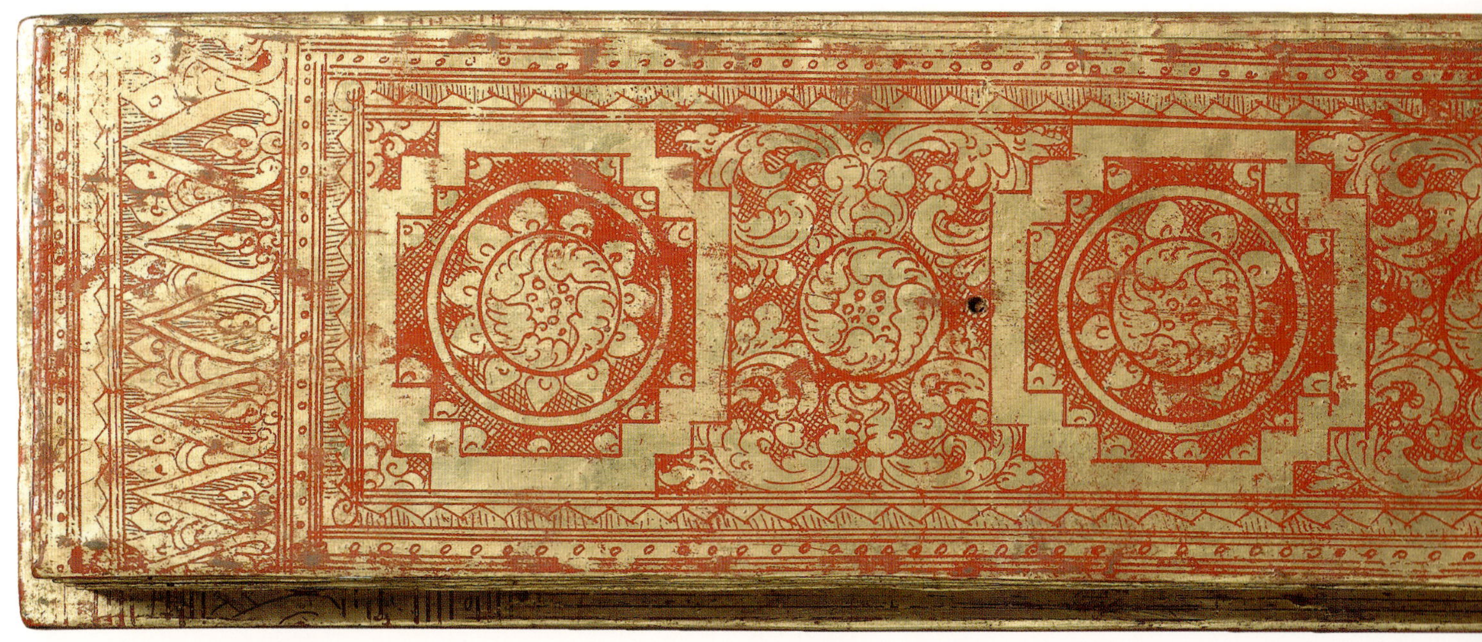

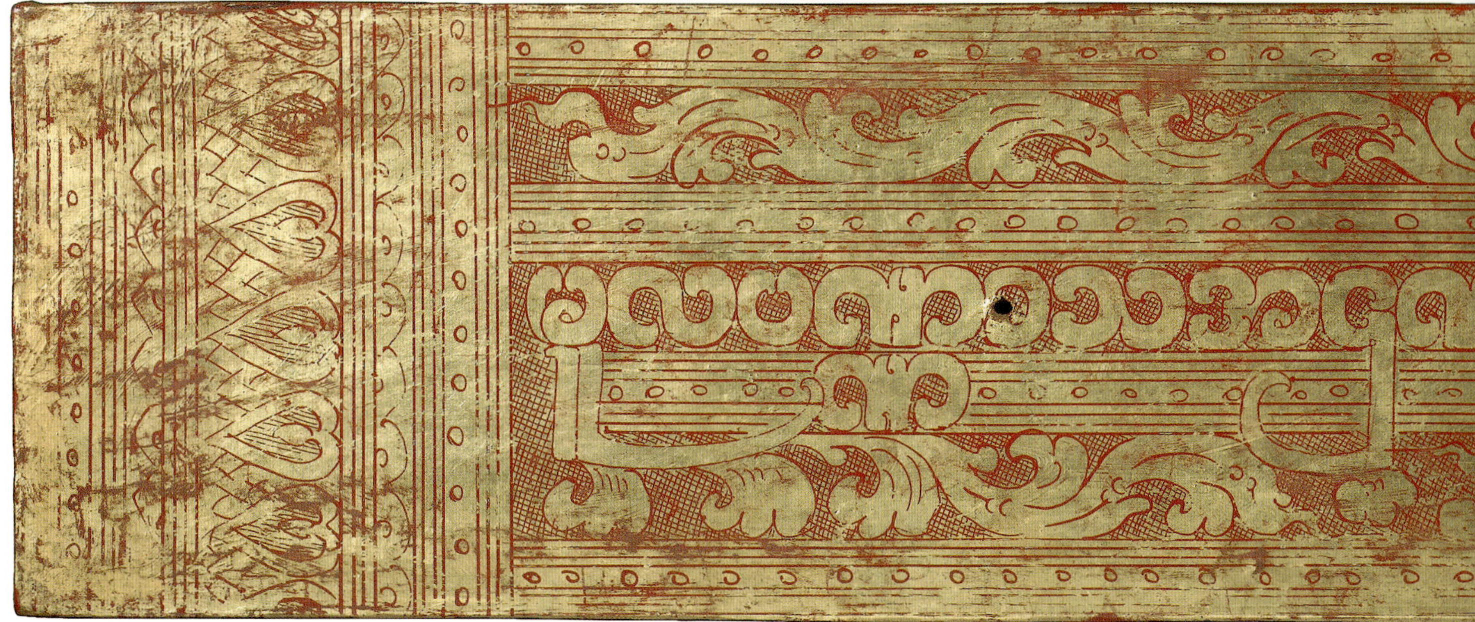

Figure 2 (pp. 4–7). Front cover, title folio, and folios with text in square Burmese script of the *Papañcasūdanī* (*Majjhima-nikāya-aṭṭhakathā*, *Mūlapaṇṇasā-aṭṭhakathā*) by Buddhaghosa. Bamboo manuscript, 9.5 x 53.5 cm, between AD 1763 and 1776.

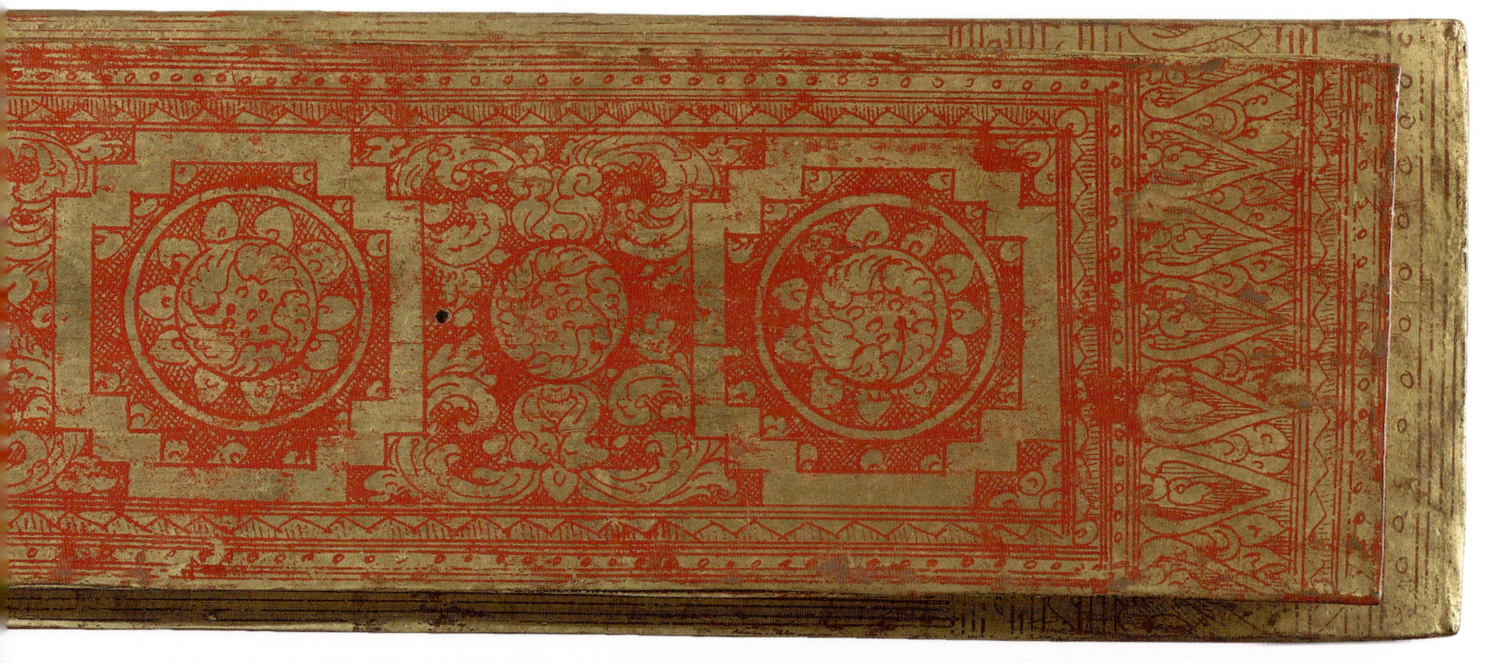

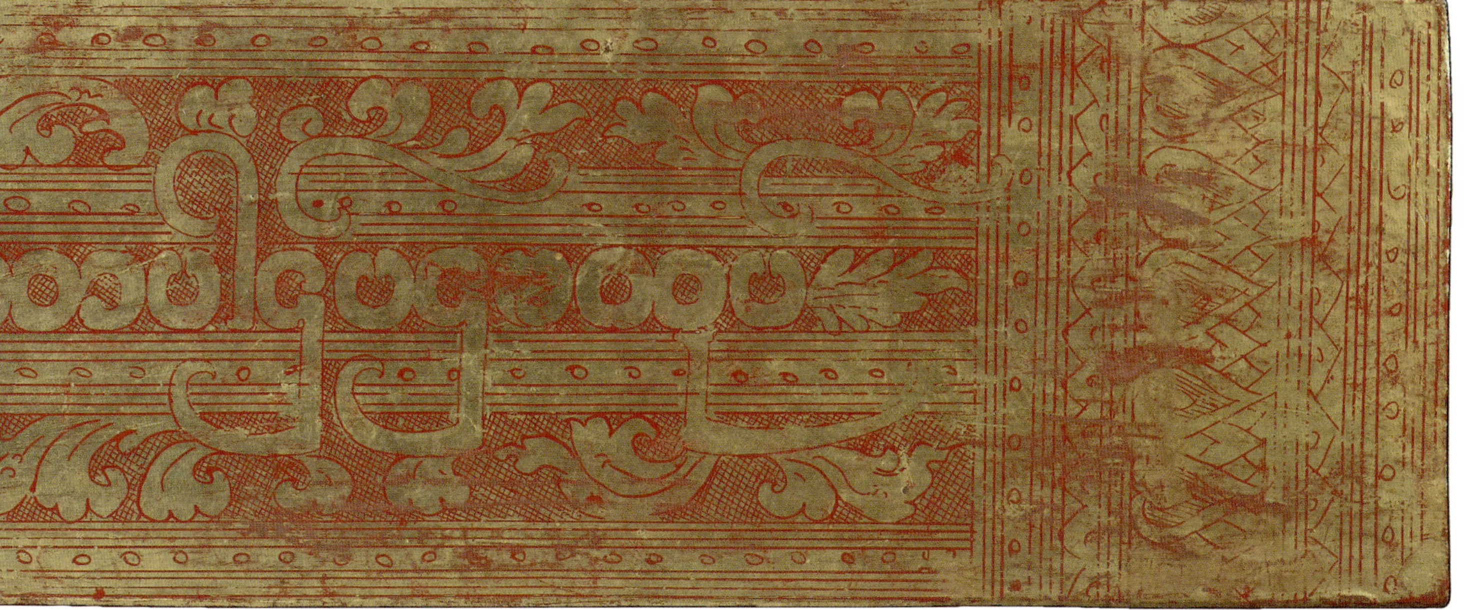

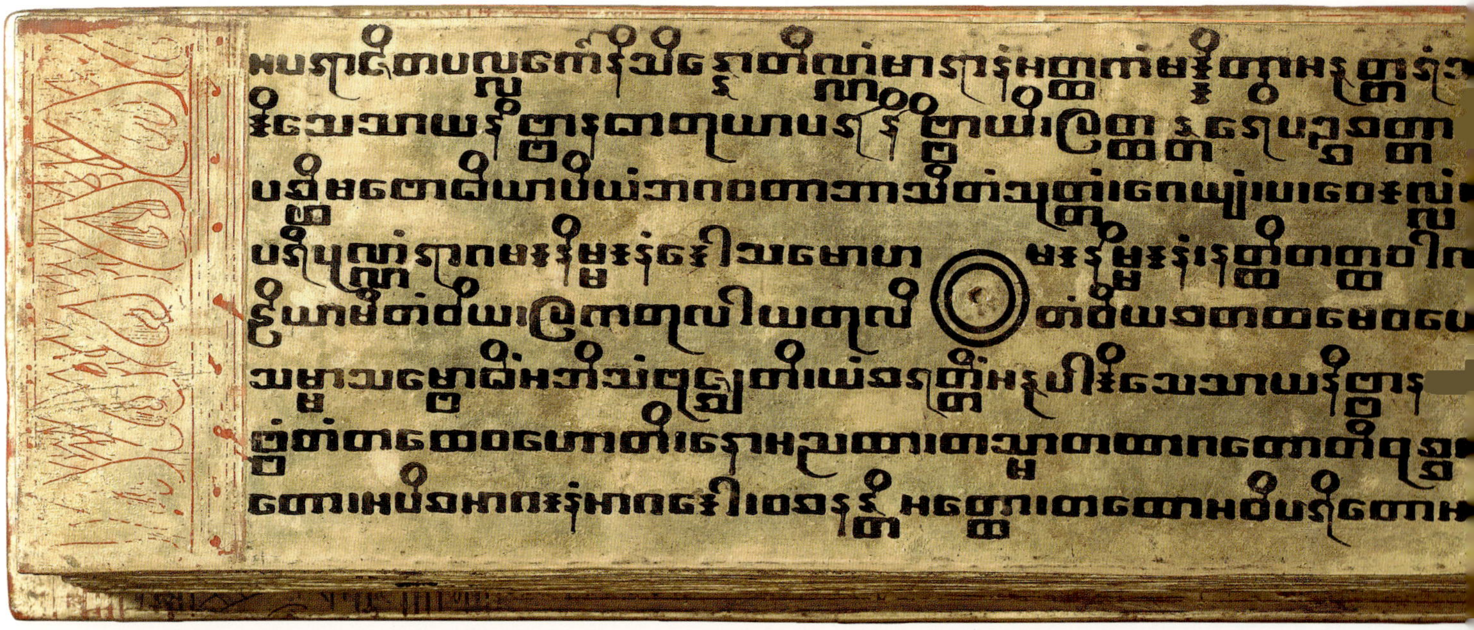

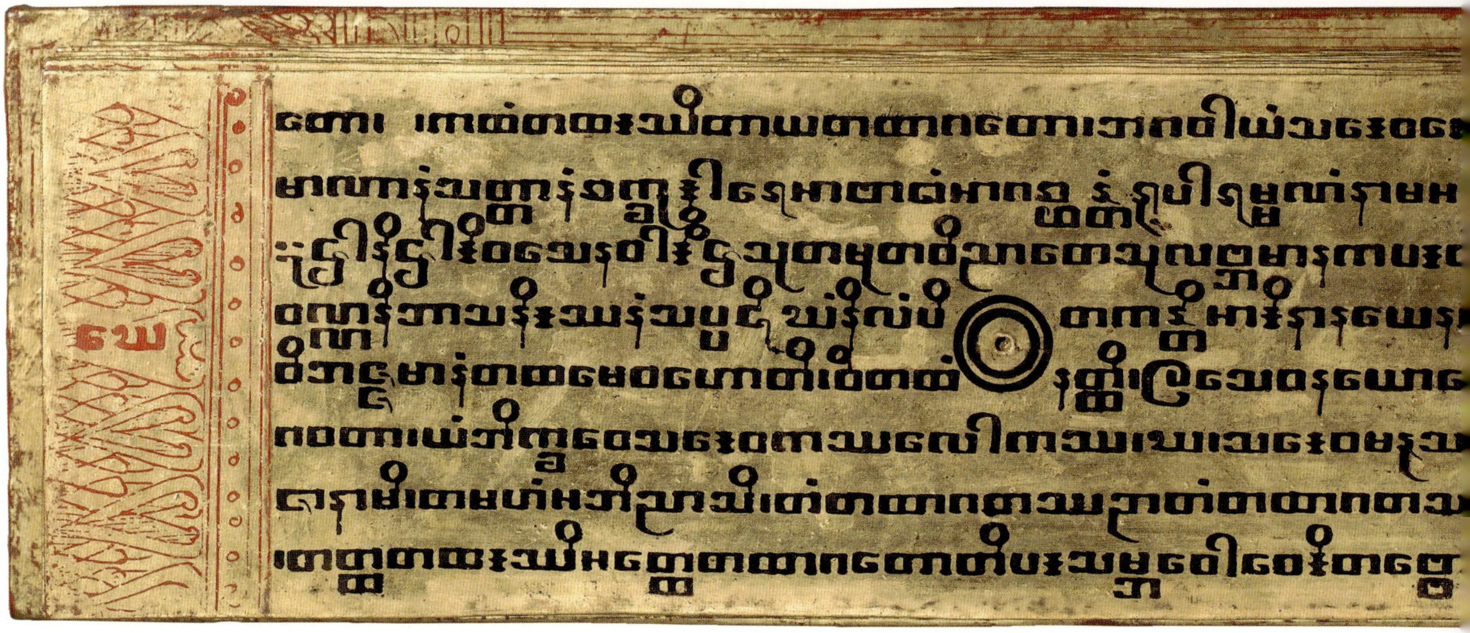

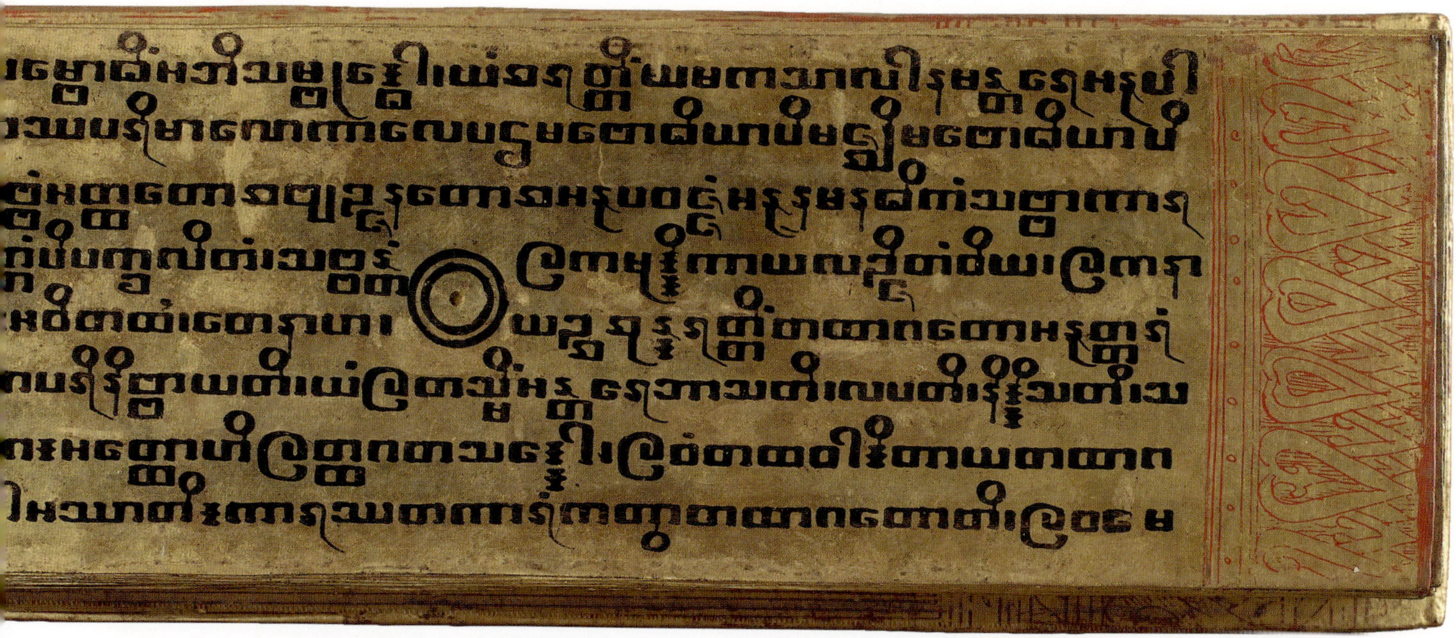

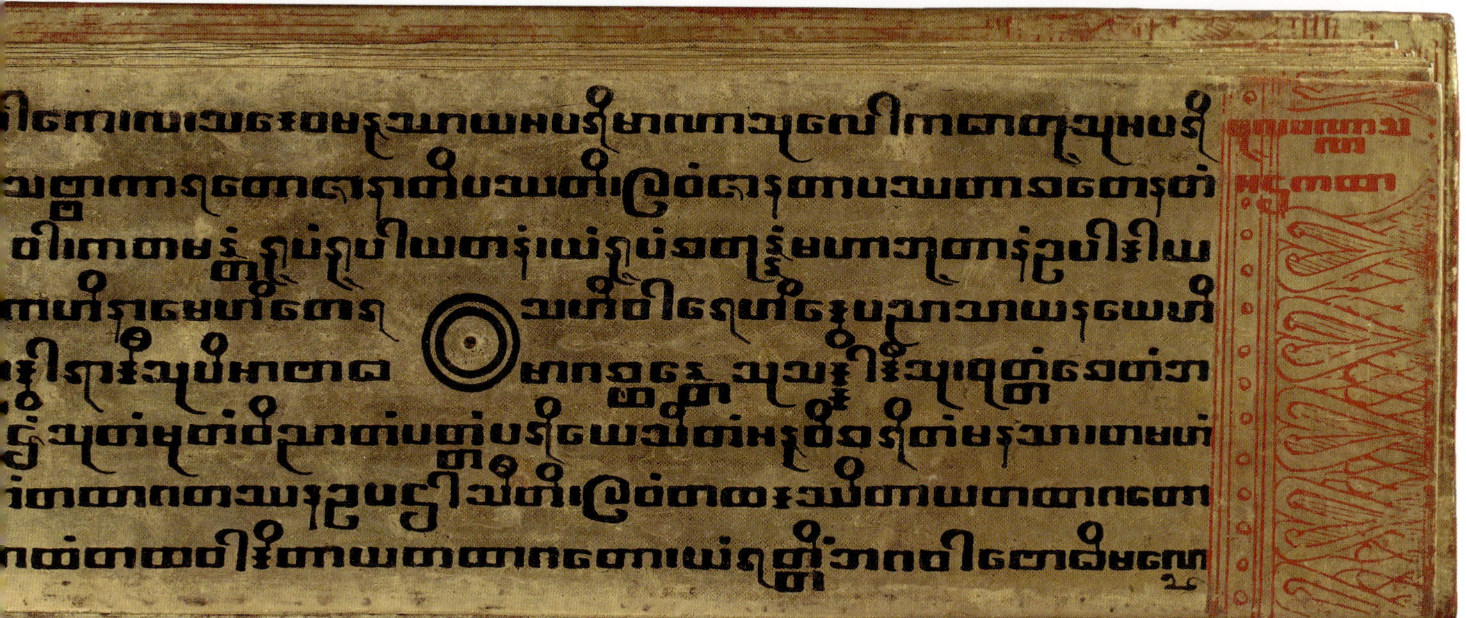

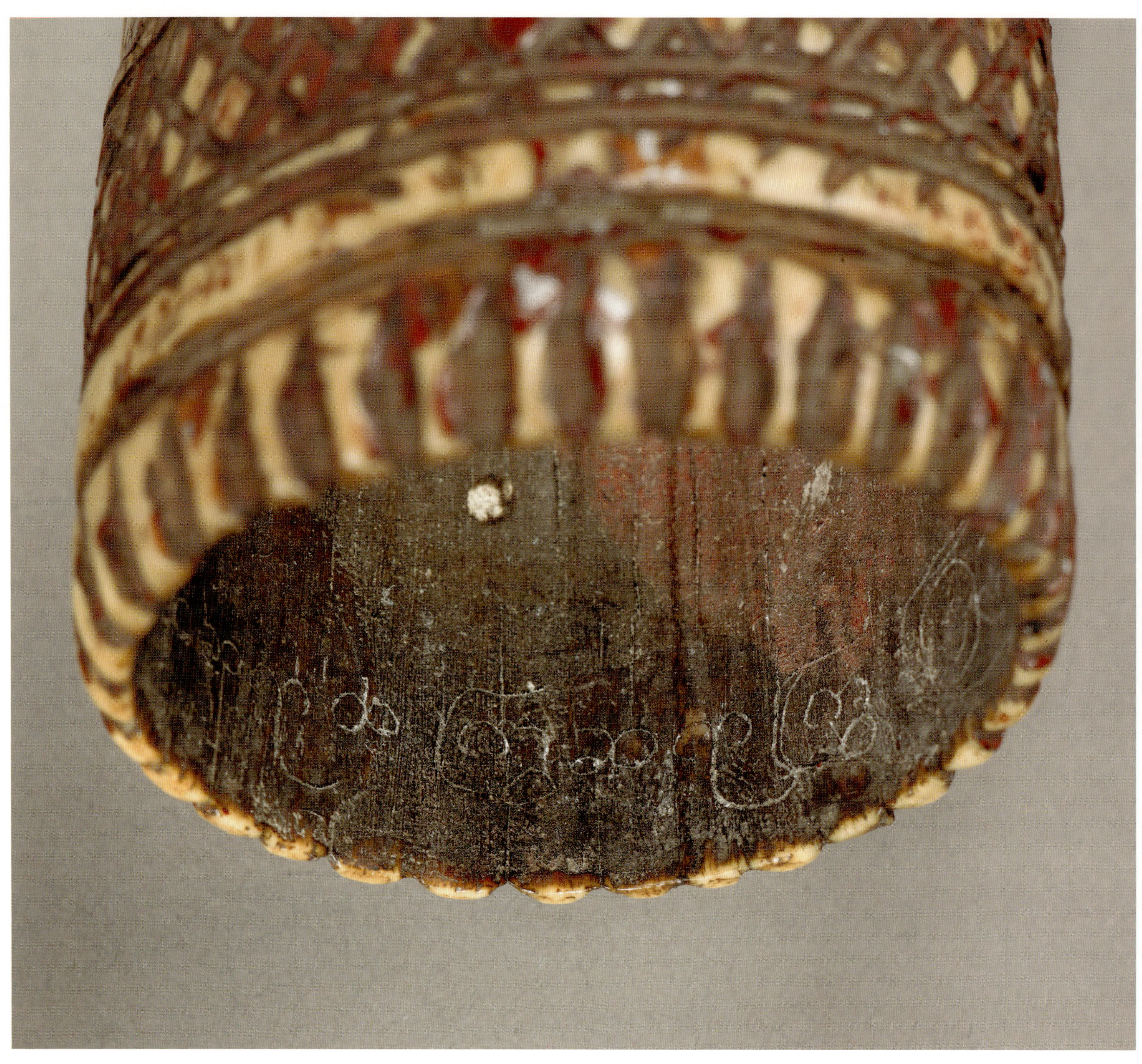

Figure 3. Inner inscription on an elephant tusk. Ivory, 34 cm. This elephant tusk was hollowed out, and the exterior was fashioned into a heptagon. It is inscribed with Burmese formulas mixed with Pāli, along with a horoscope, using very small round Burmese script. It is covered with red lacquer. It is not known how the tusk was used.

LANGUAGES AND SCRIPTS IN MYANMAR (BURMA)

Cao Thi Liêu
Librarian, Southeast Asian collections, Musée Guimet

MYANMAR is a large country in mainland Southeast Asia with an area of around 677,000 square kilometers. It is surrounded by Bangladesh and India to the northwest, Tibet to the north, China to the northeast, and Laos and Thailand to the southeast. These different borders have played an important part in its history and culture. This section is a short introduction to the history of the Burmese people.

Before the kingdom of Pagan was set up in AD 849, the Pyu and the Mon exercised political and cultural power over the whole region, and their influence was very important in the history of Myanmar.

The Populating of Myanmar (Bama or Burma)

The Pyu

According to Chinese sources, the Pyu settled in the Irrawaddy valley in the first century BC. They founded a prominent kingdom (ca. AD 78) in the north of the Irrawaddy delta with Śri Ksetra ("land of splendor" in Sanskrit) as the capital. It thrived until its destruction in AD 1057 by Anawrhata, the first Burmese king, who named it "the Pyu city." The city was later called Prome in 1825 when it was seized by the British army.

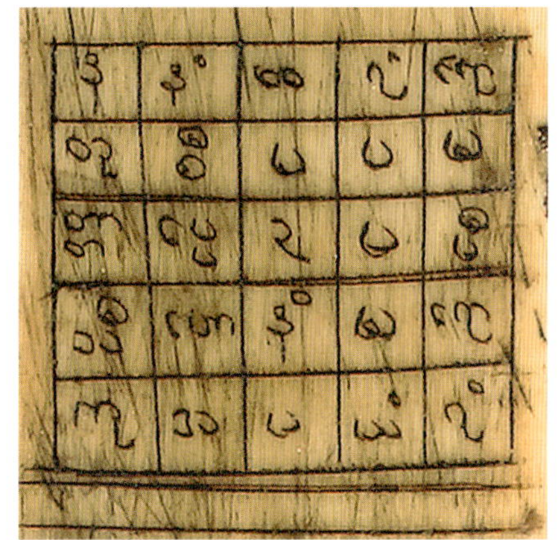

Figure 4. Horoscope diagram from the elephant tusk. Ivory, 34 cm.

The prestige of the Pyu in the region grew through trade with China and neighboring countries. In this way, they spread their knowledge of the production of silk from the silkworm and their culture and education by languages, writings, and religion, linked to Theravāda Buddhism, throughout Myanmar.

The Pyu language actually belongs to the Tibeto-Burman family of languages, which includes the Sino-Tibetan group, encompassing languages spoken in Southeast Asia, in China (Yunnan, Sichuan, Guizhou), and in the Himalayan countries such as Tibet, Nepal, and Bhutan.

An early inscription (AD 1113), the Myazedi pillar, is a jade stele in Pagan engraved with the text in four languages: Pyu, Mon, Pāli, and Burmese. It tells the story of Rājakumara, the son of King Kyanzittha (r. 1084–1112). The greatness of the Pyu declined, however, with the increase in power of the Mon and Burmese, and their rivalry came to an end when King Alaungpaya, the founder of the Konbaung dynasty, conquered the capital, Pegu (Bago in Mon), in 1758.

The Mon

According to some chronicles, the Mon people[1] of Lower Burma founded the kingdom of Thaton (or Suvaṇṇabhūmi) during the lifetime of the Buddha in the fourth century BC. Modern scholarship says that they established Thaton and Pegu (Bago) in the ninth century AD, coming from what is present-day northern Thailand.

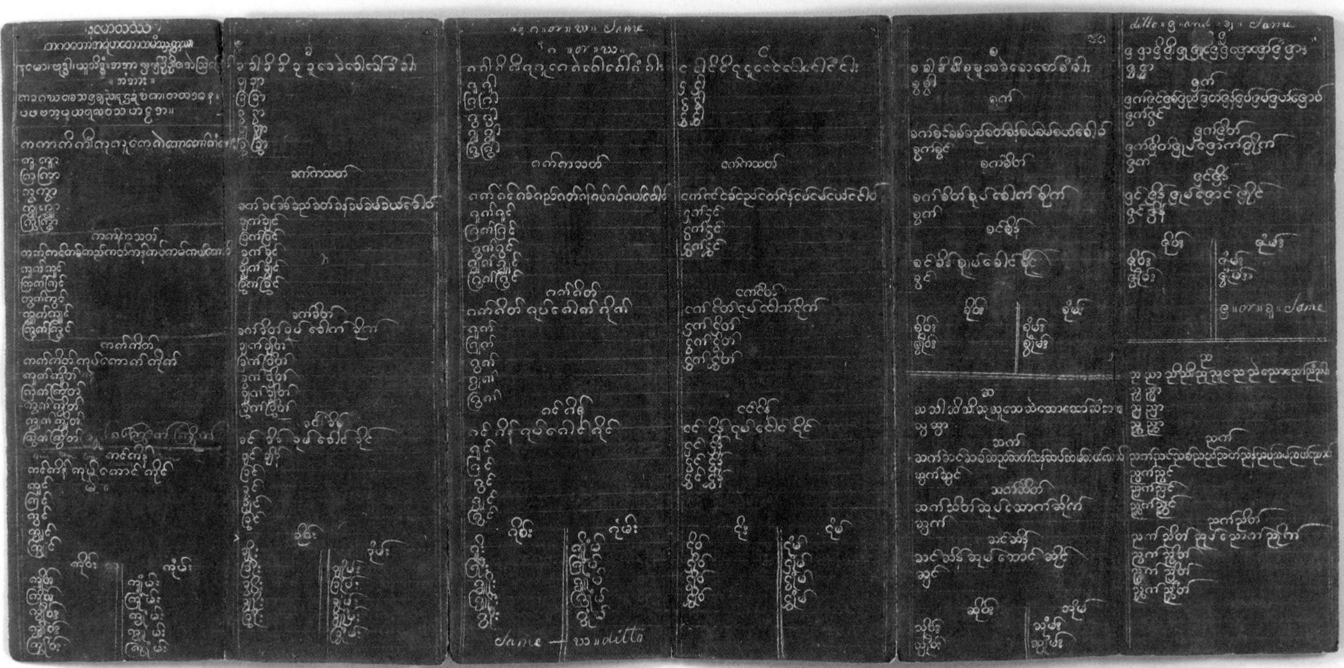

Figure 5. Mon language lessons, 19th century (?). *Parabaik* (folding black paper manuscript), 14.5 × 42 cm. The text is written using soapstone. After invocations to the Buddha, the Mon alphabet is given using the traditional order of consonants (beginning with *ka*) with all the combinations of vowels in three tones.

The political fortunes of the Mon fluctuated in parallel to those of the Burmese from the twelfth to the eighteenth century. As such, at different periods, Pegu was vying with the Burmese capital, Ava, from 1364 to 1841 and then in the south with Toungoo. The city of Pegu declined with the annexation of the Irrawaddy delta in 1755 by the Konbaung dynasty. The hegemony of the Mon ended with the fall of Pegu, without erasing the great influence of their culture throughout Burma and the neighboring countries.

The Mon culture was transmitted to Burma through their writings and language, which belongs to the Austro-Asiatic family of languages. This includes Thai, Vietnamese, and Khmer, but unlike the other languages, the Mon language does not have a tonal system. Nevertheless, unlike the Pyu language, modern Mon, which is different from old Mon, is still spoken today in Myanmar and Thailand.

The Mon script is derived from the Indian Brahmi script used for King Ashoka's edicts (274–34 BC). The same script is used by the Burmese, Karen, and Shan.

The Burmese people

The Myanmar people migrated from Yunnan (southern China) to the Irrawaddy valley, which was occupied by the Pyu, around the seventh century AD. There they founded Pagan, the first royal city, in 849. Pagan became an important city under King Anawratha (1044–77). When Pagan was defeated by the army of Kublai Khan in 1287, the dominance of Burma by the kingdom of Ava (1364–1555) alternated with the power of the Mon kingdom of Bago (1287–1540) in present-day Lower Burma, then with the Rakhine kingdom of Mrauk U (1434–1784) in the west, and finally with the Shan states that stretched into the northern and eastern regions.

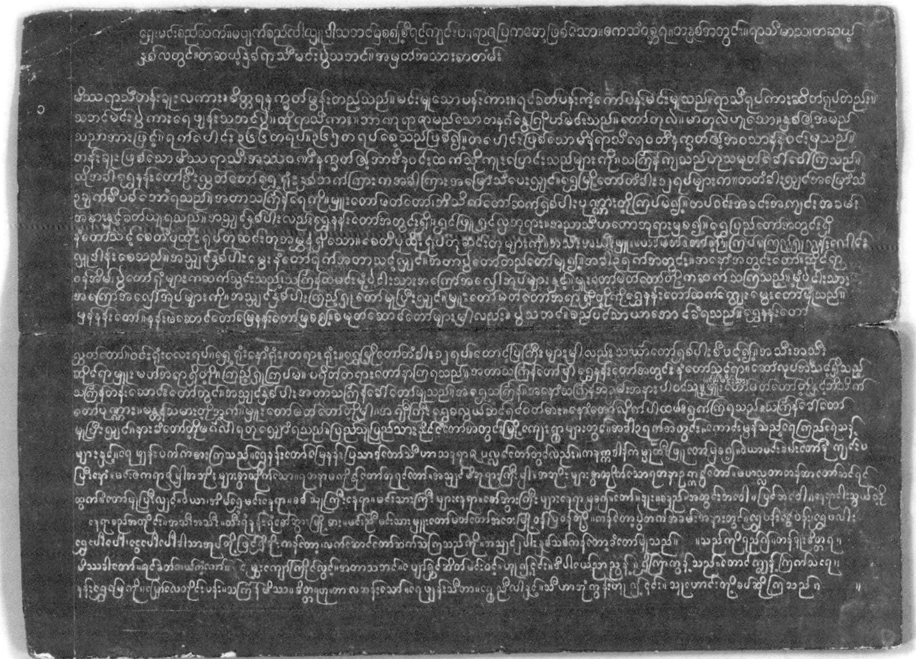

Figure 6. An early text about signs of the zodiac. *Parabaik*, panels 43 × 16 cm, ca. 1880. The text is written using soapstone. The signs of the zodiac are given with the months of the year and the festivals associated with the signs. In addition to the introduction and conclusion, twelve paragraphs detail festivities celebrated in Mandalay, beginning with Thingyan, the three-day New Year or water festival around the middle of April, when the sun is in Aries. The manuscript (MA 4810) was given to the museum by Bonvillain in 1979.

Eventually, the dynasties of Toungoo (1531–1752) and Konbaung (1752–1885) definitively marked the political supremacy of Myanmar, spreading its culture, language, and script across the whole country.

Reading and writing in Burmese

More than one hundred ethnic groups live in Myanmar—for example the Mon, the Karen, the Chin, the Kachin, and the Rakhine. These groups have been recognized by the government as the cultural and linguistic national entities of Myanmar.

Burmese is the official language and is spoken by around 70 percent of the population of over fifty million. It is a member of the Tibeto-Burman family of languages. It is a monosyllabic, tonal language with three tones: creaky, level, and heavy. Just as in all the other Southeast Asian languages, there are no declensions.

Coming from the Brahmi script system and from *nāgarī* or *devanāgarī* writing (ca. ninth century), the Burmese alphabet has no capital letters, and the consonants are pronounced with an inherent, unwritten "a," as in the first consonant, for example, က *ka* (which is also called ကကြီး *ka-gyi* or "great ka"). They are arranged in a logical order linked to the place of pronunciation of the phonemes, starting with those articulated from the back of the mouth (the uvula) for the velars, from the teeth for the dentals, and from the lips for the labials as can be seen in the following phonetic transcription:

က	*ka*	ခ	*kha*	ဂ	*ga*	ဃ	*ga*	င	*ŋa*		
တ	*ta*	ထ	*tha*	ဒ	*da*	ဓ	*da*	န	*na*		
ပ	*pa*	ဖ	*pha*	ဗ	*ba*	ဘ	*ba*	မ	*ma*		
ယ	*ya*	ရ	*ra/ya*	လ	*la*	ဝ	*ua*	သ	*tha*	ဟ	*ha*

The third row of letters are used for retroflex (or cerebral) consonants in Pāli and Sanskrit words, but they are pronounced exactly like the second row of dentals; and the second *la* is the letter for retroflex (or cerebral) *ḷ* in Pāli and Sanskrit words, but pronounced as an ordinary *l*. Some letters used for aspirate consonants in Pāli and Sanskrit are pronounced like the unaspirated letter (ဂ *ga*, ဃ *ga*; ဒ *da*, ဓ *da*; ဗ *ba*, ဘ *ba*).

By combining two signs or glyphs, like the "small ya" ျ, the "big ya" ြ, or *wa* ွ, with the consonants က, ခ, ဂ, င, ပ, ဖ, ဗ, မ, combinations which have no equivalents in the *nāgarī* script, the combinations of consonants are increased; this allows the creation of words such as

ဂျုံ	*joun*	"wheat"
ဂြိုဟ်	*jou*	"planet"
ဗျာ	*bya*	"sir"
ဗြဟ်မ		*byama* "brahman"
မုဆိုးမ	*pua*	*"dowager"*
မွန်	*mun*	"good"
ကျွန်	*chun*	"slave"
မြွေ	*mye*	"snake."

There is also an intricate vowel system consisting of open and closed syllables, which can be difficult to master.

The open syllables

The vowels /a/, /i/, /u/, /e/, /o/, and /ui/ are combined with the consonants and are marked by a sign which can be put on either side, above, or below the consonant or combination of consonants. They can also be attached to a syllable, forming a noun like ဈေး *ze* "market" or a verb such as စား *sa* "to eat." The analysis in detail of some words can explain the mechanism that unites writing and reading in Burmese.

The term စာ *sa* "text" consists of the consonant စ *sa* and the sign ာ, equivalent to /a/ of the level tone.

The noun မိုး `mo "rain" is composed of the consonant မ *ma* and the sign ို for the vowel /ɔ/ followed by the mark း for the heavy tone.

The term ရေ *ye* "water" is made up of the consonant ရ *ya* preceded by the sign ေ– for the vowel /e/. In this case, the vowel written before the consonant is pronounced after it.

Vowels and tones

The tone for each vowel is clearly indicated by the spelling. For the vowel /a/, the creaky tone (tone 1) is used for the inherent, unwritten "a"—for example က *ka* "to dance." The level tone (tone 2) uses –ာ or –ါ (the choice depends on the consonant in order to avoid ambiguous combinations), for example ကာ *kā* "a shield" and ပါ *pā* "to accompany" (the other form would make the word look like –ဟ *ha*), and the heavy tone (tone 3) uses –ာ း or –ါ း, for example ကာ း *kā* "car."

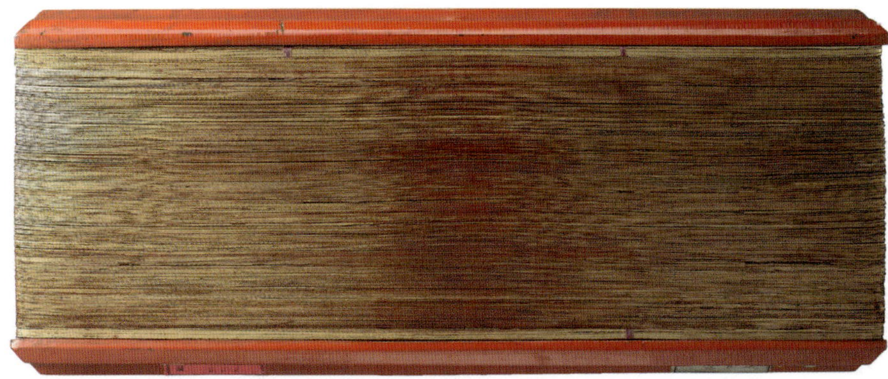

Figure 7. Pālimuttaka-vinayavinicchaya-saṅgaha. Palm-leaf manuscript, 5 × 46 cm, AD 1875. The Pāli text is by Sāriputta of Poḷonnavuva (12th century) and is a handbook dealing with the monastic discipline found in the *Vinaya-piṭaka* and its commentary. The manuscript was given to the museum by M. Hardouin in 1891.

For the other vowels (/i/, /u/, /e/, /è/, /aw/, and /o/) all three tones are written as follows:

The /i/ is written ိ (tone 1), ီ (tone 2), and ီ း (tone 3), as in သိ *thi* "knowledge," သီ *thī* "to sing," and သီး *thī:* "fruit."

The /u/ is written ု (tone1), ူ (tone 2), and ူး (tone 3).

The /i/ and /u/ are combined for the vowel /o/, with a small circle marking the first tone ို့ (tone 1), ို (tone 2), and ိုး (tone 3), as in ပို့ *po´* "escort," ပို *po* "bundle," and ပိုး *`po* "silk."

The /e/ is written ေ–့ (tone 1), ေ– (tone 2), and ေ–း (tone 3), for example လေ့ *le´* "to get used to," လေ *le* "wind," and လေး *`le* "four."

The sign ေ– combined with –ာ forms the vowel /aw/: ေ–ာ့ (tone 1), ေ–ာ် (tone 2), and ေ–ာ့ (tone 3), for example မော့ *maw* "aloft," မော်တော်ကား *motoca* "car," and မော *maw* "to be tired."

The /ɛ/ is written –ဲ့ (tone 1), –ယ် (tone 2), –ဲ (tone 3), for example နဲ့ *nɛ´* "with," နယ်, *nɛ* "region," and နဲနဲ *`nɛ `nɛ* "a little."

The closed syllables

The occlusives are formed by adding the hook to some consonants: ◌် (called သတ် *sat?* "to kill," corresponding to the Sanskrit *virāma*). This suppresses the inherent vowel "a." Examples are က် /k/, စ် /c/, တ် /t/, and ပ် /p/. The consonant is not pronounced; rather a glottal stop is added to the preceding vowel, as in လက်ဖက်, pronounced *lə phɛ?* "tea," and ဖိနပ်, pronounced *phə na?* "shoes."

The nasalization of the syllables is written by adding the sign to suppress the vowel ◌် to the consonants င /*`ŋa*/, ည /*`ŋa*/, န /*`na*/, or မ /*`ma*/, as in these nouns: ထမင်း *thə-miŋ* "cooked rice," အိမ် *aŋ* "house," and ရန်ကုန် *yan- goŋ* "Yangon."

One sign is added to the following consonants by placing it beneath them. The ဟ /*`ha/ is combined* with the sign ◌ှ as in the words ငှက် *hngɛ?* "bird," နှင်း *`hnin* "mist," and ညှပ် *hnya?* "pinch." When it is combined with ရ /*ra´*/ it gives the sound /*ʃa´*/ as in ရွှေ *ʃwe´* "gold."

The diphthongs /*aiŋ*/, /*auŋ*/, and /*wuŋ*/ are obtained by using a nasal consonant attached to a vowel ◌ိုင်, ◌ောင်, ◌ွန် as in နိုင် *naiŋ´* "country," ကျောင်း *`cauŋ* "school," and ယွန် *ywuŋ* "lacquer."

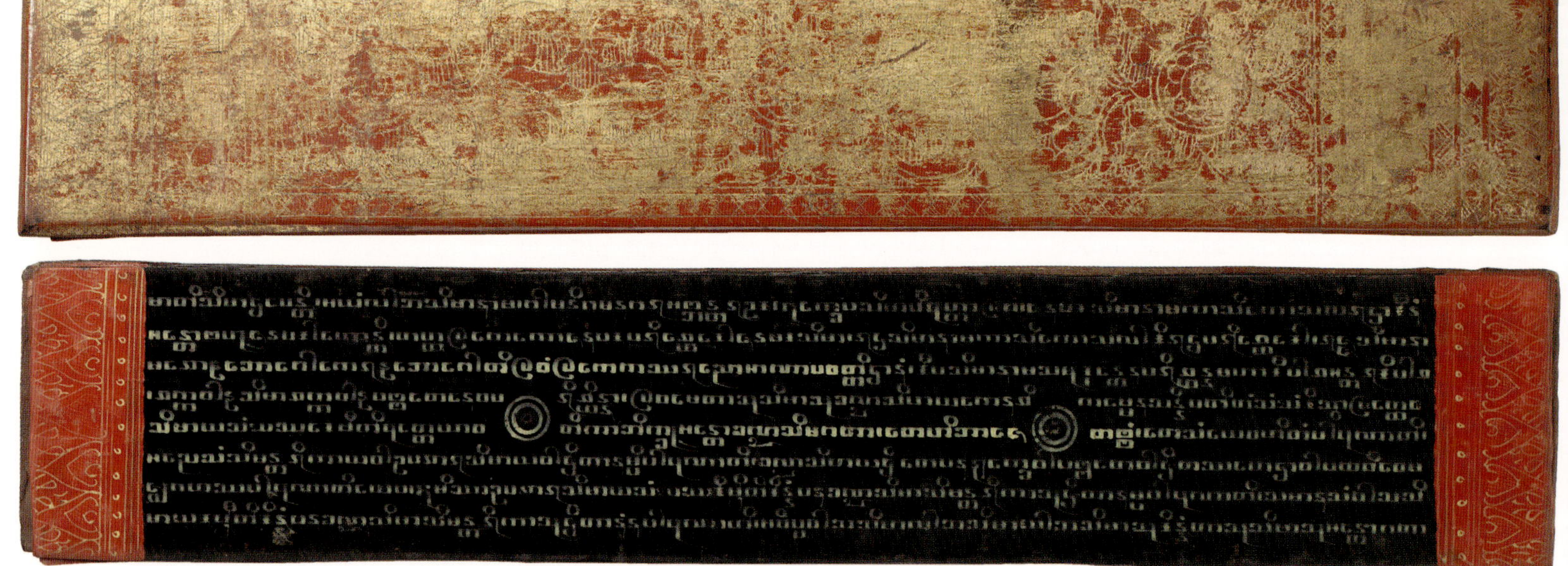

Figure 8. *Nittipakaraṇa-aṭṭhakathā* and other texts. Cloth stiffened with lacquer, 10.5 × 54 cm, 19th century (?). The text is written in small, square Burmese script using gamboge yellow. The form of the leaves is modeled on the shape of palm-leaf manuscripts. The text consists of extracts from Pāli commentaries by Dhammapāla and other commentators and paracanonical texts. The manuscript was given to the museum by M. de Bouteiller around 1890.

Syntax

Reading and writing are done from the left to the right according to a grammar that looks simple at first sight due to verbs without conjugation, nouns without gender, and invariable determiners; the complexity is linked to the spelling, with many homophones and a syntax following the order of determiner + determined, so an "inhabitant of Yangon" is said ရန်ကုန်သား "Yangon + son." Furthermore, the clause has its own construction: subject, complement, verb, and modal form.

သူတို့ အိမ် အနီးက ကျောင်းကို သွားတယ်။
θudo eiŋ´ əni´`ka cau´ `ko θwa dɛʔ
"they + house + close to + school + to go + modal for positive sentence," followed by the double sign of punctuation (။).
"They go to the school close to the house."

Due to the order of the words the subordinate clause is put before the main one:
မိုးရွာ လို့သူစာတိုက်ကို မသွားသူး။
mo´ ywa lo´ θu sa daiʔ `ko mə θwa bu
rain + as + she + post office + to + go + not
"She didn't go to the post office because it was raining."

Otherwise, proper nouns and common names are phonetically transcribed in translations of foreign literature. So it is difficult to find their correct spelling because the pronunciation and the writing form do not necessarily match. That is why it is necessary to transliterate letter by letter according to the formal conversion table of the alphabet.

In this connection, the names of the places show the real difficulty of the transcription such as the royal cities of မန္တလေး *maŋta ´`le*, which is read in French "Mandalé" and in English "Mandalay; ပုဂံ *pugaŋ*, read as "Pagan" or "Bagan"; and ပဲခူး *`pɛkhū*, "Pegu" or "Bago."

Figure 9. Leaf from *Pālimuttaka-vinayavinicchaya-saṅgaha* by Sāriputta of Poḷonnavuva (see fig. 7).

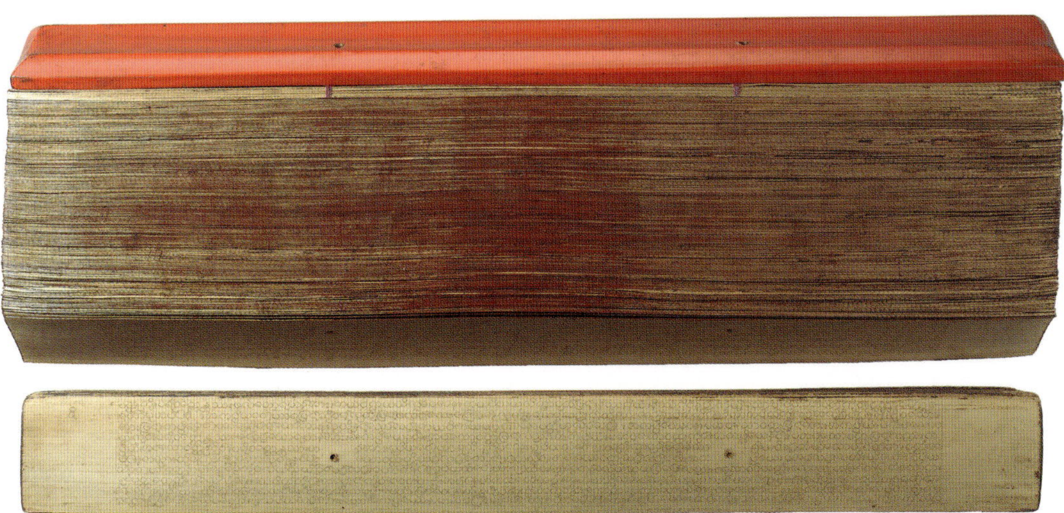

Loan words

There are many loan words from Sanskrit, Pāli, and English; these can be recognized by the way they are spelled. They are especially used for abstract, religious, and concrete vocabulary.

The following consonants that represent cerebrals are pronounced as dentals: ဋ (ṭa), ဌ , ဋ္ဌ (ṭha, ṭṭha), ဍ (ḍa), ဎ (ḍha), ဏ (ṇa), and ဠ (ḷa). They are only used in religious and philosophical words. Many superimposed consonants are used in religious terms, abstract ideas, and titles.

Religious words

ဓမ္မ (=ဓမ်မ) Pāli *dhamma* Buddhist Law
ဗုဒ္ဓဘာသာ (=ဗုဒ်ဓဘာသာ) Pāli *buddhabāsa* Buddhism
နိဗ္ဗာန် *nɛʔbaŋ* (Pāli *nibbāna*)

Abstract words

စိတ္တ (=စိတ်တ) Pāli *citta* becomes စိတ် *seiʔ* "spirit" in Burmese.
သဒ္ဓမ္မ (=သဒ်ဓမ်မ) Pāli *suddhamma*, သ *θaʔda* "faith."
ဒုက္ခ (=ဒုက်ခ) Pāli *dukkha*, "pain"

Titles

ဘုန်ကြီး *poŋ`ci* or "great glory," meaning "monk"
ရာဇာ *raza* king, ရာဇ္ဇာကုမာရ် *Razakumaʔ*, "King Rajakumara"
မိဖုရား *`mibuya´*, "queen"

Loan words from English are often phonetic transcriptions, for example:
မော်တော်ကာ: *mɔtɔ`ca*, "car"
အင်ဂလိပ် *ingəleiʔ*, "English"
ဂျပန် *jia´paŋ*, "Japan"

And the calendar months:
ဇန်နဝါရီလ *jaŋnawari-la* "January"
ဧပြီလ *epri-`la* "April"
ဩဂုတ်လ *əgouʔ-`la* "August"

These names of months are from the Gregorian calendar. The Burmese calendar is based on the lunar and solar system with a number of days that can vary between twenty-nine and thirty each month, as in Tabodwe (roughly equal to January/February), Kason (April/May), or Tawthalin (August/September).

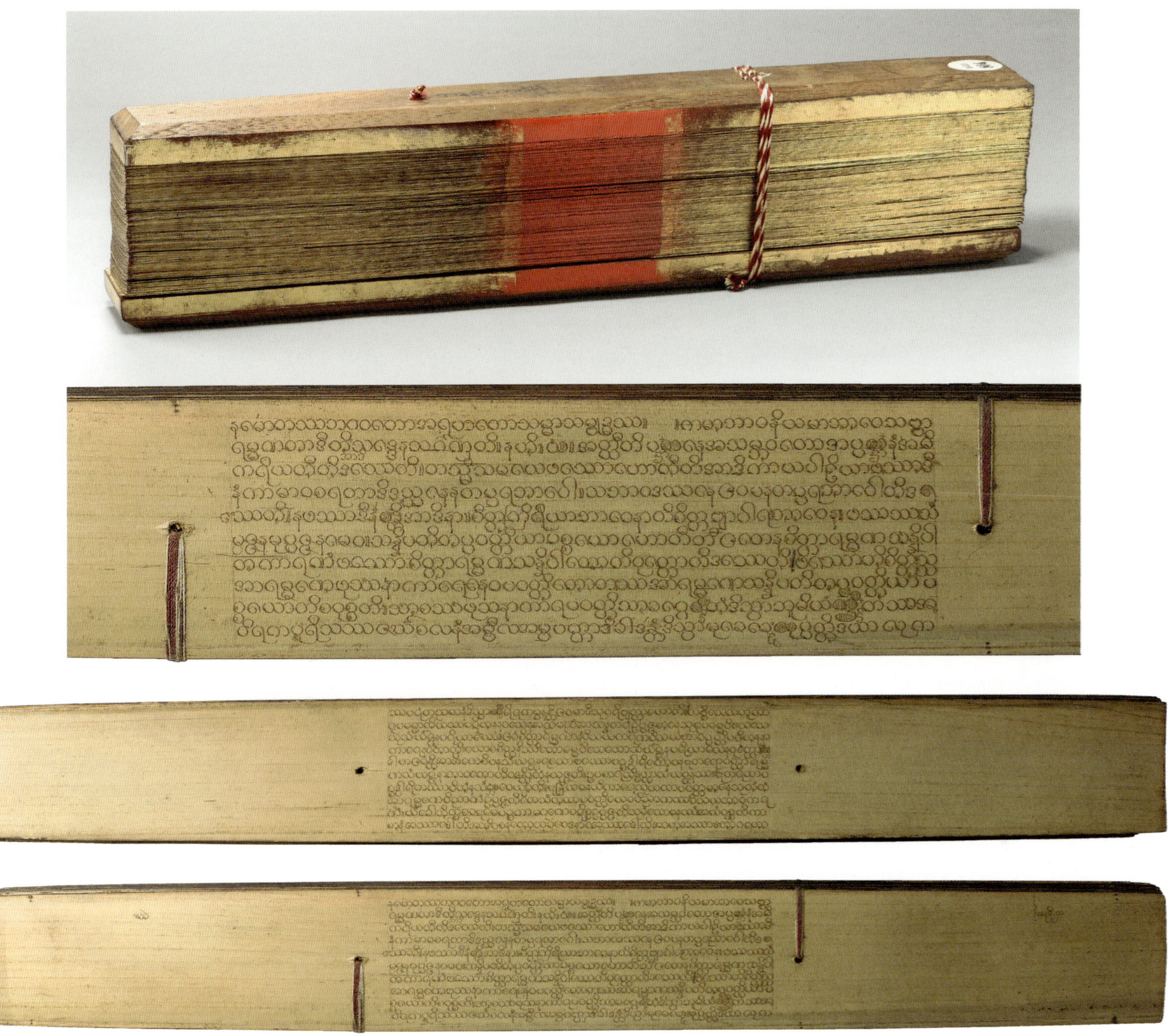

Figure 10. *Dhammasaṅgaṇī-anuṭīkā*, Palm-leaf manuscript, 6 × 49 cm, AD 1842. This text is a subcommentary on the *Abhidhamma-piṭaka*, the third collection of the Buddhist Pāli canon.

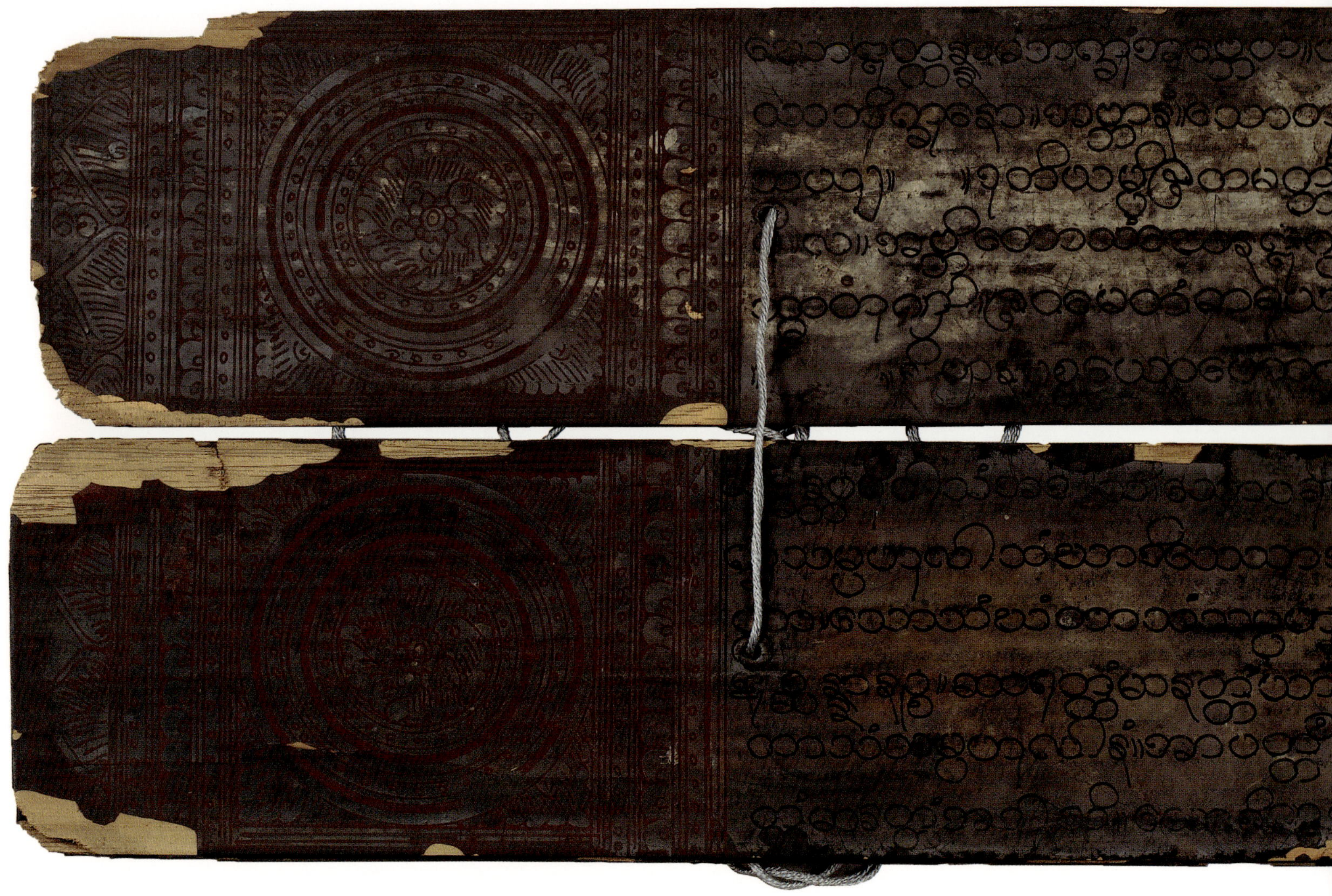

Figure 11. Fragment of a Mon *kammavācā*. Palm-leaf manuscript, 53.5 × 8 cm 18th century (?). *Kammavācā* ("verbal acts") manuscripts contain texts used for legally binding acts of the Buddhist monks. These palm leaves are covered with a layer of silver that has oxidized. Decorative elements are in vermillion. The text is in black in round Burmese script.

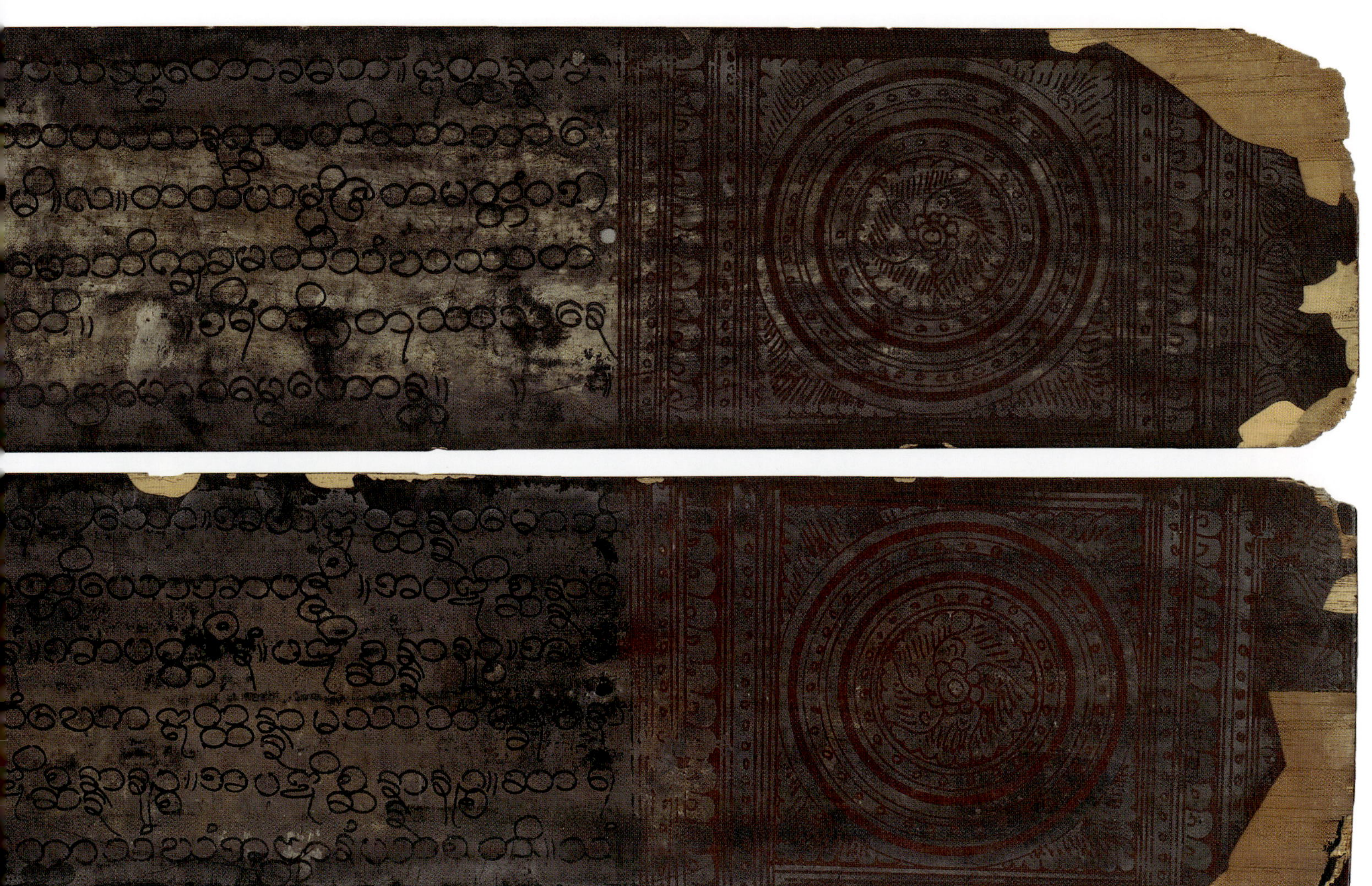

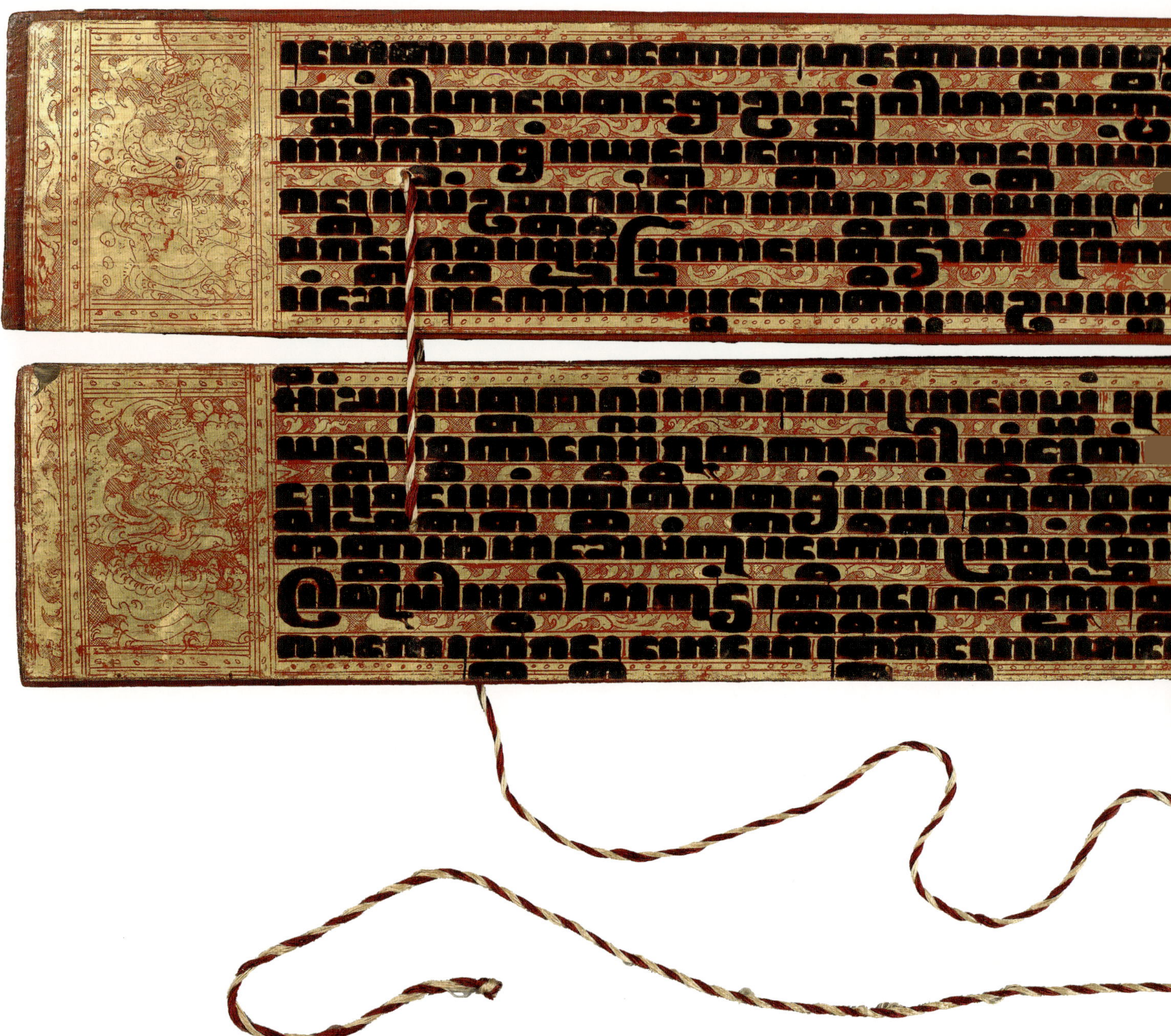

Figure 12. *Kammavācā*, Thin, lacquered metal sheets, 10 × 53 cm, 19th century (?). The material used for traditional *kammavācā* manuscripts can vary, but the general appearance is the same: the material is covered in lacquer, which is gilded and decorated using vermillion, and the standardized texts are written in black lacquer using the "tamarind seed" script, so called because the large letters resemble the seeds of the tamarind fruit. This script is no longer used today. *Kammavācā* manuscripts are usually made up of approximately fifteen leaves and contain the texts of the ordination ceremony and other official acts for procedures such as the robe ceremony at the end of the rains retreat.

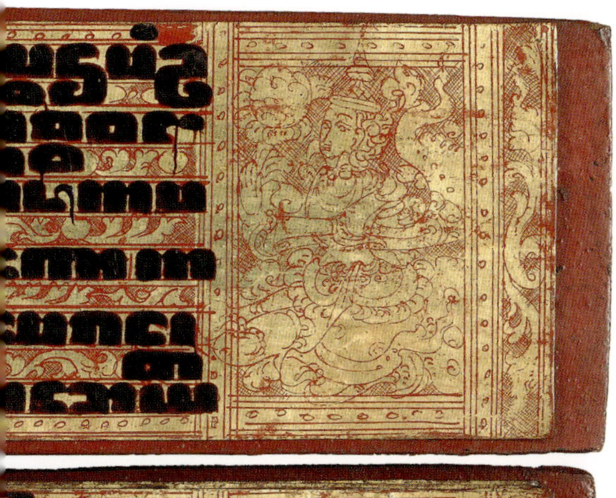

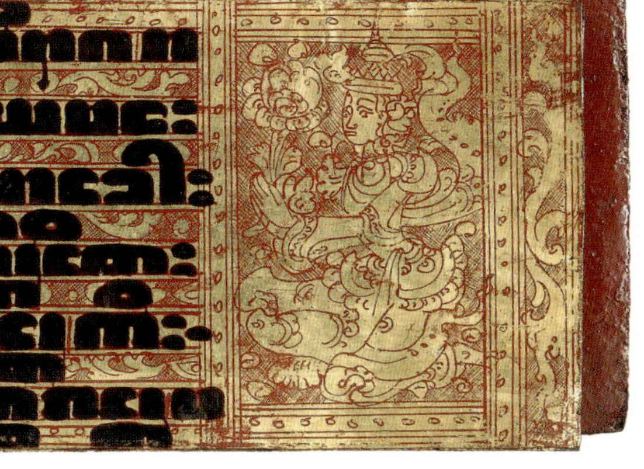

The Spread of the Burmese Script

In addition, we can note that some ethnic groups in Myanmar, such as the Karen and the Shan, have adapted the Burmese system to their languages and writings, which can be found in palm-leaf and paper manuscripts. For instance, Karen is a good example of the linguistic similarity. The Karen language, spoken by almost one million people living in Myanmar and in northern Thailand, belongs to the Tibeto-Burman group, with the same alphabet but without these consonants: ဇ *za*, ဓ *dha*, ဗ *ba*, ဈ *jha*, and ည *ŋa*, as well as the Pāli letters ဋ *ṭa*, ဌ *ṭha*, and ဍ *ḍa*. The system of consonants and vowels (five tones) is sometimes different with respect to pronunciation—for example, ယ *j*, *ʒ*, z instead of *ya*.

Glyphs and other signs added to some consonants increase their number: the sign –ှ to ဟ /*ha*/, the –ျ to ယ /*ja*, *za*/, ြ to ရ /ra/, –ၠ to လျ /*la*/, and finally –ွ to ဝ /*wa*/.

The vowels in Karen language are less numerous:

/a/	is written	–ါ	as in	ကါ	∂/*ka*/
/i/	is written	–ိ	as in	ၡိ	/*ʃi*/
/ö/	is written	–ၢ	as in	လၢ	/*le*/
/ü/	is written	–ု	as in	ပု	/*pî*/
/u/	is written	–ူ	as in	ထူ	/*thu*/
/e/	is written	–့	as in	–တ့	/*te*/
/æ/	is written	–ဲ	as in	ဘဲ	/*bæ*/
/o/	is written	–ိ	as in	မိ	/mo/
/aw/	is written	–ီ	as in	နီ	/*nɔ*/

The five tones of Karen language are noted by signs put after the consonants:

Tone 1 ၢ်	as in	မိမိၢ်	*maw maw*	"mother"
Tone 2 ာ်	as in	နာ်	*na*	"to believe"
Tone 3 း	as in	ကူး	*ku*	"to cough"
Tone 4 ၣ်	as in	သံၣ်	*ti*	"comb"
Tone 5 ၤ	as in	မစၤ	*mesa*	"to help"

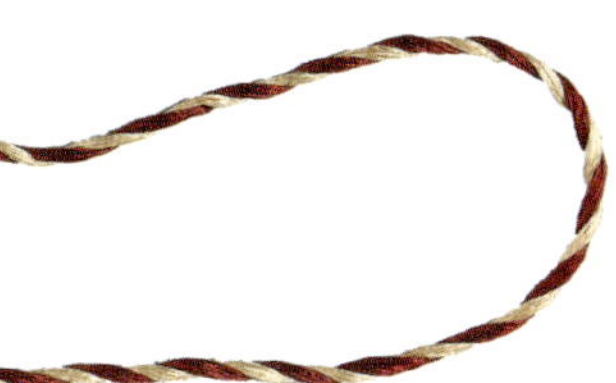

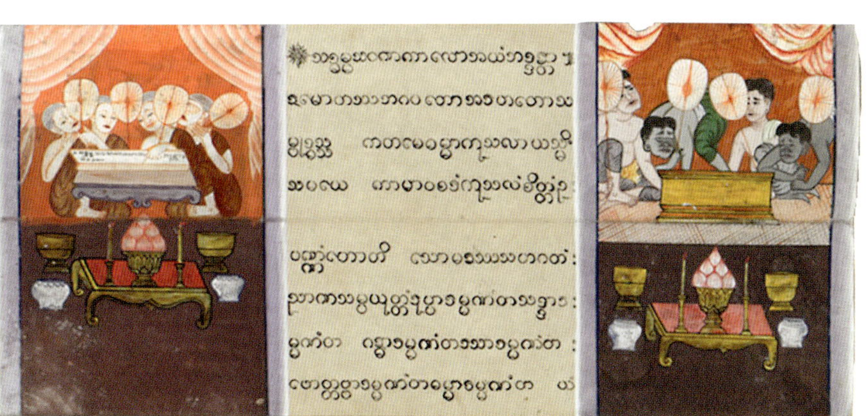

Figure 13. Abhidhammā-ṭīkā. White *parabaik*, 66 cm long, 19th century. The text is written in Pāli and Shan, using the Burmese script. The manuscript is about past lives of the Buddha (*jātakas*), and the placement and style of the illustrations are very similar to Siamese manuscripts from the same period.

So even though both languages belong to the Tibeto-Burman group, which makes them close, the Burmese and Karen languages have kept their own traits.

Pronunciation of Burmese

The following explanation of the letters used for the pronunciation of Burmese is taken from *A Burmese-English Dictionary* (Stewart et al.).

Vowels

a open syllables, palm; elsewhere the same sound shortened
i open syllables, *ea*ger; elsewhere pin
u open syllables, t*oo*; elsewhere put
e French *é*lève
ɛ in open syllables, French élève; elsewhere well
ɔ l*aw*
o French *eau*
ei *ei*ght
ou bolt
au down, sound
ai fine
ə *a*bove

Consonants

b, d, g (as in *go*), h, j, k, l, m, n, nh (as *gn* in French *digne*), p, r, s, t, w, y (as in *you*), z approximately as in English. Aspiration of k, s, t, and p must be avoided.

c an intimate combination of *t* and *y*, resembling the initial consonantal sound of *tulip* (British) or the *ch* of *cheese* made with the tip of the tongue touching the lower teeth.

ŋ when initial as *ng* in *singer*; when final, a nasalization of the preceding vowel

θ *th*in

ð *then*

ʃ *sh*ake (no rounding of the lips)

h following a consonant indicates aspiration of that consonant, as in *kh*, *sh*, *th*, *ph*, *ch*. Preceding a consonant, it indicates that that consonant is a breathed consonant; thus, *n*, *m*, *l* are voiced consonants while *h*, *hn*, *hm*, *hl* are breathed consonants (*hl* being like the *ll* in *Llandudno*)

ʔ is a throat consonant as in the Cockney or the Glasgow pronunciation of *water* as waʔer. See the explanation under Tones.

Tones

"Tone" is here used to describe four of the five categories of sound found in Burmese. The fifth, or neutral (as in *a*bove), tone is regarded as nontonal.

1. The *creaky* tone (or tone one): This is pronounced with an intermittent voice, falling from a relatively high initial pitch and ending in a weak closure of the glottis. Marked by ´ following the syllable, as in *sauŋ´* "to wait."
2. The *level* tone (or tone two): A syllable in this tone is low pitched relative to adjacent syllables. No fall of pitch is permissible. Lightly stressed in comparison with syllables in other tones belonging to the same combination. Level tones are left unmarked in the phonetic transcriptions, as *sauŋ* "blanket."
3. The *heavy falling* tone (or tone three): This is high pitched at the start and falls steeply. Pronounced in a "breathy" voice ending in a "fade out." Heavily stressed. Marked by ` preceding the syllable, as *`sauŋ* "harp."
4. The *abrupt* tone (or the glottal stop): This is rather higher in pitch than the creaky tone. It terminates in a throat consonant produced by an abrupt closure of the glottis. Accompanied by much greater effort and constriction of the larynx than the creaky tone. Marked by ʔ following the syllable, as *sauʔ* "to be steep."

Note

1. The Mon are also referred to by the term Talaing, but they consider this term to be pejorative.

Bibliography

Bernot, Denise, et al. *Dictionnaire birman-français*. 15 vols. Langues et civilisations de l'Asie du Sud Est et du monde insulindien. Paris: SELAF/Peteers, 1978–94.

Cornyn, William S., and John K. Musgrave. *Burmese Glossary*. Program in Oriental Languages Publications, ser. A, no. 5. Washington: American Council of Learned Societies, 1958.

Harvey, G. E. *History of Burma*. London: Frank Cass & Co. Ltd, 1925.

Phayre, Arthur P. *History of Burma*. London: Susil Gupta, 1967.

Stewart, J. A., C. W. Dunn, and Kin Maung Lat. *A Burmese-English Dictionary*. Part 1. London: Luzac & Co., 1940.

U Thi Ha and Daw Thida Moe. *Trilingual Illustrated Dictionary English-Myanmar-Karen*. Yangon: Today Publishing House Ltd., 2004.

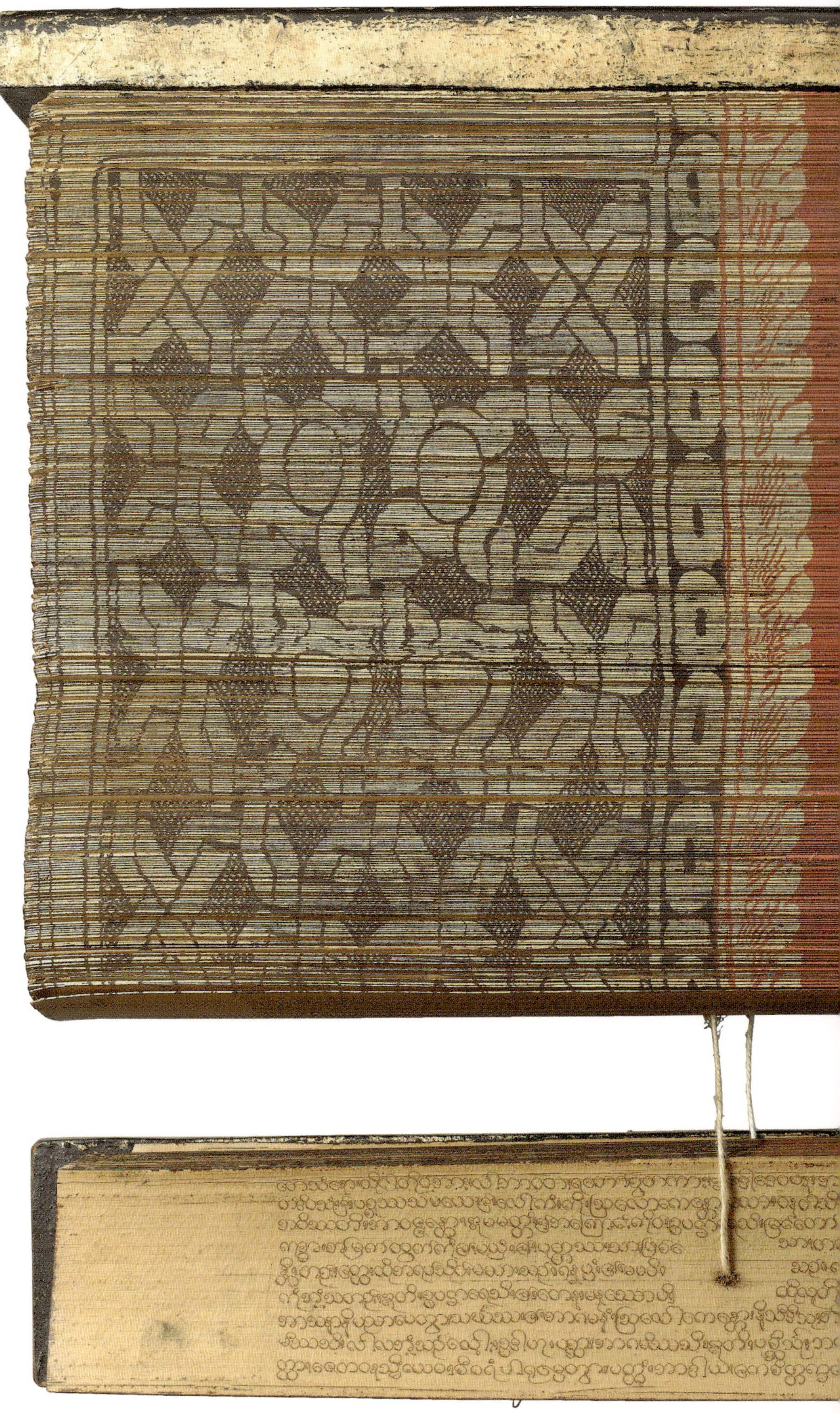

Figure 14. Dhammapada-aṭṭhakathā nissaya. Palm-leaf manuscript, 6 × 47.5 cm, second half of 18th century. This is a word-for-word translation from Pāli into Burmese of the commentary on the *Dhammapada* (*The word of the doctrine*), a collection of verses attributed to the Buddha. The unusual design using gold, black, and vermillion on the edges of the leaves is especially beautiful.

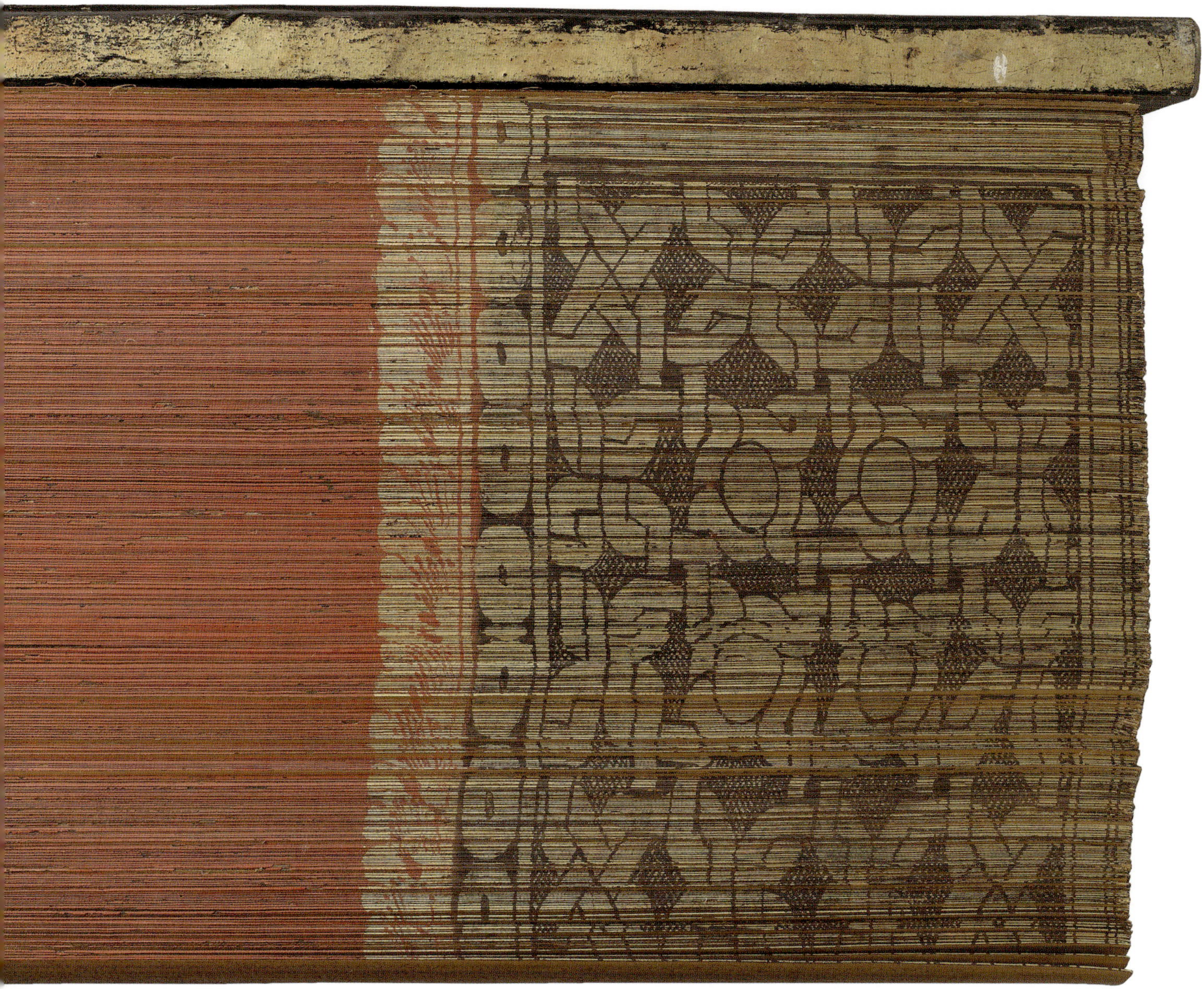

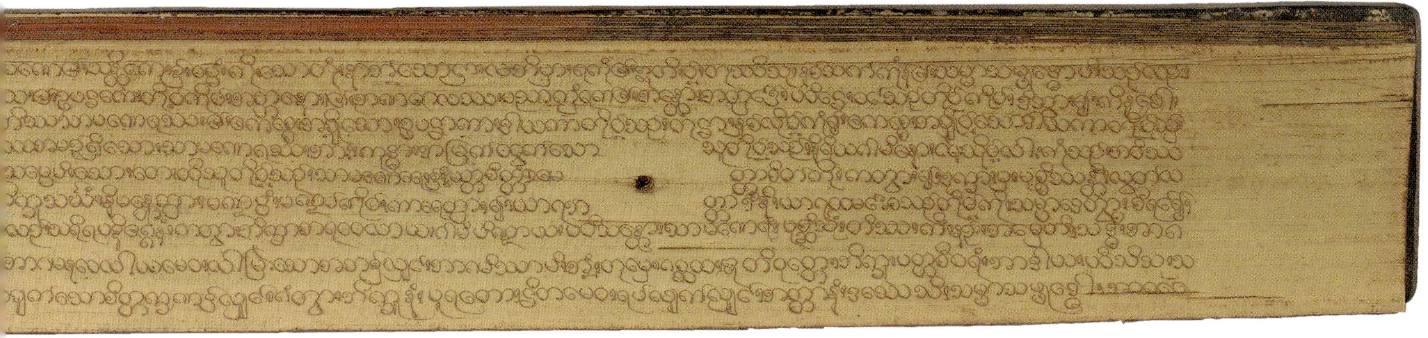

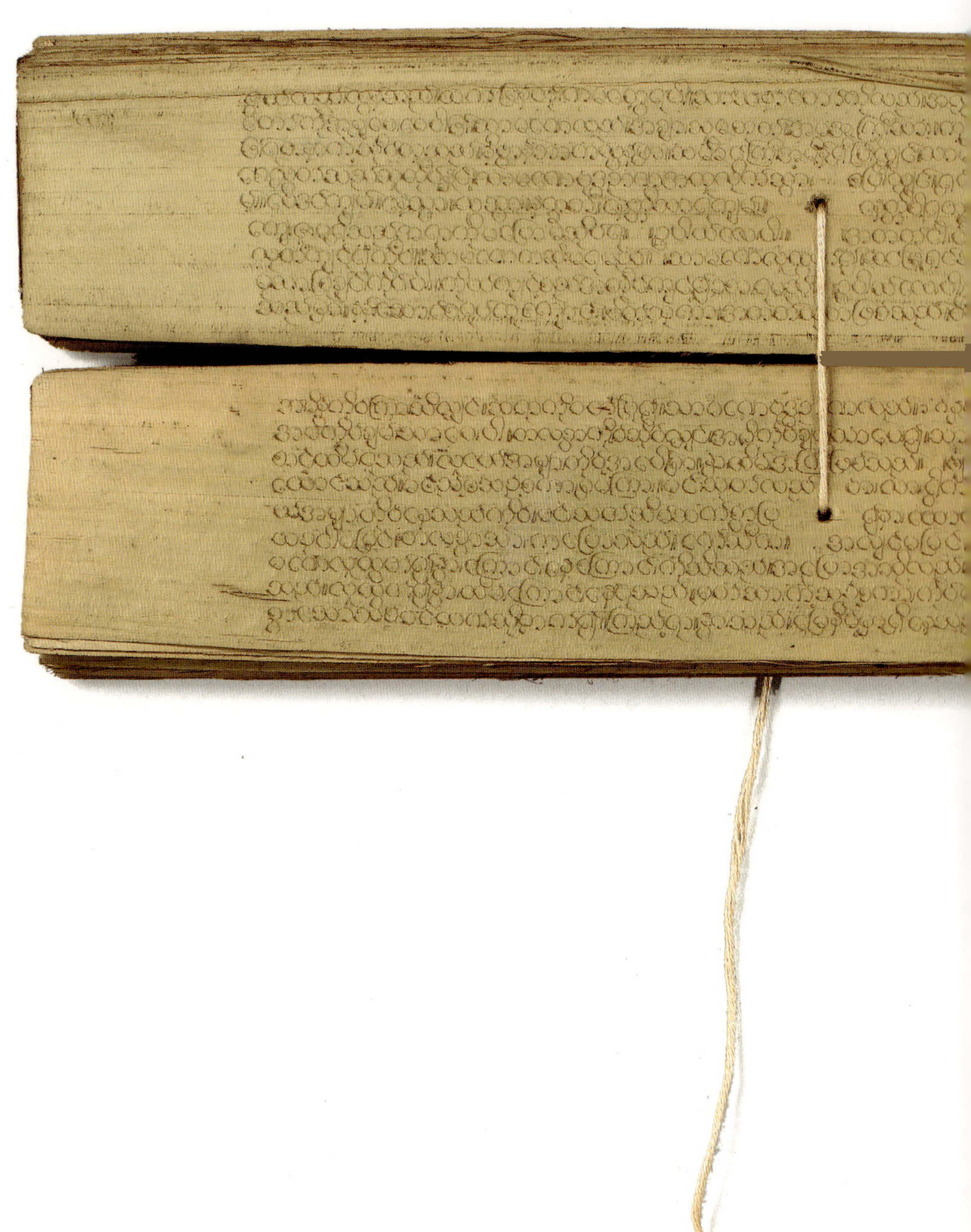

Figure 15. Untitled manuscript. Palm-leaf manuscript, 49.5 × 6 cm, 19th century (?). It is not uncommon for leaves to be missing from palm-leaf manuscripts, as is the case for this manuscript. This can make it very difficult to identify the text. This text is about a high official on a mission to collect taxes.

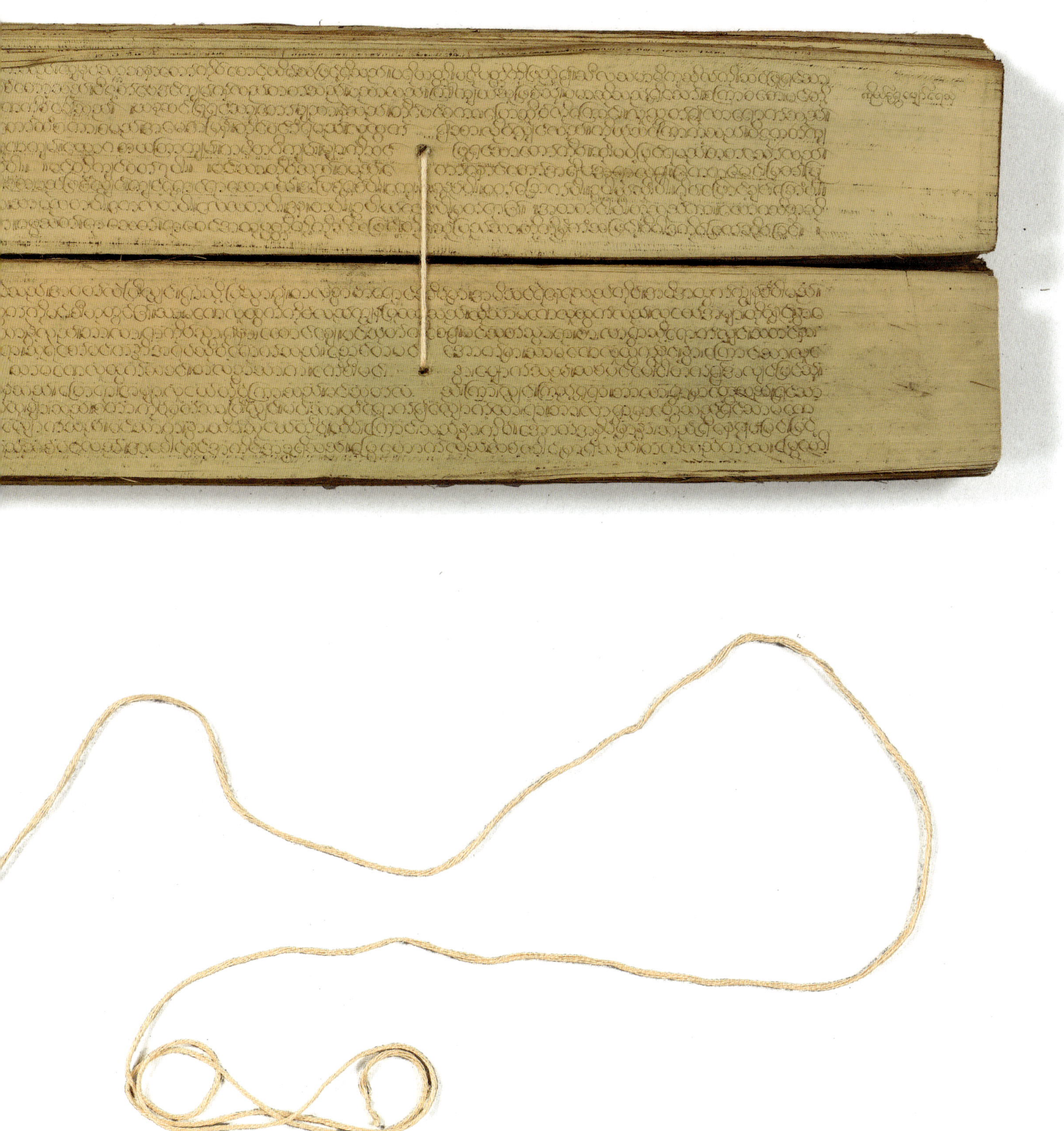

BURMESE BOOKS: *Forms and Materials*

Francis Macouin
Former General Curator Librarian, Musée Guimet

UP TO the nineteenth century, almost to the end of the Konbaung dynasty (1752–1885), a Burmese book was generally a manuscript—typically one made of palm leaves. The use of printing presses came from the West and was only gradually introduced during the nineteenth century.[1] As in India and Southeast Asia, palm leaves were commonly used. The leaves of the talipot (*Corypha umbraculifera*) were used as the trees supplied leaves of good quality and the right size for written texts. For administrative documents (correspondence, horoscopes, etc.), leaves of the palmyra palm (*Borassus flabellifer*) were used. The quality of these leaves was not as good, but the tree also supplied large quantities of products such as jaggery (made from palm juice).

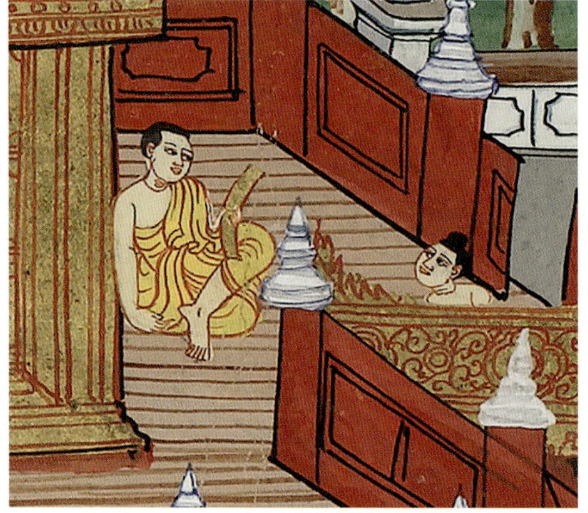

Figure 16. Monk reading a manuscript. *Parabaik* detail (MA 4807), late 19th century.

Palm leaves had to be prepared before use. The process generally followed the following steps: First, the palm fronds were cut while still fresh and boiled in water to eliminate the oozing resin. They were then dried and wrapped in packages of twelve leaves. To be made suitable for writing on, they were carefully scraped, and then they were finally cut to the required dimensions.

The manuscript is made up of loose, oblong rectangular leaves, approximately five to six centimeters high and around fifty centimeters long. These manuscript leaves are called *ola*, a word of Tamil origin. The number of lines on an ola rarely numbered more than a dozen on one side because they were so narrow. The text is inscribed in horizontal lines using a metal stylus that is supported underneath by the nail of the left-hand thumb and held in the right hand almost perpendicular to the leaf. To guide the writing, lines are traced using a mixture of turmeric and water. The letters are not cut deeply into the leaf, and as a result both sides of the leaves can be used. The letters are not easy to see, so in order to read the text, a mixture of soot and the gum of the *Dipterocarpus grandiflorus* tree is applied to the leaves and remains in the shallow incisions of the letters. The letters then stand out as the black pigment in the letters contrasts with the light brown of the palm leaf. Texts and even illustrations are usually inscribed in this manner, but manuscripts are also found where the text is written using ink, in which case a bamboo quill is used.

Two holes are pierced a third of the way in from the edges of the leaves in order to insert small bamboo sticks to hold the leaves together, or strings are often inserted to tie them together. Manuscripts vary in length from a few leaves to hundreds of leaves. They are usually numbered in the upper-left corner of the verso side of the leaves, which is convex due to the natural curvature of most of the palm leaves. The folios do not use numerals but an earlier method that employs consonants in alphabetical order combined with vowels—twelve vowels being available for each consonant.

The written leaves are often protected at the beginning and end by several blank leaves that can be sewn together or by slightly larger wooden covers. The covers are often made of wood from the red cotton tree (*Bombax ceiba*). They may be decorated with lacquer, lacquer and gold leaf, lacquered carvings, and so on. Exceptional manuscripts sometimes had the edges of the leaves covered with lacquer. During the Konbaung period, gold leaf on the edges of the leaves indicated that there was a connection with the royal family. If the gold leaf was broken by a large red band in the middle, it showed a connection with a court official. The lacquer came from a different tree than the one used in China. In Burma, the tree that was tapped to collect its resin was the *Gluta usitats* (or the *Melanhorroea usitata*) from the *Anacardiaceae* family. When the resin is used in its natural state, it produces black lacquer, the color that appears when the resin solidifies. When the resin is mixed with cinnabar (red mercuric acid) it produces red lacquer. The decoration on the manuscripts can include a more elaborate procedure, with designs that mix black and red lacquer as well as gold. For more prestigious usage, the palm-leaves could be lacquered on both sides. In such cases, black ink or gold lettering was used to write the text.

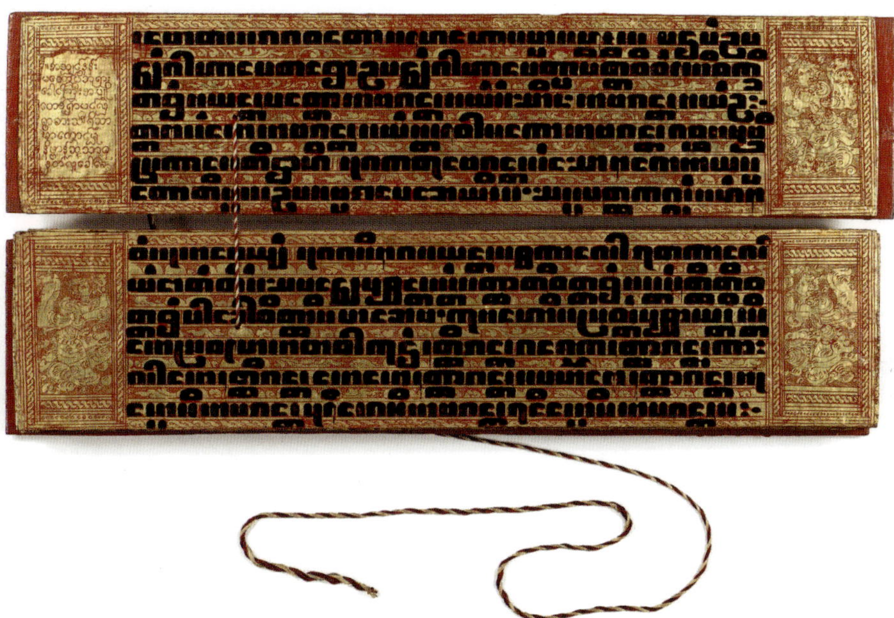

Figure 17. Kammavācā. Stiffened cloth covered in lacquer, 12.5 × 53 cm, 19th century (?).

When the size of the manuscript was not limited by the use of palm leaves, it could be bigger, mainly by using other materials, making the leaves taller without the general form and structure being changed. Leaves could be made of cloth or a thin lattice of bamboo which was covered in lacquer on which the text was written using gamboge (yellow pigment). Royal manuscripts are often of this type. The ink used to write royal manuscript of the canon (*Tipiṭaka*) was made using ashes of cloth mixed with water, resin from the margosa or neem tree (*Azadirachta indica*), and gall from carp (*Cirrhina mrigala*).

A special category of manuscripts that requires some explanation is that of the *kammavācā*. They are exceptionally beautiful and quite common. The name means "vocal [legally binding] acts," and the texts in them are used by the monks for procedures such as ordination. These manuscripts were offered to men when they ordained as monks in order to celebrate this solemn act of the monastic community. They often

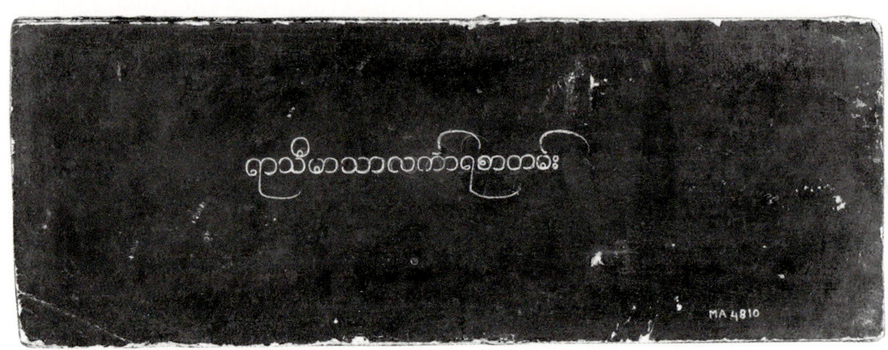

Figure 18. Cover of the manuscript on the zodiac. *Parabaik*, panels 43 × 16 cm, ca. 1880.

include eight extracts (*khandaka*) from the Vinaya-piṭaka, the section of the Pāli canon dealing with monastic discipline. Their production is for the most part stereotyped and showy, but they are set apart by their use of archaic lettering, called "tamarind-seed letters." They are comprised of around fifteen leaves or metal plaques and two covers. Nineteenth-century examples are usually made of lacquered cloth, but they could also use lacquered metal, woven bamboo strips, or even ivory. The decoration covered the entire surface, and at the end of the nineteenth century it

Figure 19. Students attending a lecture. Some of them have *parabaiks*. *Parabaik* detail (MA 4806), late 19th century.

Figure 20. Student with a *parabaik* under his arm (MA 4806). *Parabaik* detail, late 19th century.

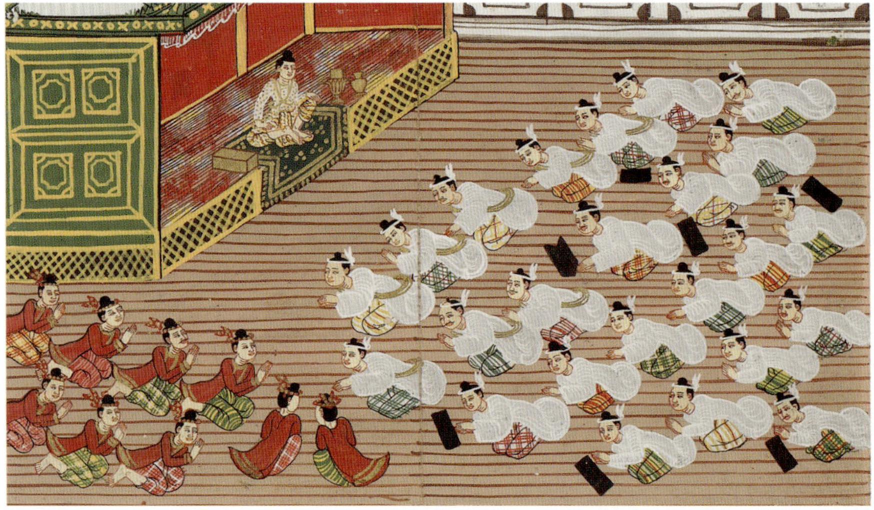

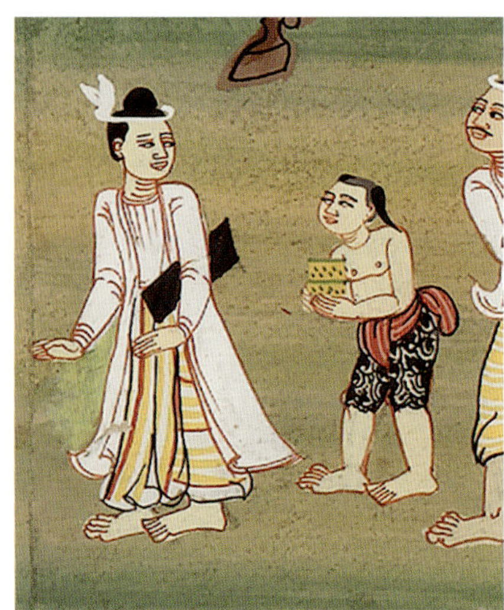

was composed of cinnabar-colored lacquer and gold. The letters used a thick lacquer that resulted in rather large, raised letters written on six lines.

Even though paper was not the main product used in writing, it was far from being unknown. A local artisanal production process still exists today, especially in the Shan states in eastern Burma. The raw material is still used (or was formerly used) in Korea, Japan, and Java to make high-quality paper. The product in question is the bark of the paper mulberry (*Broussonetia papyrifera*), which is native to Burma. It grows to a height of ten to fifteen meters, reaching its maximum height in only seven to eight years. There are no plantations of the trees in Burma; the bark is simply collected in natural forests. The bark is then treated to produce the paper. It is cut up, beaten, boiled with lime and ashes, and then washed. The pulp is then spread out on a cloth frame and dried. The paper obtained by this process is fairly thick and strong, if a little coarse. Paper is also made from bamboo.[2]

The handmade paper is used to make accordion-style books known as *parabaik*s. They keep the long rectangular form of *kammavācā* manuscripts, but they can be folded to open horizontally or vertically and can measure several meters. The thick paper makes it possible to use both sides.

There are three main types of *parabaik*. For the first type, the text is written in black ink with red highlights on paper that retains its natural color, or, for more prestigious texts, paper that is whitened. This whitening treatment is prepared by mixing chalk with the gum of the margosa tree; this is applied and then polished using seeds from a liana vine.

The second type of *parabaik* is coated with a black covering using carbon powder boiled in "rice water" and fish glue, or with leaves of a type of catjang. The black surface is written on using soapstone pencils, making it possible to erase the text and reuse the *parabaik*, much like a slate. The black *parabaik*s were used mainly for practical work: to take note of ephemeral information, to make rough drafts, or for plans, tattoo designs, and so on.

The third type of *parabaik* consists of illustrated manuscripts that can extend to a length of approximately ten meters. These date from the Konbaung period and seem to be exclusively produced in royal ateliers. Even so, they continued to be produced some time after upper Burma was annexed by the British (1886).

*Parabaik*s, especially illustrated ones, were sometimes protected by decorated covers that could be made of stamped leather, carved wood that was lacquered and studded with colored glass, or a raised design made using a mixture of lacquer and other material such as cinders from rice balls or sawdust (the *thayo* technique). The manuscripts could be enclosed in a flexible envelope of canvas reinforced with bamboo slats and covered with another piece of cloth. Luxurious manuscripts were kept in protective coffers that could be of lacquered wood that was sometimes encrusted with colored glass. These coffers could even be placed in cabinets similarly decorated.

One singular production in Burma is woven ribbons that were wrapped around the manuscripts. Designs and texts were woven into the ribbons. The texts were dedicatory formulas, names of donors, extracts of Pāli texts, and so on. Chests and cabinets were used to preserve the manuscripts. Michael Symes saw the royal library in Amarapura in 1797 and reported on the cabinets there.

It was the usual practice to have the entire Pāli canon copied for the king at the beginning of a new reign. Mindon, who reigned from 1853 to 1878, had three copies made, beginning in 1856. One was made using gold lettering on lacquered palm leaves; the second was inscribed on

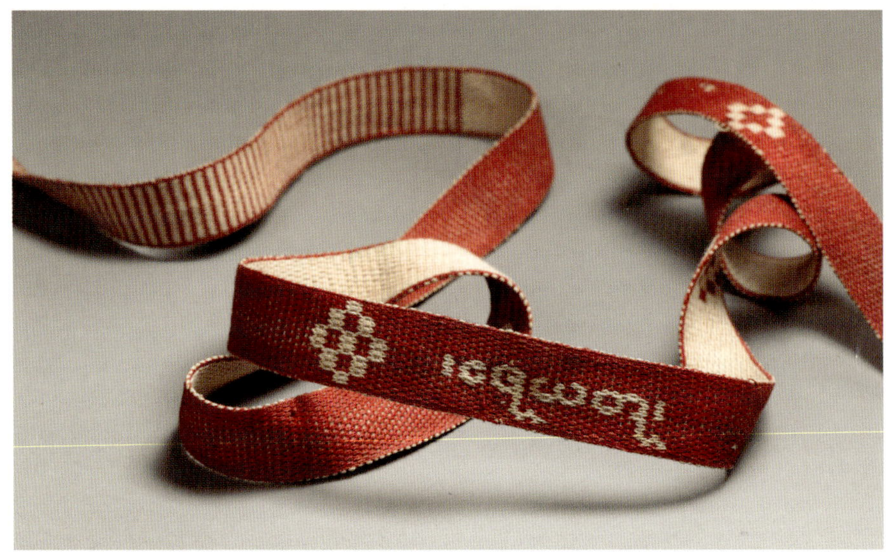

Figure 21. Woven ribbon (စာထုပ်ကြိုး *sā-thup-krī:*), 450 cm, second half of the 19th century. Hand-woven ribbons were used to tie manuscripts after they were wrapped in a cloth. Texts were woven into the ribbons and included the name of the text, the name of the donor of the manuscript, where they lived, their status, and texts in Pāli. The term *sazigyo* (စာစည်ကြိုး) is often used for these ribbons, but that term means a twisted string made smooth by rubbing it with red ochre wax. The string was tied around the middle of the manuscripts to keep the leaves in order. The word visible in the photo is the title, *Jeyatu* (ဇေယတု), "to conquer." The text is about good omens and so on.

plain palm leaves; the third was written on palm leaves using ink. The manuscripts were housed in specially built libraries. The library in Mandalay, which no longer exists, was built between 1857 and 1862, and in 1864 the canonical texts of previous reigns that had been in Amarapura up till then were placed in it.

Manuscripts made of dried palm leaves are vulnerable and subject to deterioration through normal use. This means that palm-leaf manuscripts written before the eighteenth century are very rare. To preserve the texts and to have copies for general use, it was necessary to regularly copy the texts. This desire to preserve the religious texts by having them copied in order to insure their survival was reinforced by the desire to perform a pious action. The texts contained the Buddhist doctrine (*dhamma*, Skt. *dharma*), one of the three jewels alongside the Buddha and the community of monks (*saṅgha*). It was therefore important to preserve the texts. To make doubly sure, the texts were engraved on stone, following the earlier practice. In China, for example, in order to establish an authorized, effective text and to make it public, the classic texts were engraved on stone pillars installed in the center of the capital as early as the Han dynasty (AD 175).

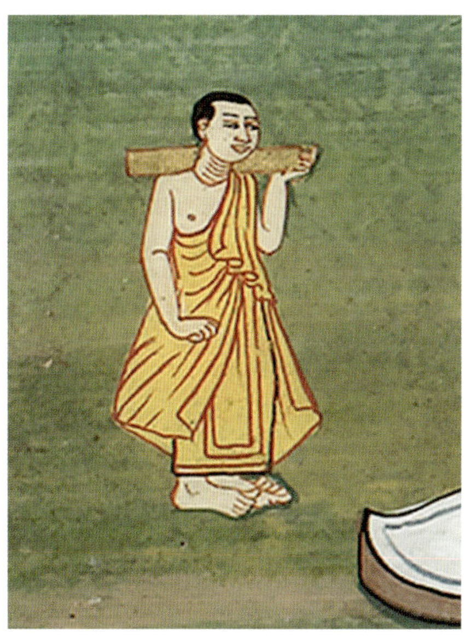

Figure 22. Monk carrying a manuscript on his shoulder. *Parabaik* detail (MA 4807), late 19th century.

The most famous example in Burma was initiated by King Mindon, the founder of Mandalay, in a project that lasted from 1860 to 1868. The Pāli canon (*Tipiṭaka*) and a few paracanonical texts such as the Milindapañha were engraved on 729 marble steles, which were each approximately five feet tall. They are housed in small pagodas arranged in three concentric enclosures around the Mahālokamārajin Ceti, also known as the Kuthodaw Pagoda. The engraved letters were made visible by painting them with gold ink. Inspired by this example, several other projects had texts inscribed on stone; for example, the Pāli commentaries and subcommentaries (*aṭṭhakathās* and *tīkās*) were engraved on stones at the Sandamuni Pagoda beginning in 1913. And in the same spirit, the canon was engraved on wood that was then gilded—texts that are preserved in the Yadana Man Aung Temple in Yawnghwe. The canon was not printed on paper until around 1900 by Philip H. Ripley, the son of an Armenian who was adopted by King Mindon. The tradition of using and writing manuscripts gradually declined, leaving the dissemination of texts—even the most sacred—to the printers.

Notes

1. The first Burmese font was made in Rome in 1776 for the printing of Father Carpani's *Alphbetum Barmanun* and the works of other Catholic missionaries. In Burma itself, printing only began in 1816.
2. Handmade paper is still made using bamboo or rice straw. It is used by gold beaters.

Bibliography

Bollée, W. B. "Some Less Known Burmese Pali Texts." In *Pratidānam*, edited by J. C. Heesterman, G. H. Schokker, V. I. Subramonian, 493–99. The Hague, Paris: Mouton, 1968.

Herbert, Patricia. "Burmese Court Manuscripts." In *The Art of Burma: New Studies*, edited by Donald M. Stadtner, 89–102. Mumbai: Marg, 1999.

———. "Scarlet, Gold, and Black: The Lacquer Traditions of Burma." In *The Art of Burma: New Studies*, edited by Donald M. Stadtner, 103–16. Mumbai: Marg, 1999.

Lowry, John. *Burmese Art.* London: H. M. Stationery Office, 1974.

Maung Wun. "Notes on Burmese Manuscript Books." *Journal of the Burma Research Society* 33, no. 2 (1950): 224–29.

Quigly, Elizabeth Pauline. *Some Observations on Libraries, Manuscripts and Books of Burma, from the 3rd Century A.D. to 1886, with special reference to the Royal Library of the last Kings of Burma; with pen sketches by the Author*. Foreword by Than Tun. London: Arthur Probsthain, 1956.

Singer, Noel F. "Kammavaca Texts: Their Covers and Binding Ribbons." *Arts of Asia* 23, no. 3 (1993): 97–106.

———. "Palm Leaf Manuscripts of Myanmar (Burma)." *Arts of Asia* 21, no. 1 (1991): 133–40.

Singer, Noel F. "The Peimpathara Parabaik." *Arts of Asia* 18, no. 6 (1998): 128–37.

U Thaw Kaung. "Myanmar traditional Manuscripts and their Preservation and Conservation." In *Selected Writings of U Thaw Kaung*, 255–88. Yangon: Myanmar Historical Commission, 2004.

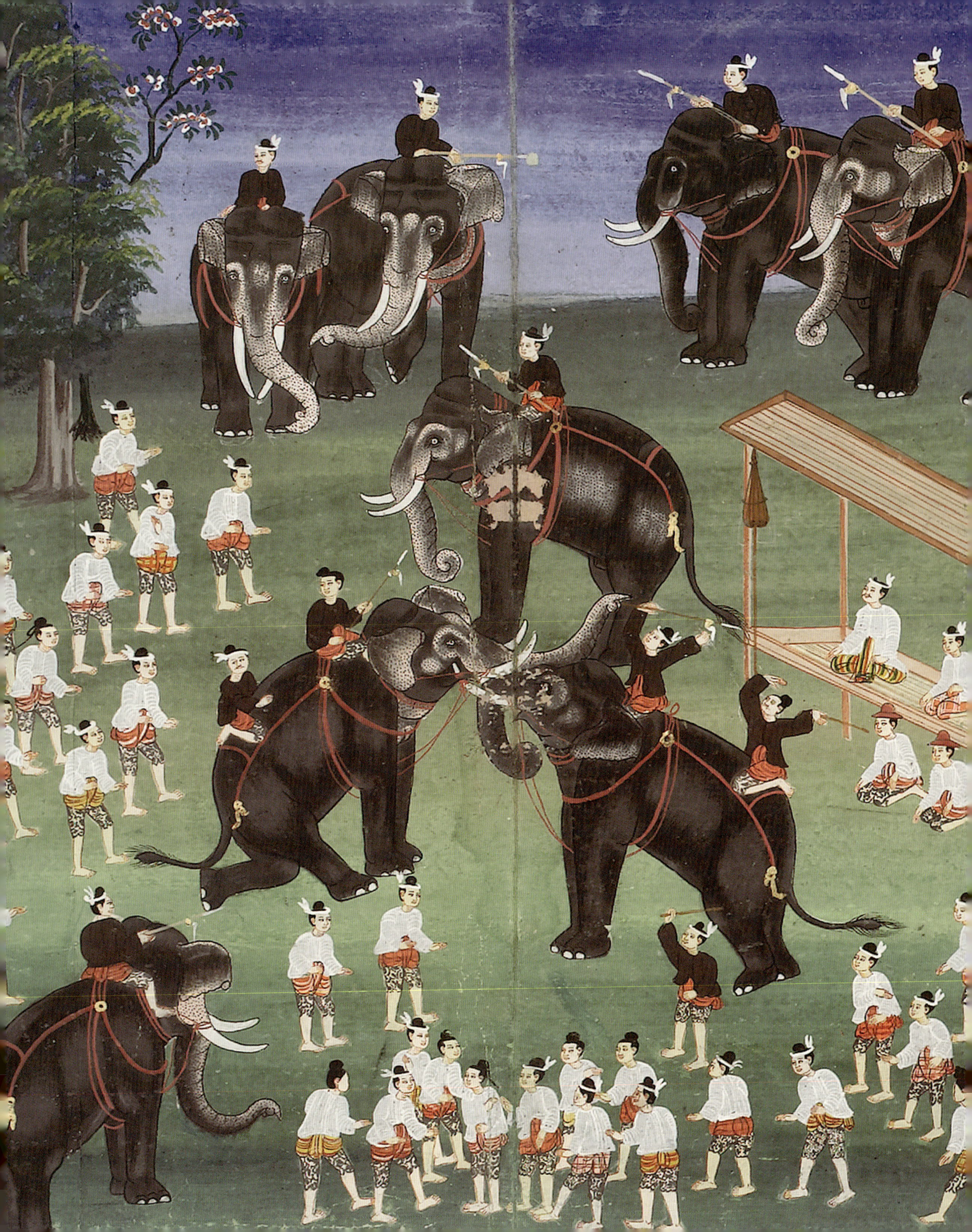

THE PAGEANTRY OF A VANISHED KINGDOM: *The Collection of Parabaiks in the Musée Guimet*

Pierre Baptiste
Senior Curator, Southeast Asian collections, Musée Guimet

Figure 23. Training elephants to fight (MA 1661).

THE frenetic conquests of the first Burmese monarch of the Konbaung dynasty (1752–1885) added to the prestige of a court that was established in the plains of the Irrawaddy valley around the present-day cities of Sagaing and Mandalay, as did the various types of foreign influence that flourished there and insured the development of a highly refined culture. The founder of the dynasty, King Alaungpaya (1714–60), set up an impressive policy of expanding his rule that led to the Burmese army attacking Ayutthaya in Siam (Thailand), but it was there he met his death. It was his son, his second successor, Hsinbyushin (1736–96), who managed to sack and reduce to ashes the prestigious Thai capital in 1767. The capture of a city that ranked among the most brilliant in Southeast Asia had an undeniable influence on the Burmese court—not only because of the prestige that came from such a conquest but also with respect to Thai arts, which were at their height and which contributed to the flourishing of Burmese arts. At the same time, through victories in the north over the Chinese, Hsinbyushin established a peace treaty with Emperor Qianlong (r. 1736–95), a treaty that was signed by his generals in 1770.

On the western front, unfortunately, the same push to expand the rule of the peacock throne towards the Indian kingdom of Manipur came up against British interests in the region and led to the Anglo-Burmese wars a half century later, wars instigated by the powerful East India Company, which had already managed to annex all of India. King Bagyidaw (1784–1846) suffered the first defeat at the hands of the English in 1826. It was a defeat he never got over because he knew, perhaps, that it was irreversible. Indeed, his successors could only watch their empire decline, unable to do anything about it.

The Anglo-Burmese wars (1824–85) rang the death knell of the dynasty, which ended in 1885 when English troops entered Mandalay. King Thibaw (1859–1916), the last Burmese king, surrendered and was exiled to Ratnagiri, near Mumbai, India. The plundering of the British army, the long neglect of the colonial authorities before the Archaeological Survey of India took over preserving the country's heritage, and bombing during the Second World War did not spare the last royal capitals of Burma, cities where many civil and religious monuments were concentrated in the second half of the nineteenth century. Sagaing, Ava, Amarapura, and Mandalay had each in turn been the principle residence of the Burmese kings of the Konbaung dynasty, and many monasteries surrounded enormous royal palaces where the pageants of the court had retained all their brilliance, up until the time that the British ended it all.

It is therefore especially precious to have preserved here and there some of the manuscripts containing Burmese art in the form of miniatures painted in vivid colors and showing many of the aspects of the festivals of that epoch. In these *parabaik*s, the pages, which are folded in accordion style, include colorful description of religious ceremonies, festivals, hunting, parades, and audiences that marked the life of the court and the inhabitants of the capital during the time of King Thibaw (r. 1879–1885). Slowly turning the panels of thick paper made from tree-bark pulp, we can dream of the palaces and temples that have disappeared but are shown here in great detail—in places shown in relief through the use of gouache and gold leaf. Moreover, we can think of these delicate, anonymous people whose clothes and gestures are distinct, depending on the rank or the role played by each of them, reflecting a society that had a harmonious and clearly controlled hierarchy. We know that the Konbaung court carefully oversaw all aspects of social life, and many Western travelers in the eighteenth and nineteenth centuries were astonished by the profusion of sumptuary laws laid down by the Burmese kings to regulate in very fine detail the position of each person in society and the privileges they were granted or refused. For example, there are illustrated treatises giving in great detail the clothes to be worn by courtiers as well as the humblest individual, for whom any ostentation was forbidden. All of society was centered on the king, who ruled over it with the aid of his close family members and an aristocracy whose lineage was strictly recorded in the documents in the royal archives.

The Guimet Museum has the good fortune to possess a few examples of these very rare illustrated manuscripts that are difficult to preserve in Burma due to the humid climate and voracious insects. Some of them were acquired in the 1950s (MA 565 in 1949, MA 1661 in 1955); the details of how they came to France are not known. Others were donated more recently (in 1979) by the Bonvillain family (numbers MA 4806 to 4813) in memory of Philibert Bonvillain (1852–1916), a French engineer who resided in Mandalay between 1875 and 1885. These manuscripts were offered to the engineer by King Thibaw because of the close ties he made in the court in connection with the projects he supervised. These included setting up an iron foundry, building a royal residence in Western style, a steam ship, and a railroad—projects he supervised from Mandalay, having learned Burmese. He was preparing a Burmese grammar and dictionary. We know that two of the illustrated manuscripts (MA 4806 and 4807), which he brought back to France after evading the English invasion, were made by one of the king's artists.

Parabaik MA 4806 has a beautiful cover (fig. 25) made of lacquered paper with high reliefs of animated figures that are probably from the Rāmāyaṇa and which are enclosed in garlands of leaves. Inside the manuscript, there are eighteen scenes in yellow borders in portrait format with the

Next page, from top:

Figure 24. *Parabaik* MA 4806, folded.

Figure 25. Lacquered covers of *parabaik* MA 4806.

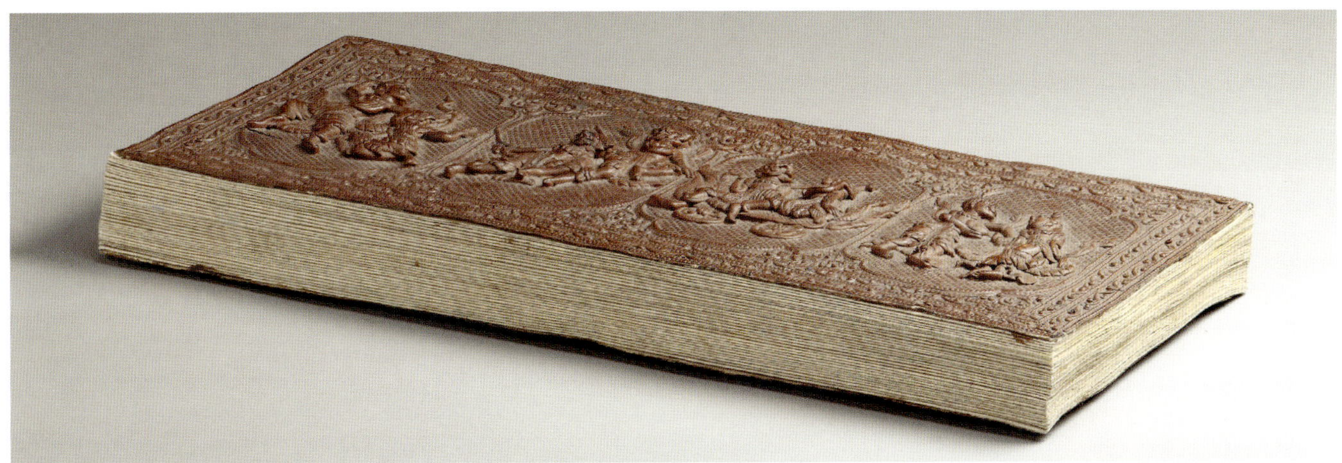

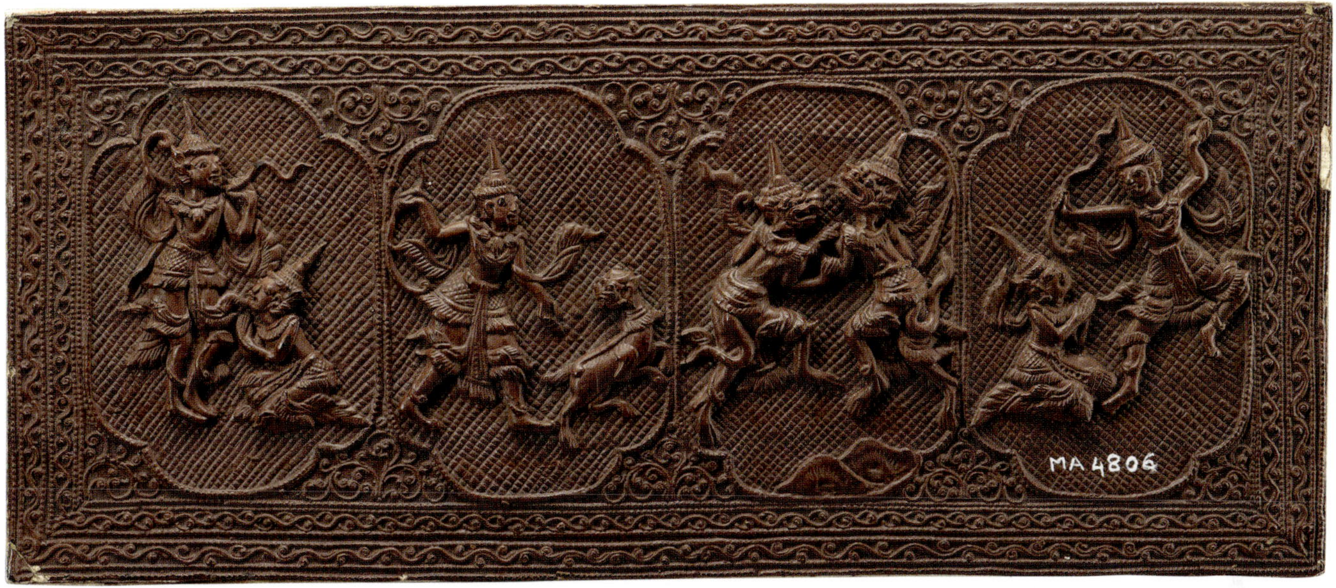
MA 4806

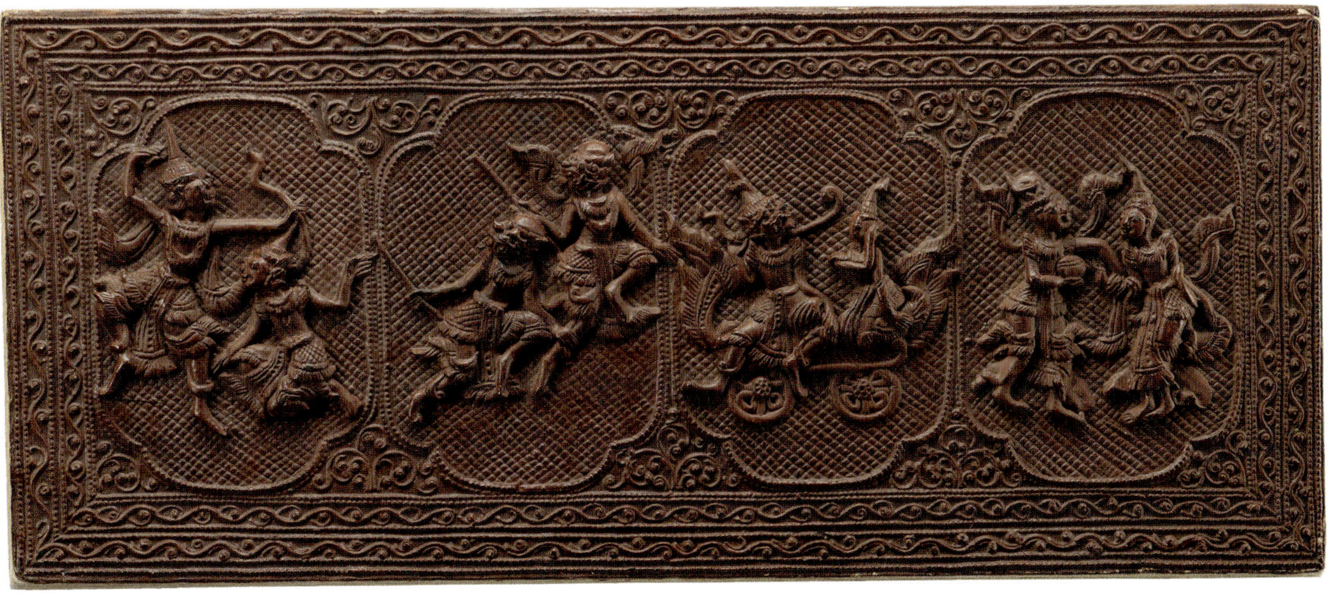

scenes taking two, four, six, or eight leaves. The first scene (fig. 26) shows an assembly for a "monk's festival" (according to the title); it seems to correspond to funeral rites for the head of a monastery, judging from the pageantry that is depicted. The catafalque is highly decorated, with receding pinnacles and with a *kinnara* and *kinnarī* (beings who are half-human, half-bird) on either side. It is set off by posts holding up the canopy inside the enclosure for the cremation. Chariots used in the procession are close by, near the guardian's tent. Exceptionally, cremations of this type, organized long after the death of the head monk, were occasions when the entire community could participate in the festivities.

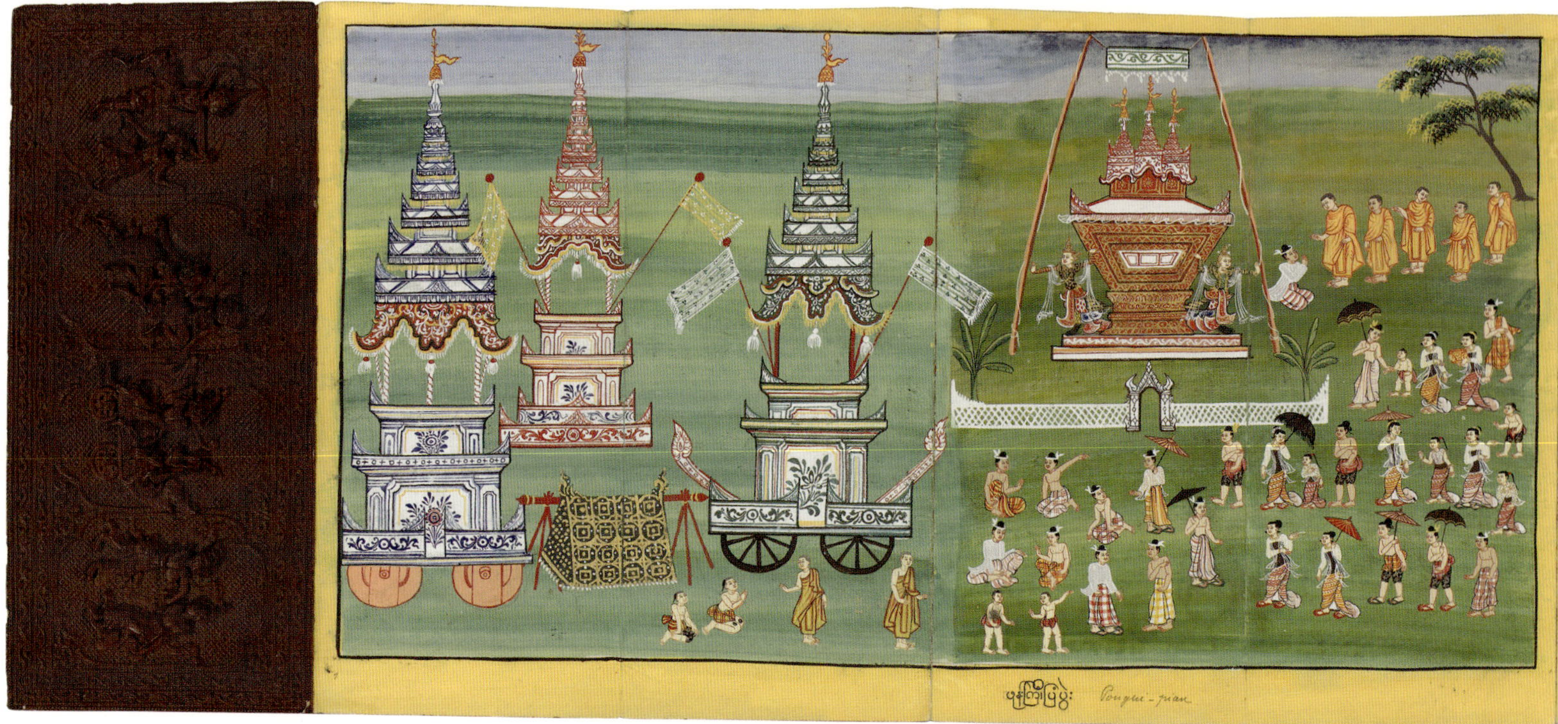

Figure 26. Funeral of a monk.

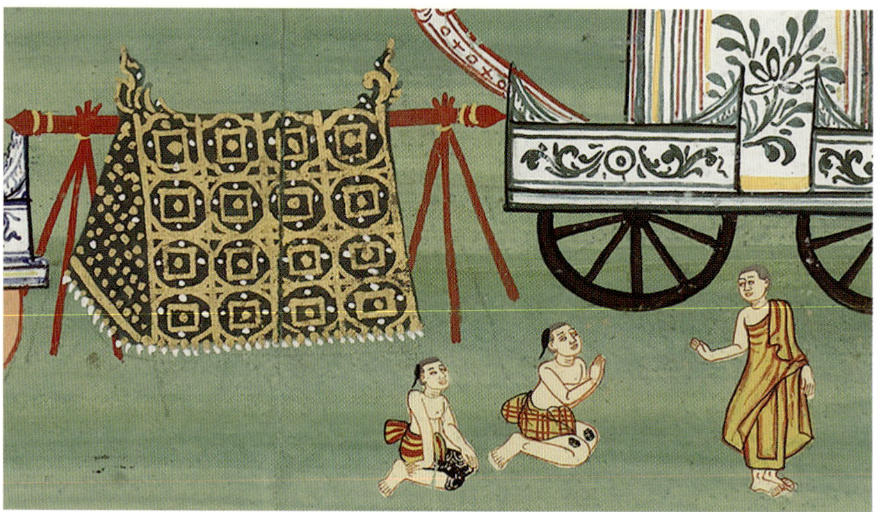

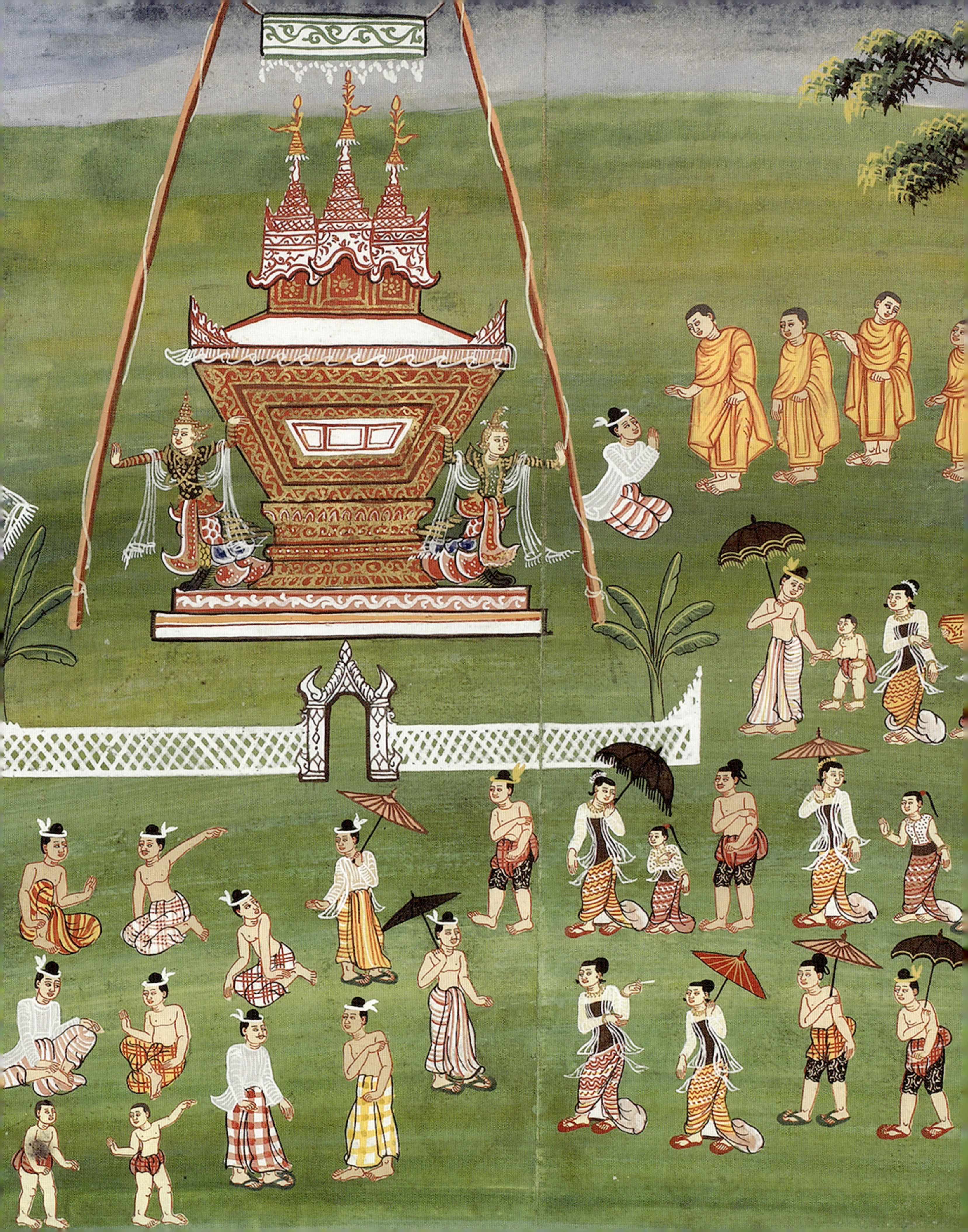

The second scene (fig. 27), which takes up eight leaves, shows the royal "water festival with a regatta." This took place at the time of the Burmese New Year (Thingyan) in the month of April. There was a great celebration when the royal barge and the boats of all the various groups went down the river. Spectators are shown along the riverbank enjoying the procession and the nautical games.

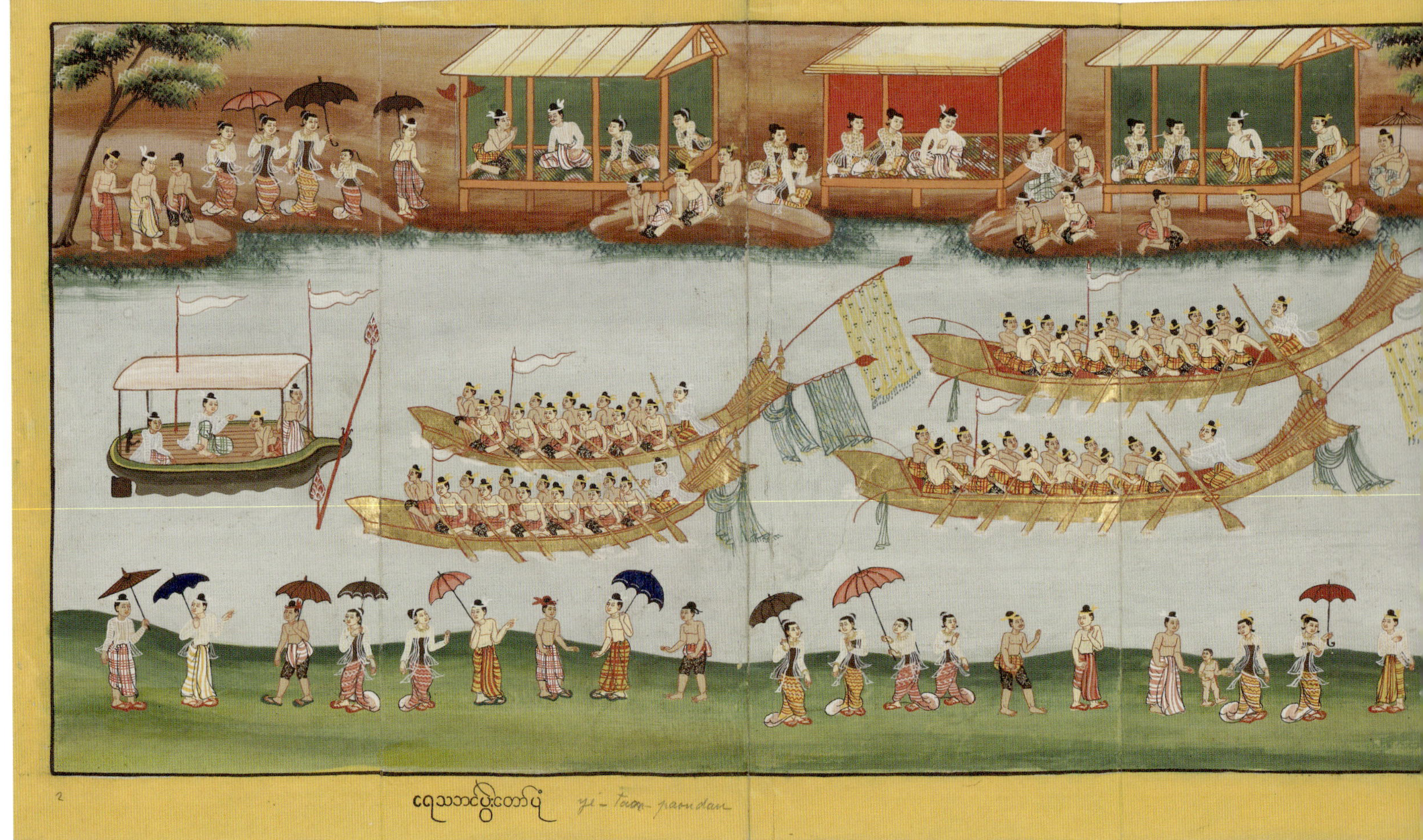

Figure 27. Royal water festival.

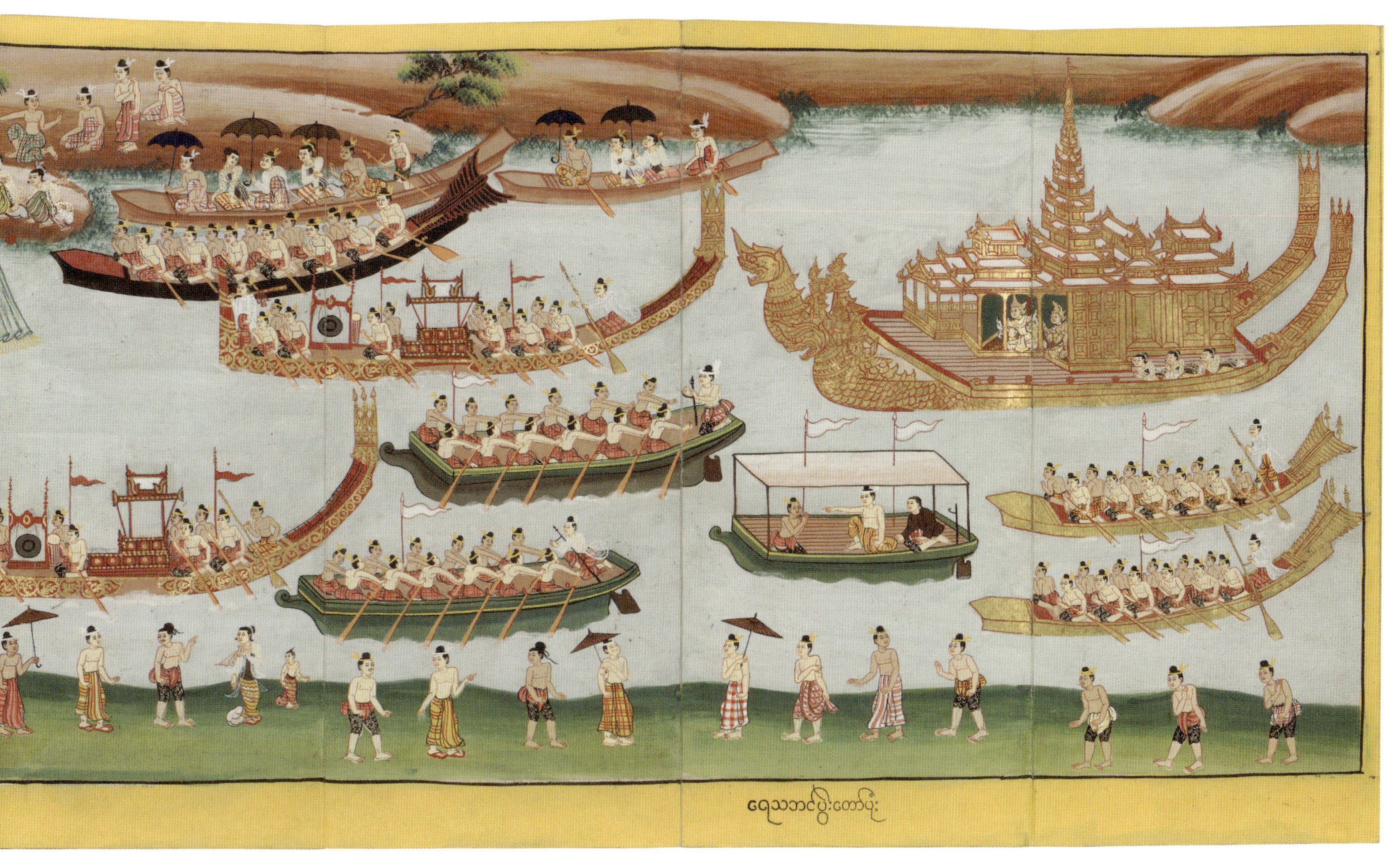
ရေသဘင်ပွဲတော်မိုး

Another type of entertainment is illustrated in the third scene (fig. 28), which is described as showing the "spectacle of the Inaung play," a theatrical play that incorporates song, dance, and comedy interludes. It came to Burma from Thailand, and the Burmese adapted it into their own tradition at the end of the eighteenth century. The king and queen, protected from the sun in a pavilion, watch the play outside with the courtiers seated on either side. In front of the actors seated on chairs, a cockfight is being held.

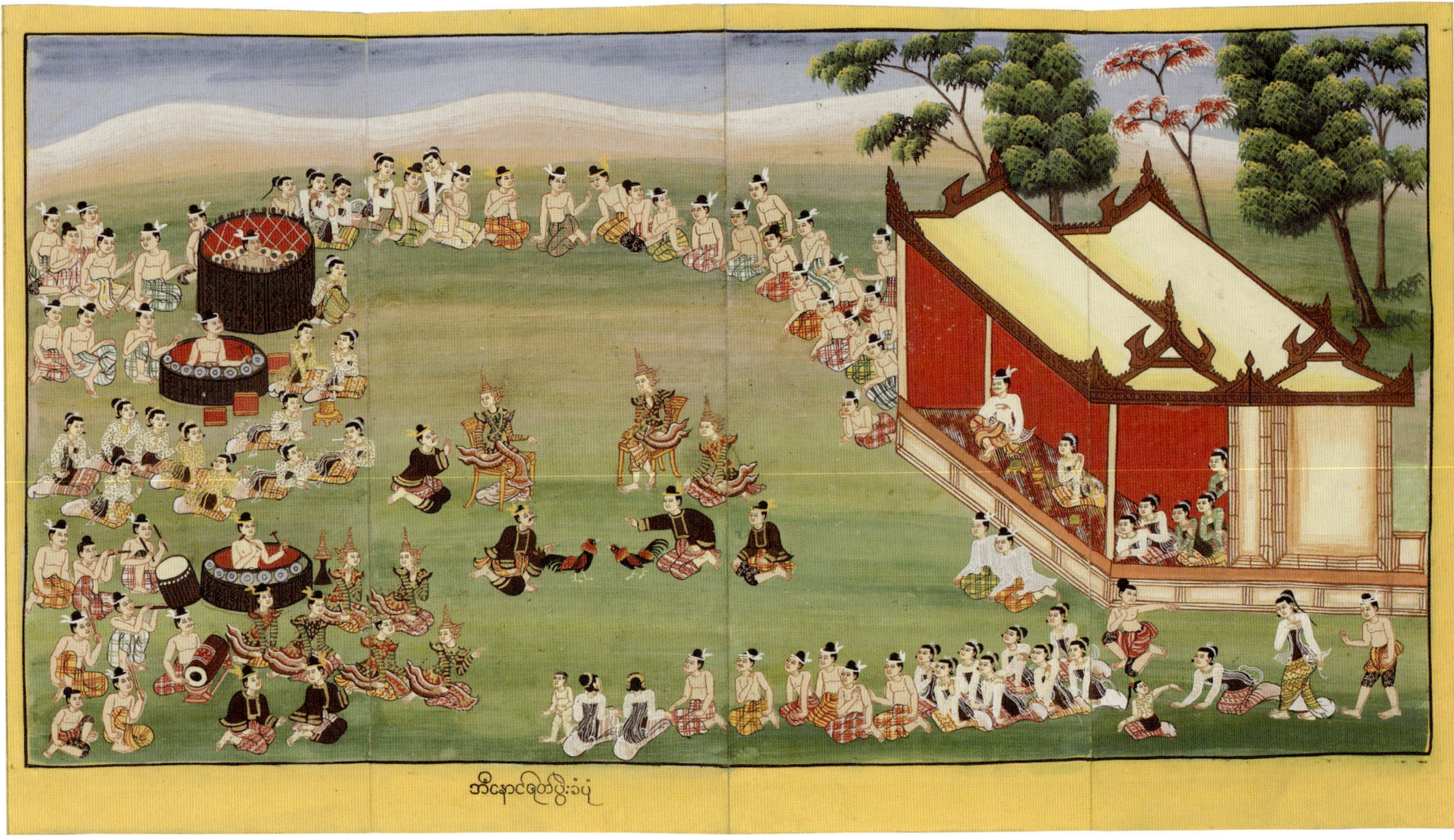

Figure 28. *Inaung* performance.

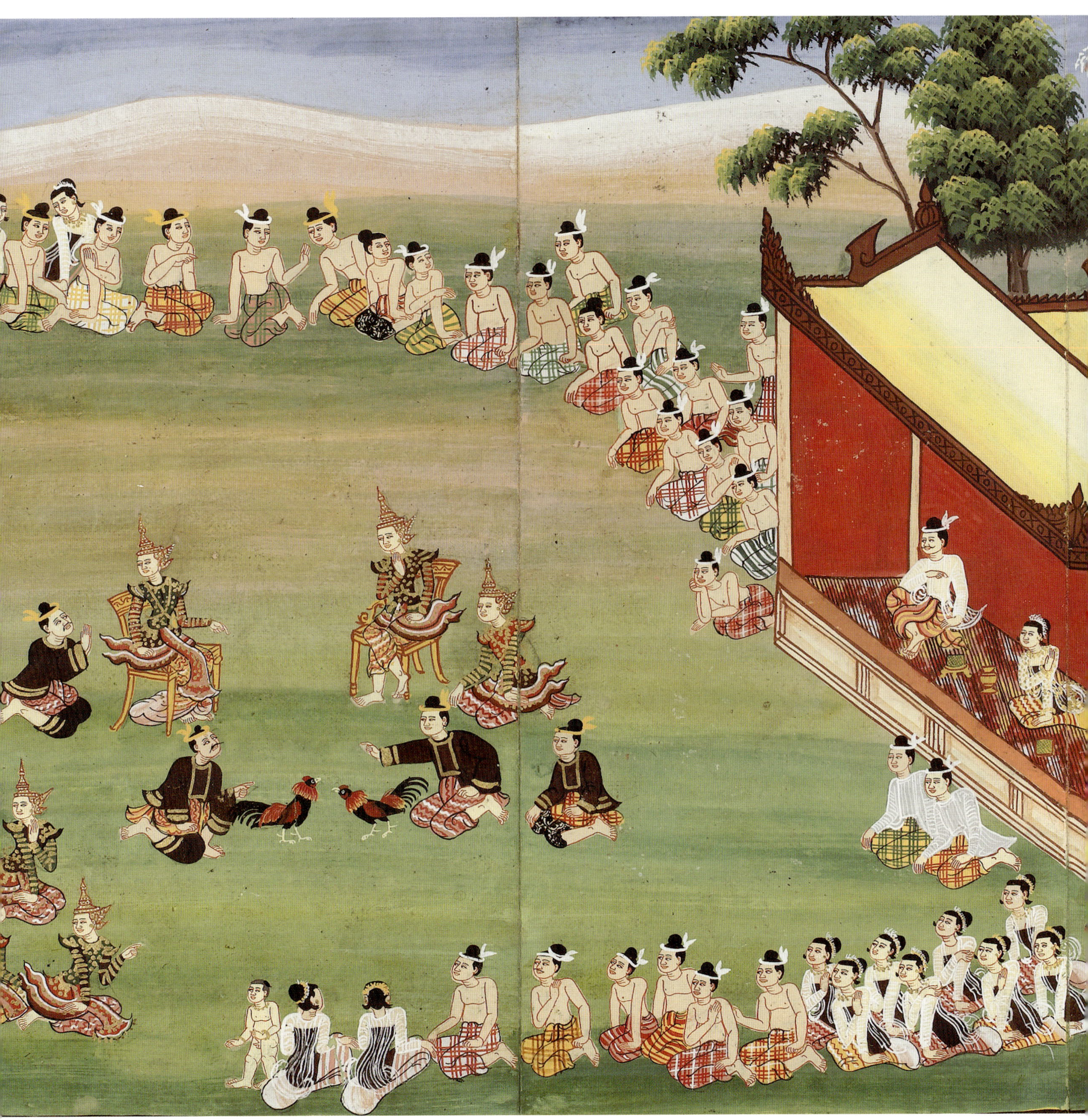

The next four leaves (fig. 29), captioned "entry of the elephants in the training enclosure," show in minute detail the structure of brick and wood. It no longer exists today, but similar enclosures can be still seen in Thailand, especially in the former capital, Ayutthaya, which was sacked by the Burmese. Elephants are also the subject of the next scene (fig. 30). Here they are seen being trained for combat in the countryside. The Burmese army was well known for the efficient use of elephants, which made a major contribution to the success of the conquests of Alaungpaya and Hsinbyushin.

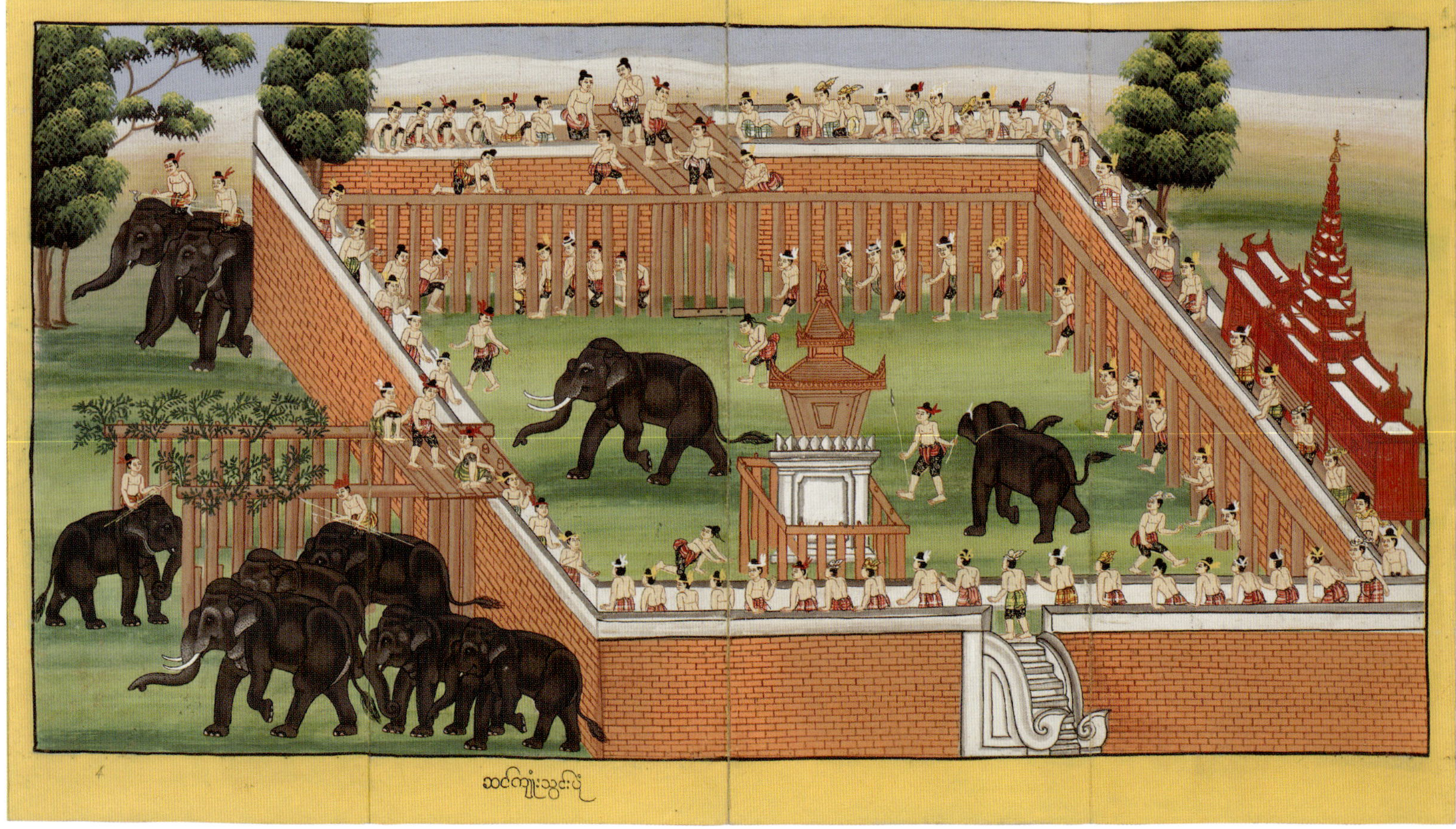

Figure 29. Enclosure for training elephants.

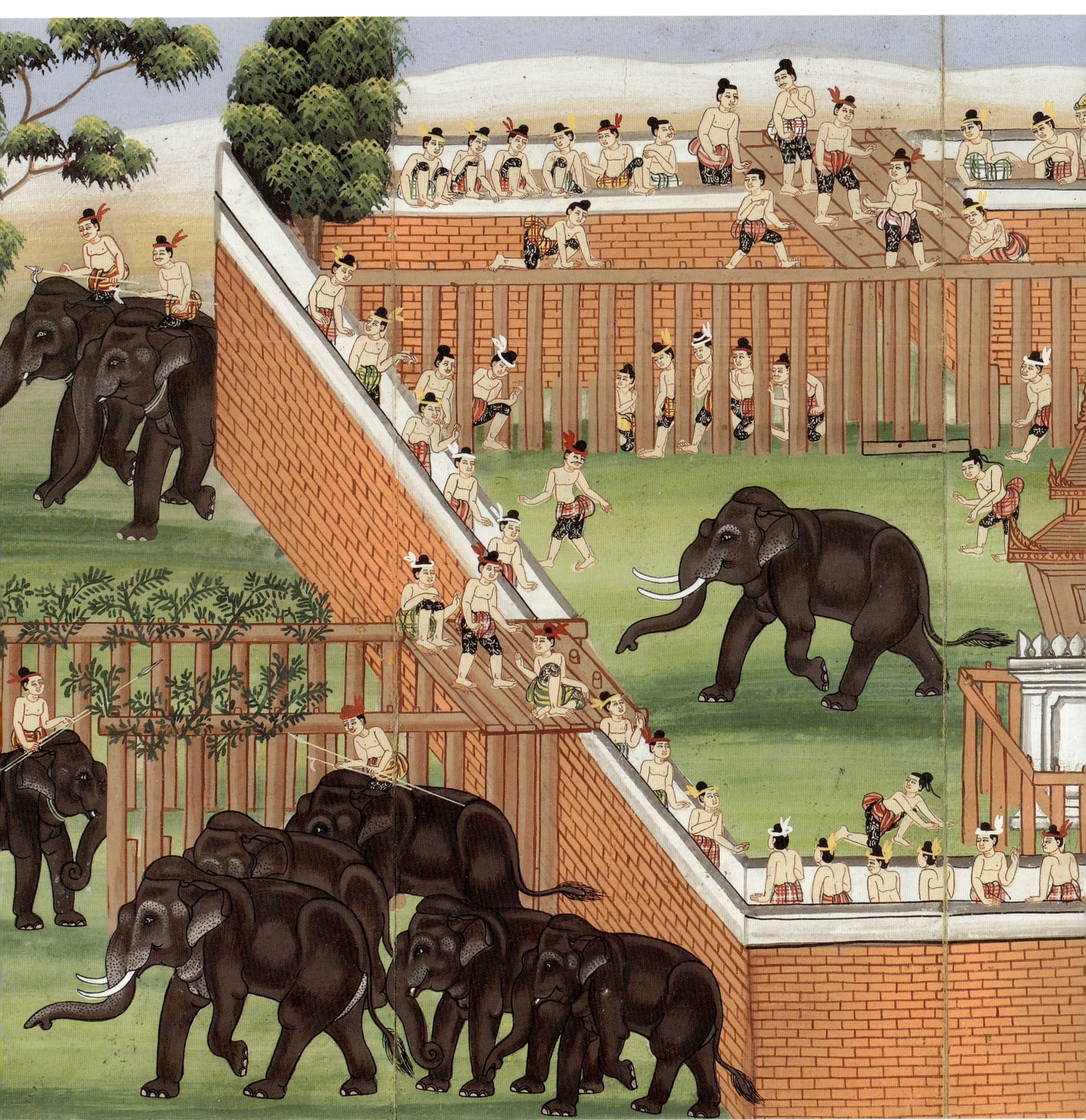

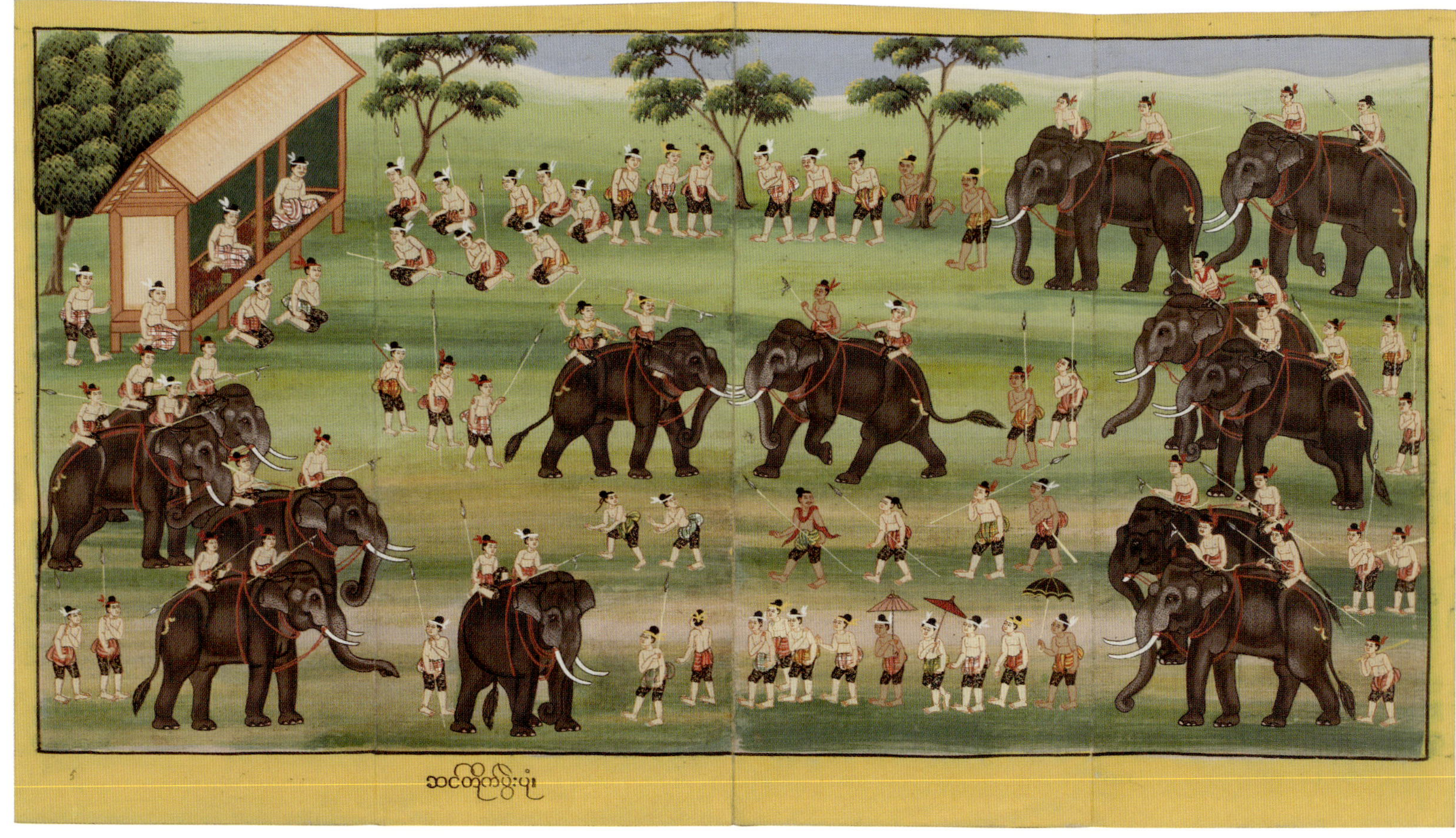

Figure 30. Training elephants in the countryside.

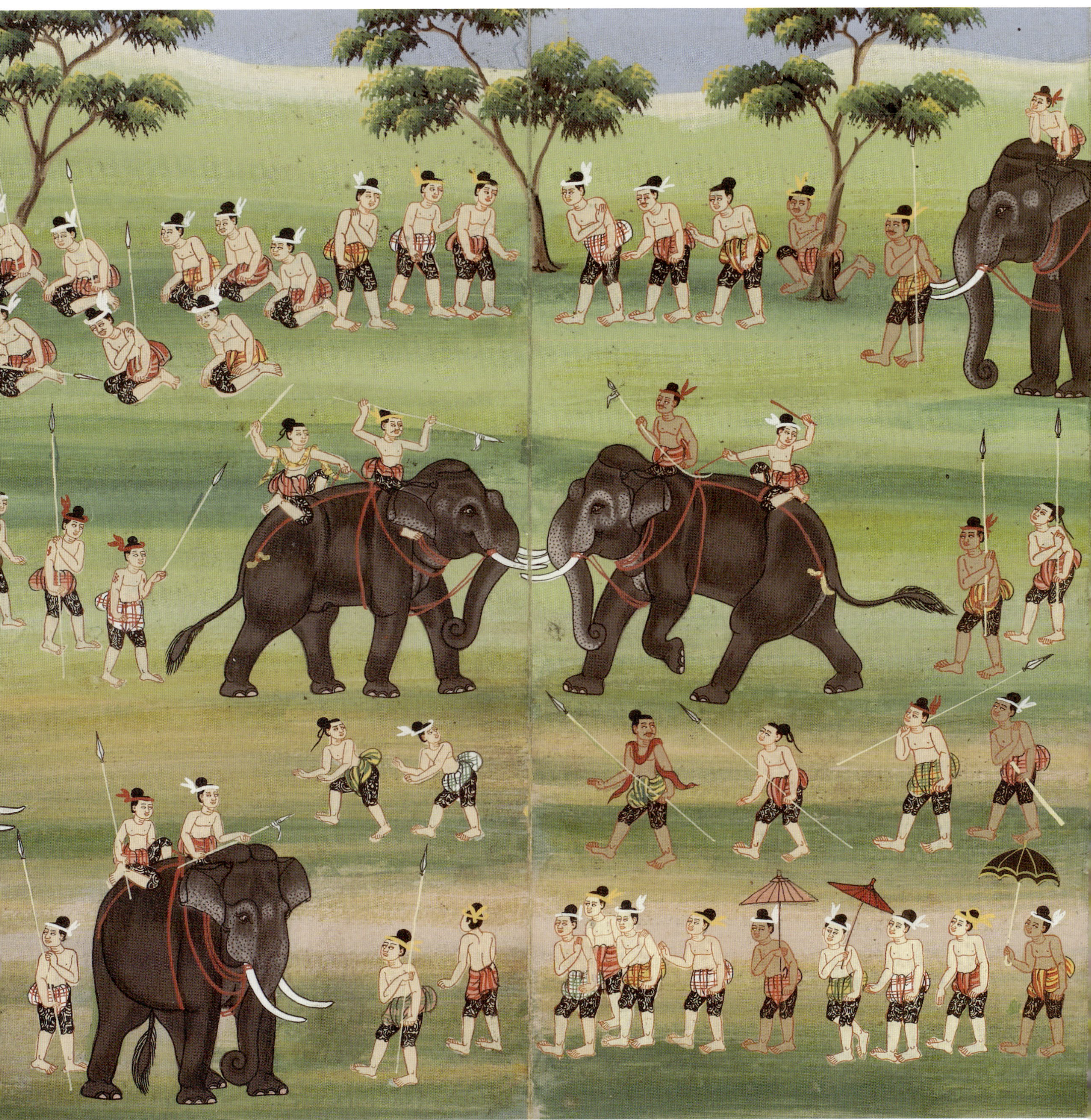

In the next scene (fig. 31), a pagoda festival (*paya pwe*) is shown. These are held in conjunction with a religious anniversary and include shows with dance, theater, and music concerts given outside; they resemble a festival and a country fair combined. In the scene in the *parabaik*, the beginning of the *pwe* is shown—the moment when everyone gathers together and takes offerings to the monastery.

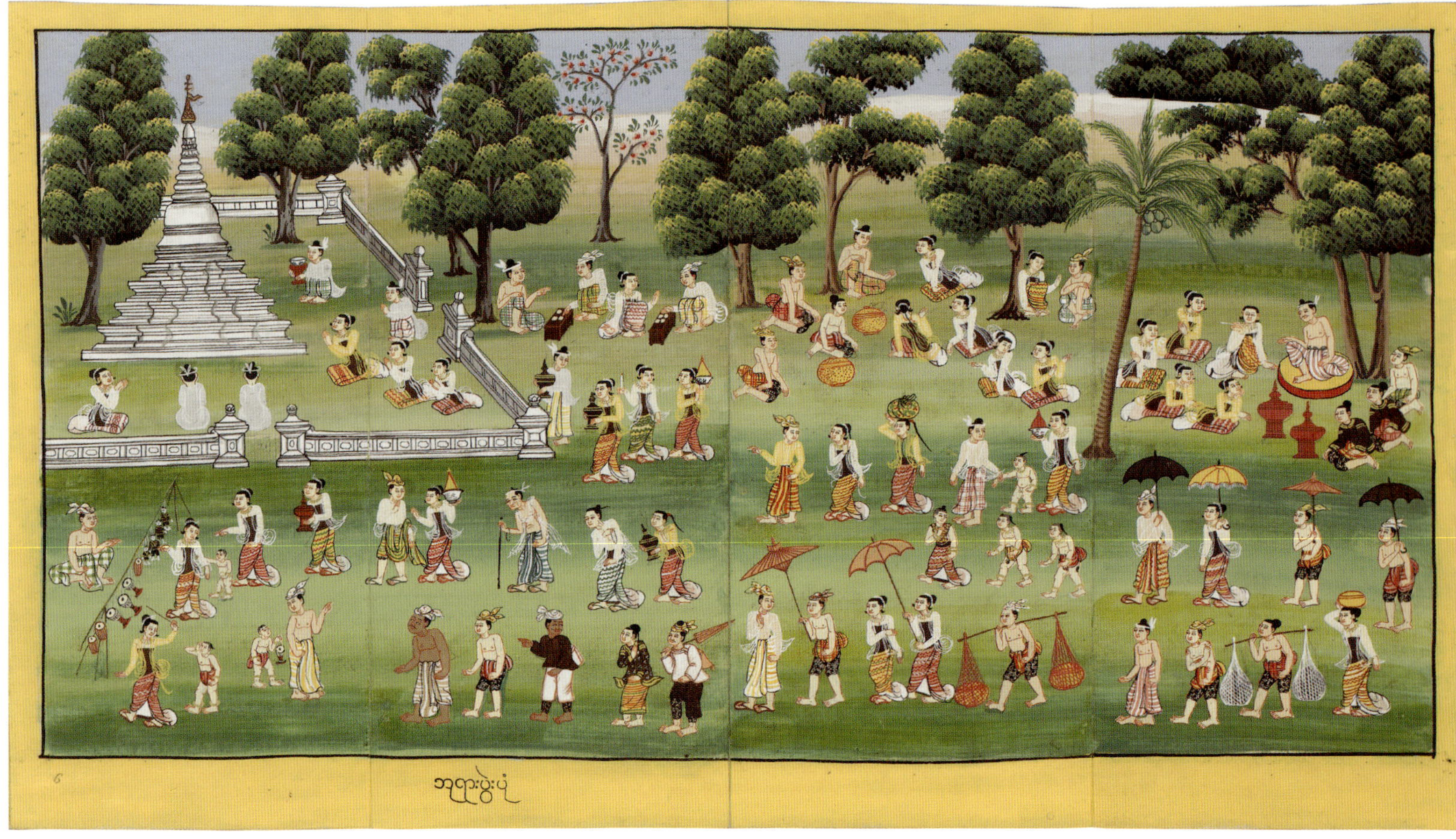

Figure 31. Gathering at the start of a pagoda festival.

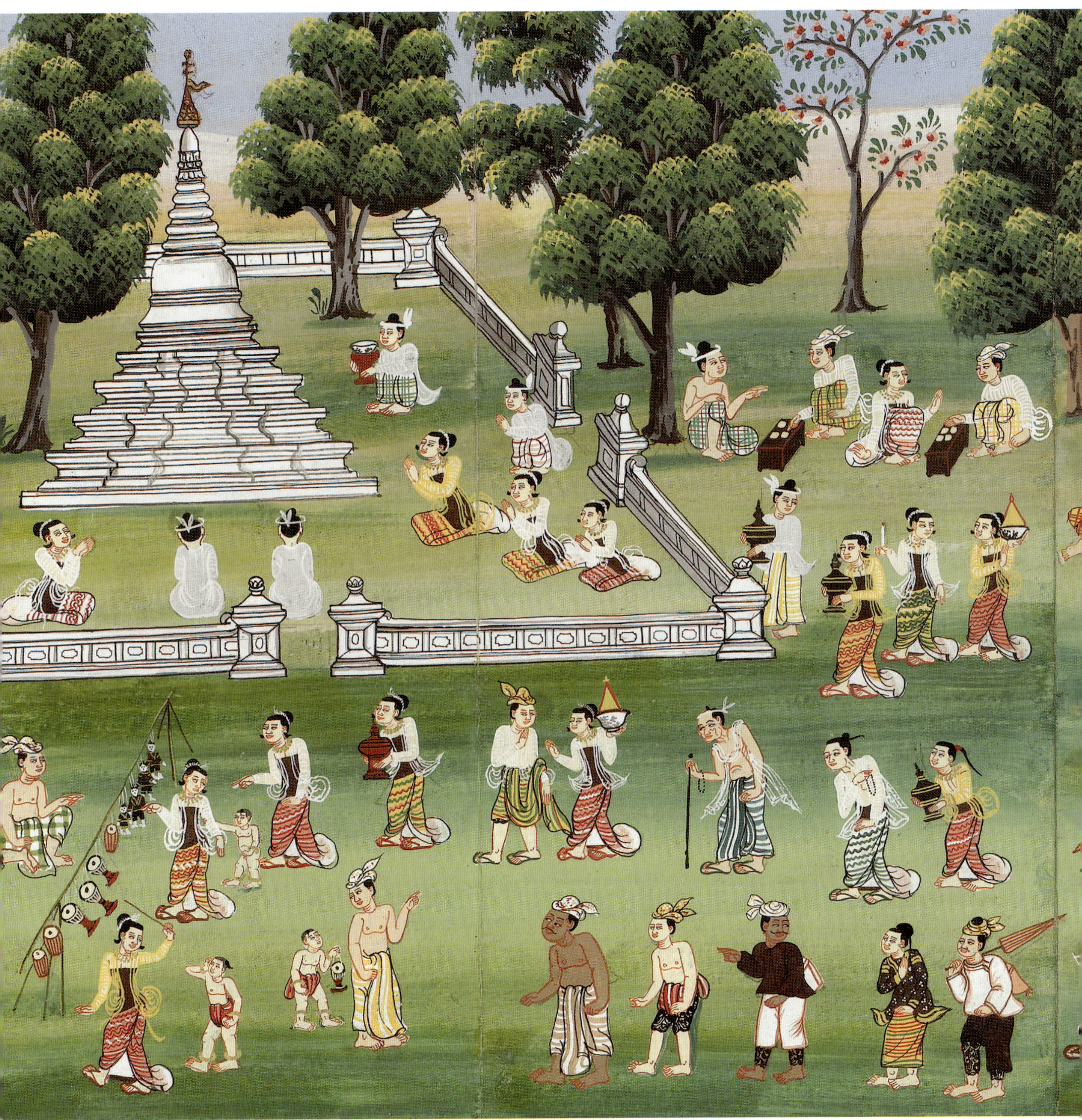

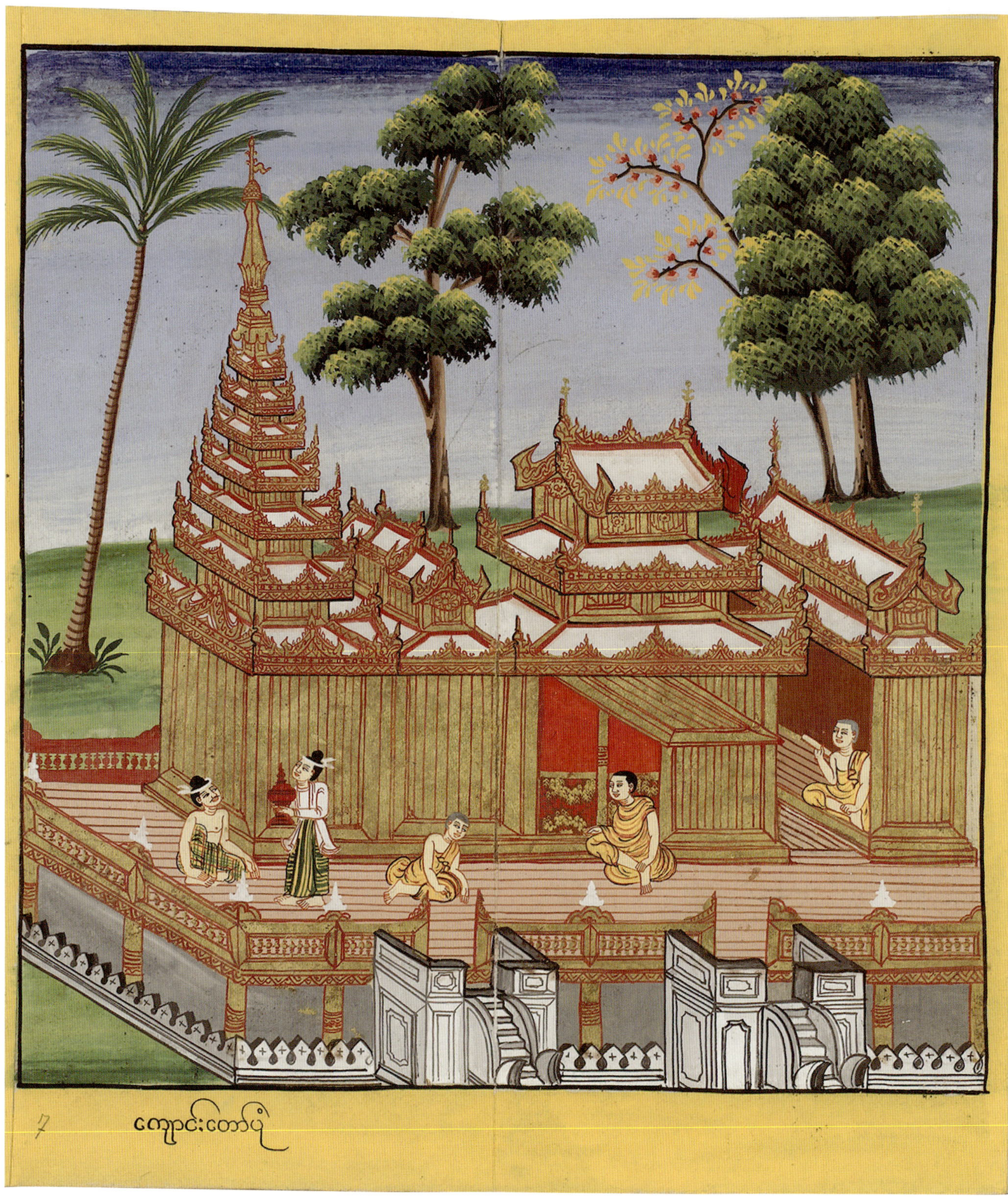

Figure 32. Lay people with offerings for the head of a temple.

The following scene (fig. 32) shows a "royal temple" (*kyaung daw*) where lay people are coming with offerings for the head of the monastery. The scene is shown in fine detail, but it is reduced in size in order to include everything. This is a type of scene that is typical of the Mandalay period, and the Guimet manuscript is a fine example.

Like elephants, horses were also important for the prestige and effectiveness of the Burmese army. They are depicted in the next two scenes. In the first one (fig. 33), we see horses being exercised. In the second scene (fig. 34), we see a polo festival (*bali yeik pwe*), a festival that existed before the British invasion and which probably goes back to the eighth century, introduced through the contact between Sassanian Iran and the Tang dynasty (AD 618–907).

Figure 33. Cavalry exercises.

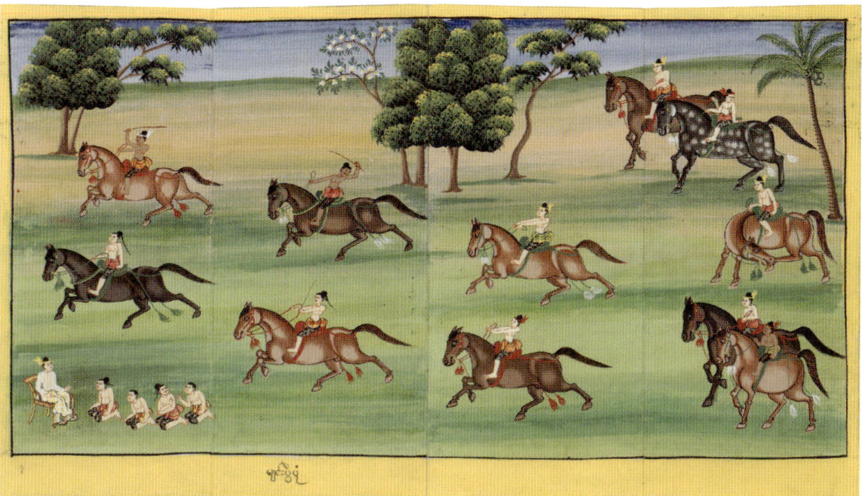

Figure 34. Polo festival.

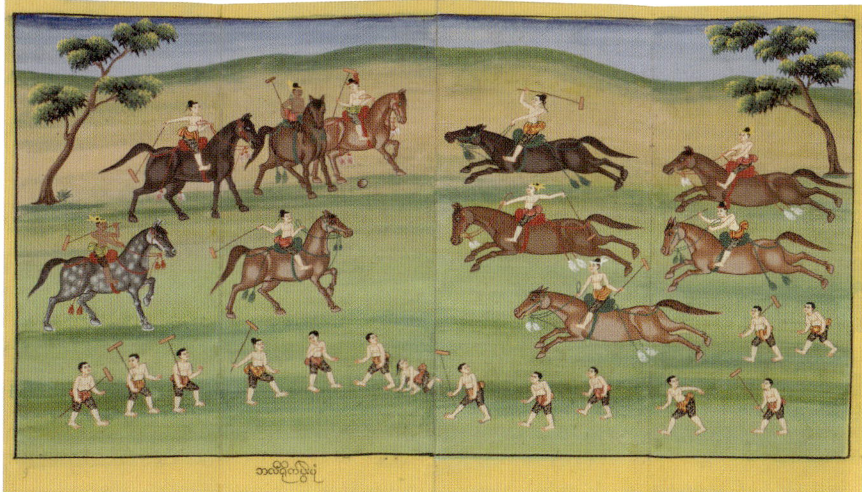

An "audience of ministers and officers at the court" is shown in the next four leaves (fig. 35). This is a modest example of the royal pomp in the palace when the king and queen, dressed in shining attire, presided over the court, seated on elevated thrones resembling pedestals and looking like inaccessible idols. Photographs of the throne room in the Mandalay palace were taken before it was destroyed in the Second World War. It was a vast room opening to the east with a large terrace where the ministers (seen in the manuscript on the right, facing north) and the officers (on their knees and in a symmetrical formation in front of the south aisle) gathered. The throne room can be recognized by the high tower with tiered spires, flanked by two long wings with columns and covered by richly decorated, gilded roofs adorned with stylized peacocks. The scene in the manuscript only shows characteristic aspects of the throne room, which is lit by large cut-glass chandeliers that were imported from India and that show the ever-increasing influence of the East India Company in this part of Southeast Asia. It obviously impressed the artist who painted these images.

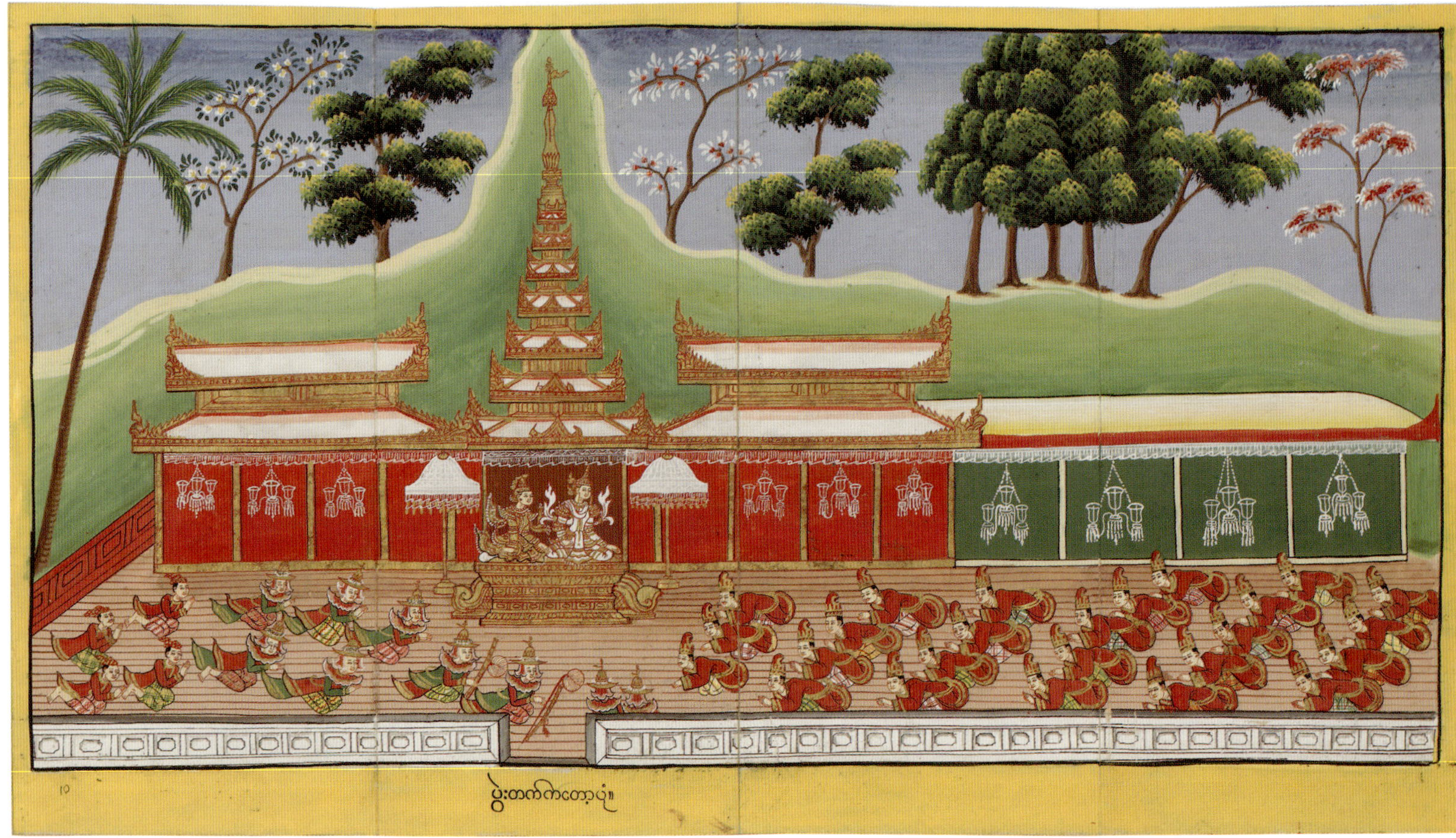

Figure 35. An audience before the king and queen.

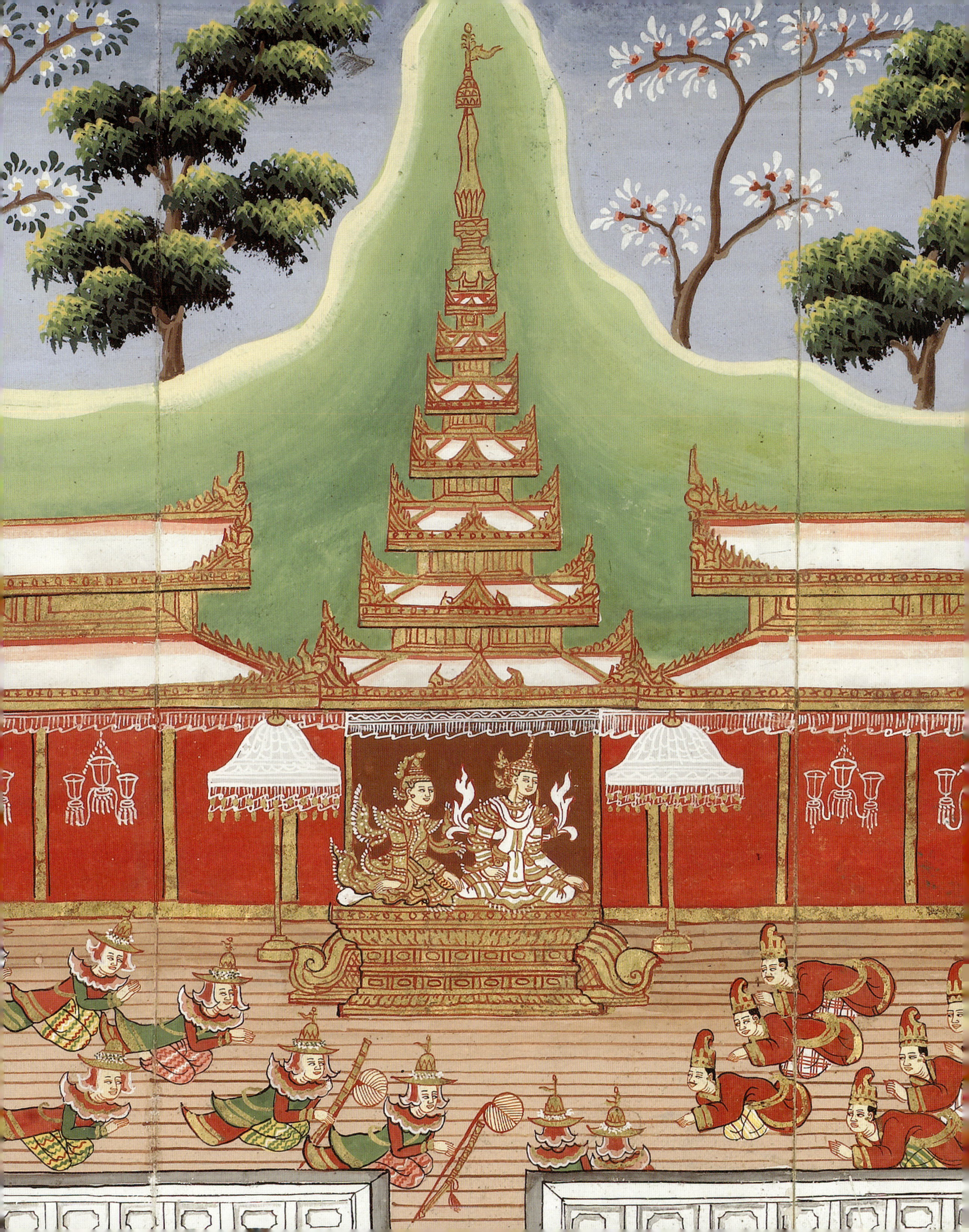

The last eight scenes, which take up twenty-six leaves, depict the life of the court officials and their training. Figure 36 shows a "military school," where the students are using their schoolbooks, which are black *parabaiks*. In figure 37, a "prince and his guard" seem to accompany a student (perhaps the son of a noble) whose white clothes and *parabaiks* are identical to those of young would-be students. The next scene (fig. 38) is more developed and shows "naval school maneuvers" under the watchful eye of the king, who is dressed in a uniform and seated in a sumptuous royal barge, shown here in great detail. The barge was preserved in the palace moats long after the king was exiled, no longer of any use. Then comes the "transfer of the entire royal school" (fig. 39). The king participates in the event, enthroned on a rich palanquin and accompaniedbyhisminsters,officers,andthecavalry,andtheyarefollowed by figure 40, which shows "the arrival of a minister" with his rich retinue. The last scenes are less formal, showing "archers practicing" (fig. 41), "cavalry training with javelins" (fig. 42), and ending quite logically with a court ceremony where the army swears allegiance (fig. 43), and they are seen "going to the beach to dig for water."

Figure 36. Military school.

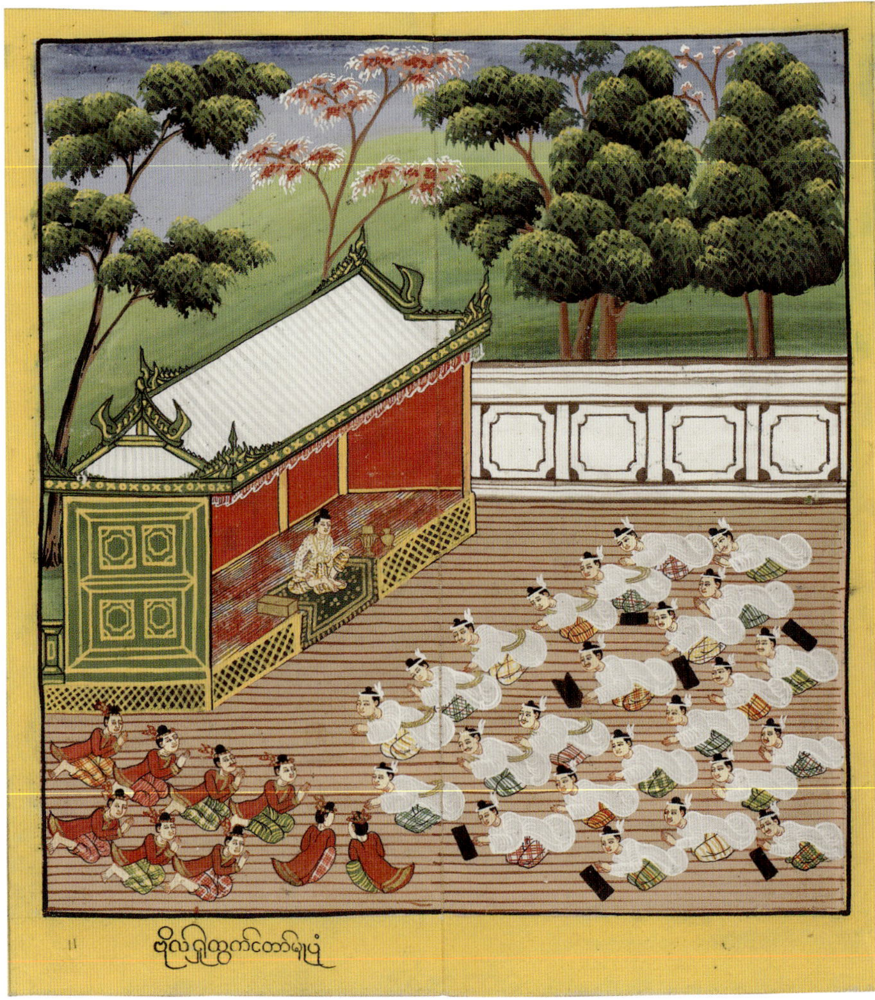

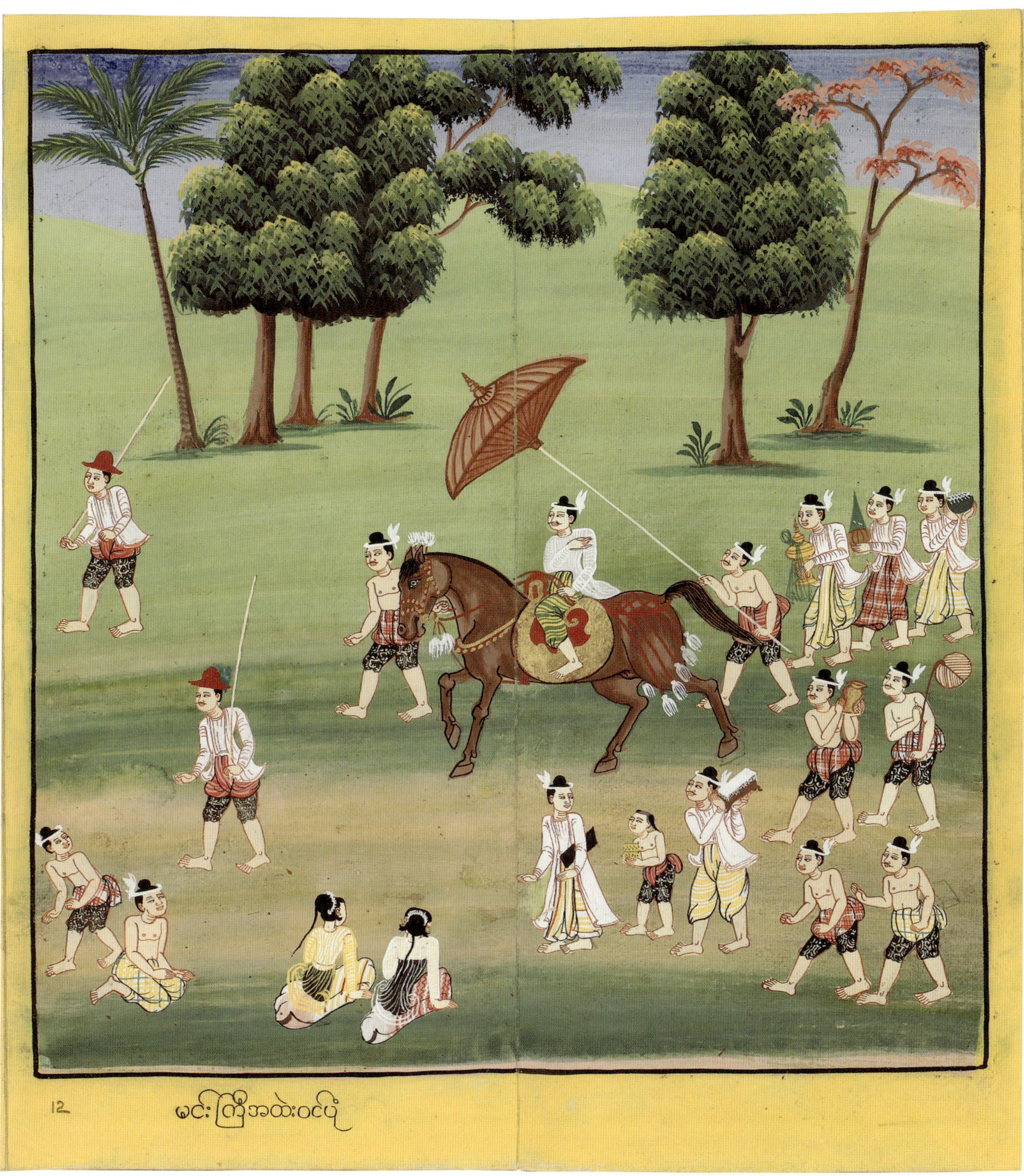

Figure 37. A prince and his guard accompanying a student.

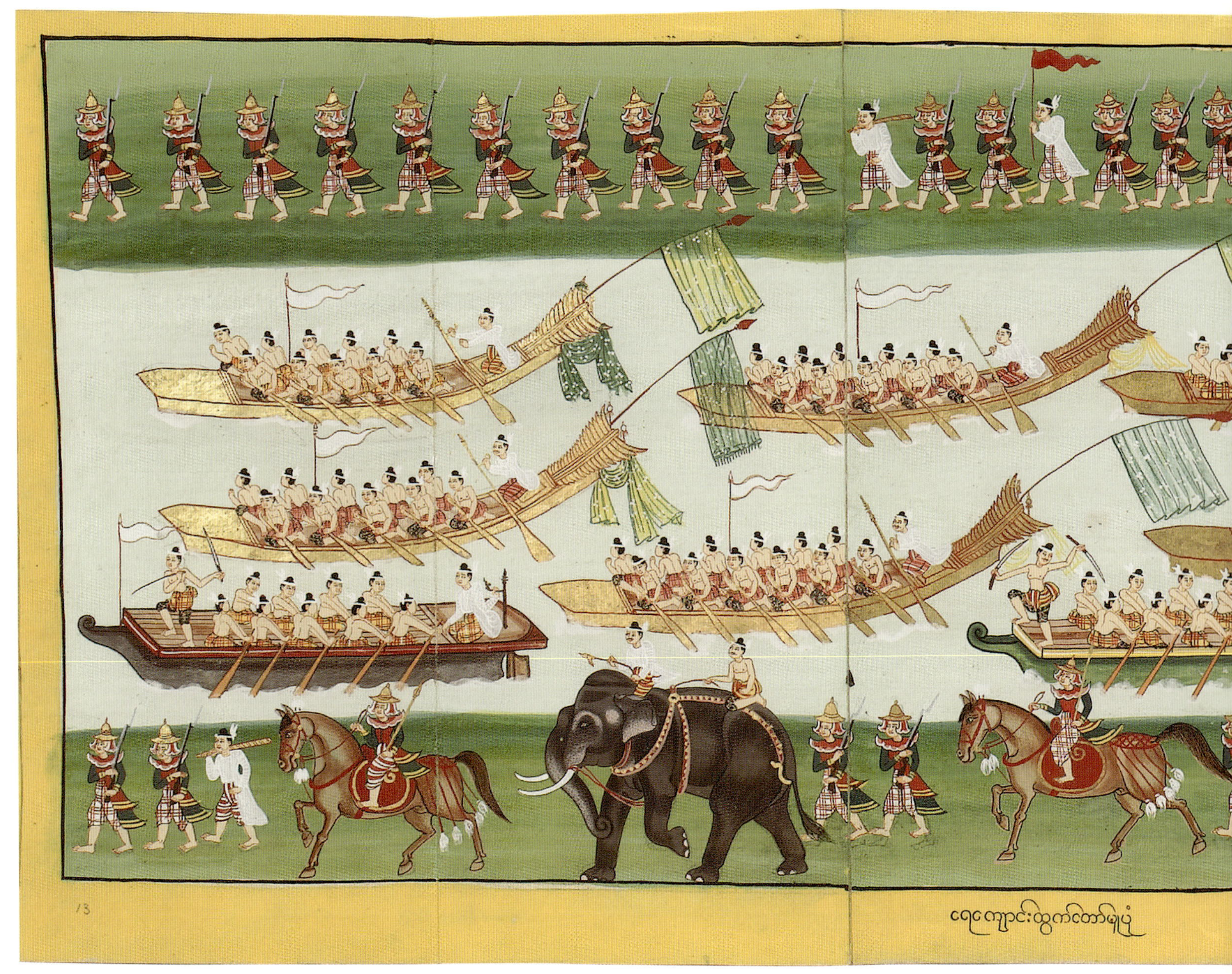

Figure 38. Naval maneuvers under royal supervision.

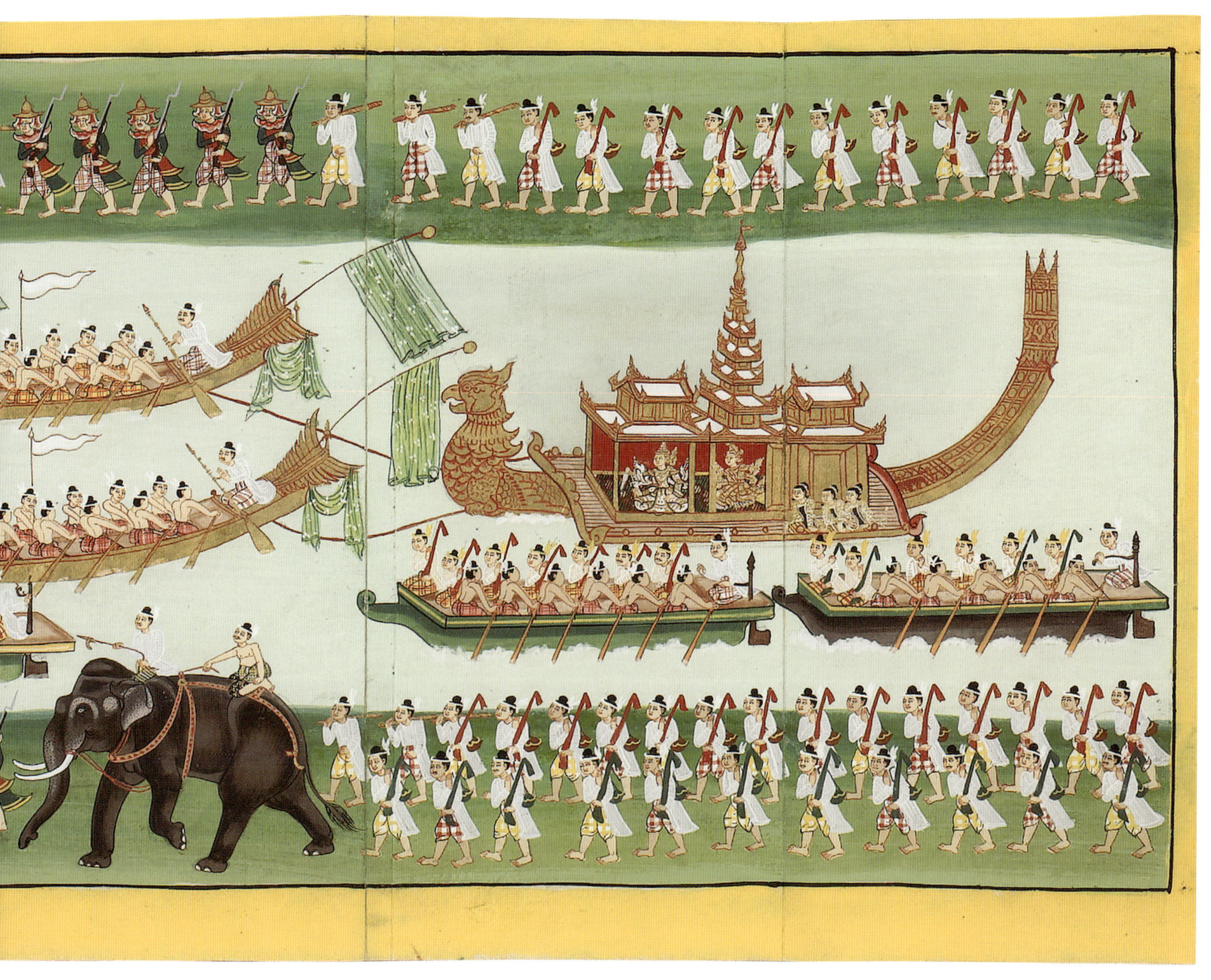

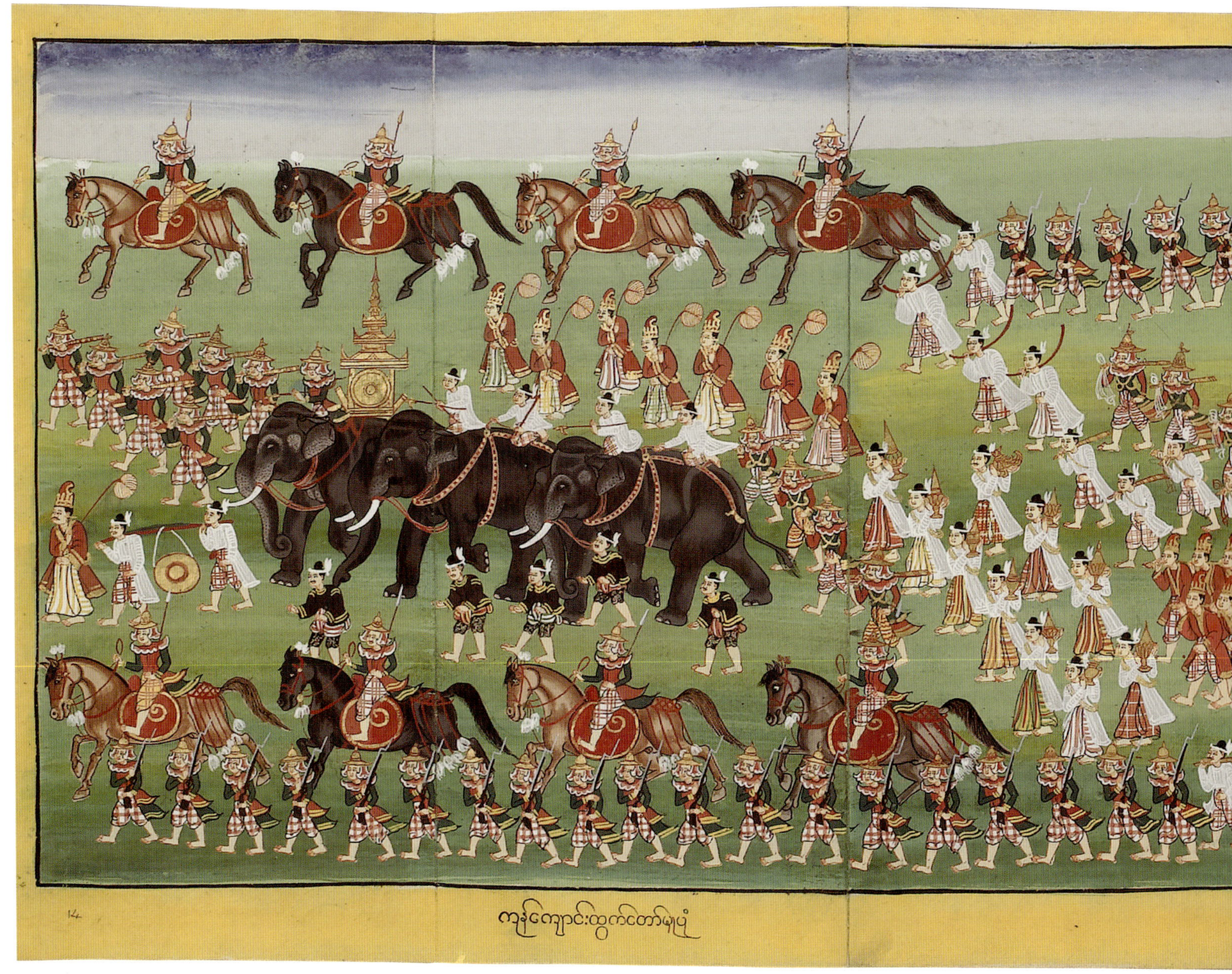

Figure 39. The king on palanquin, accompanied by his ministers, officers, and cavalry.

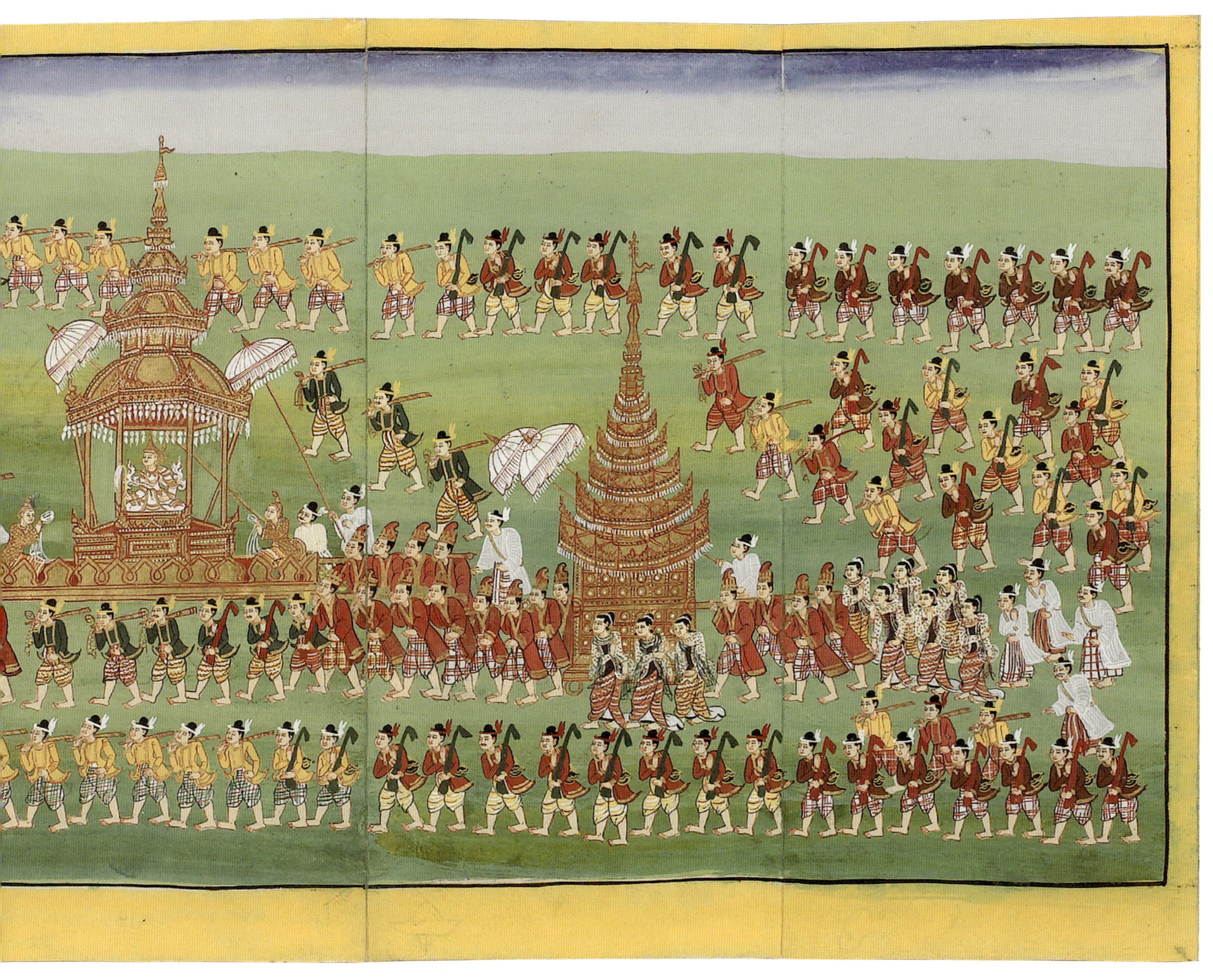

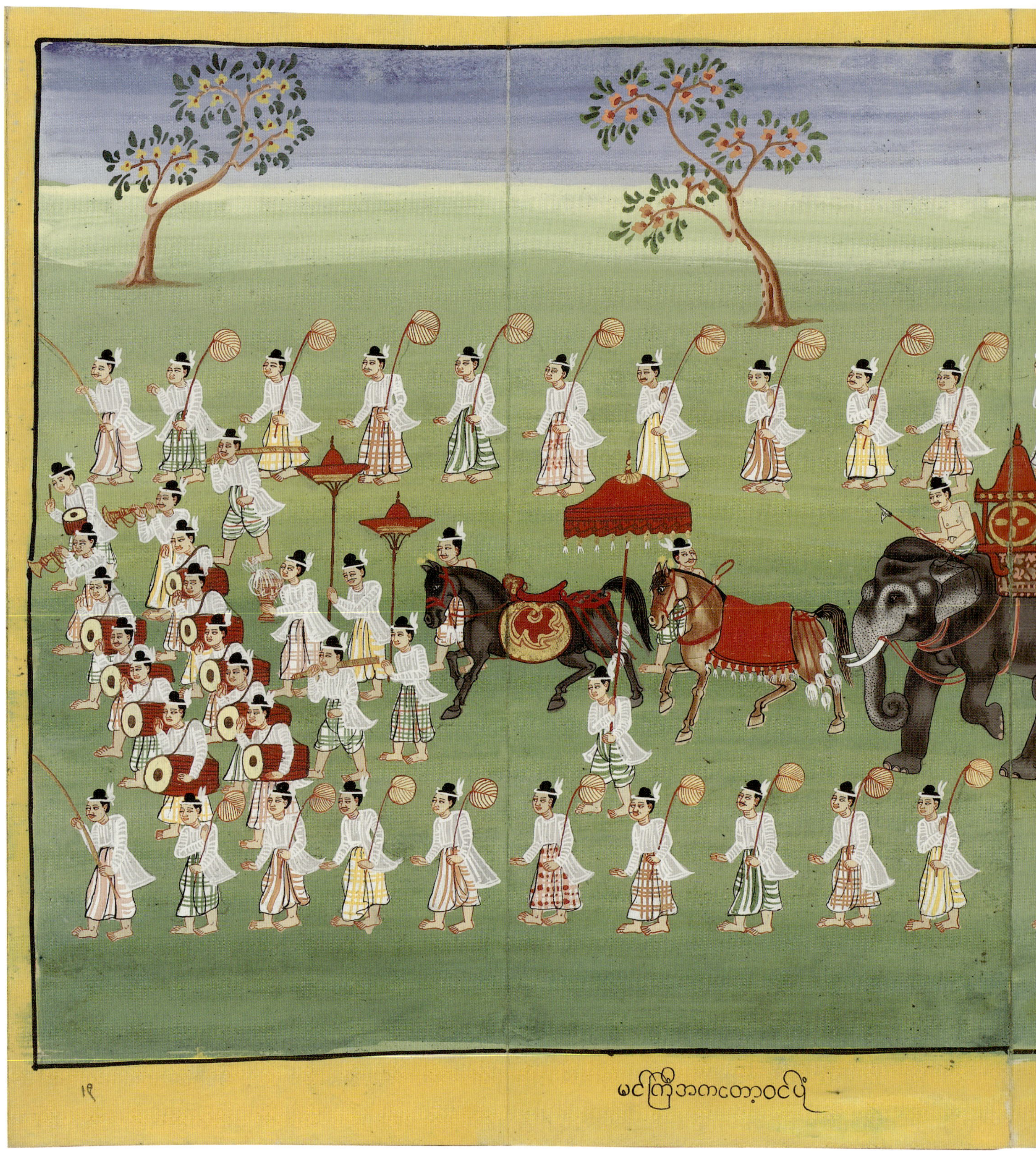

Figure 40. Arrival of a minister.

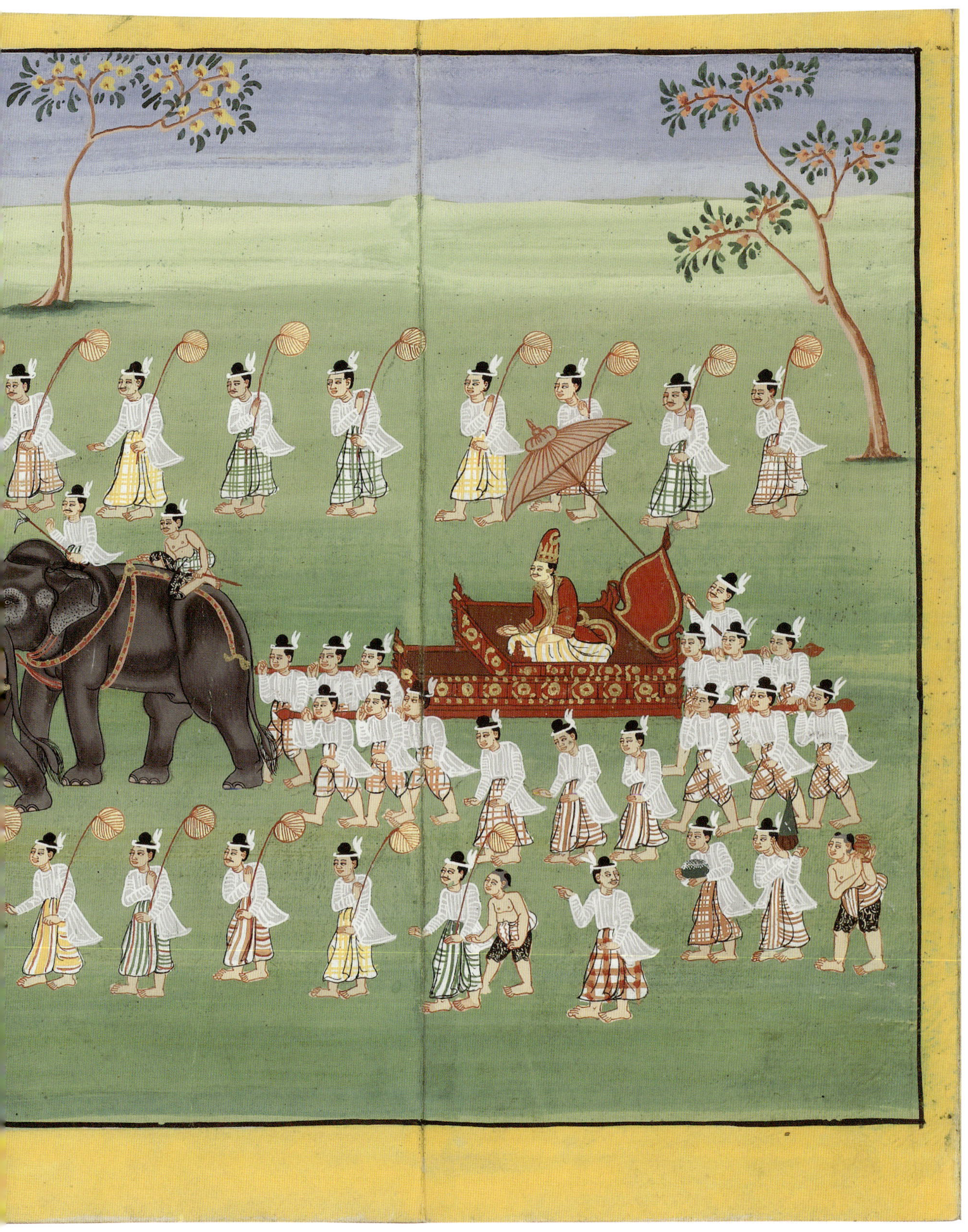

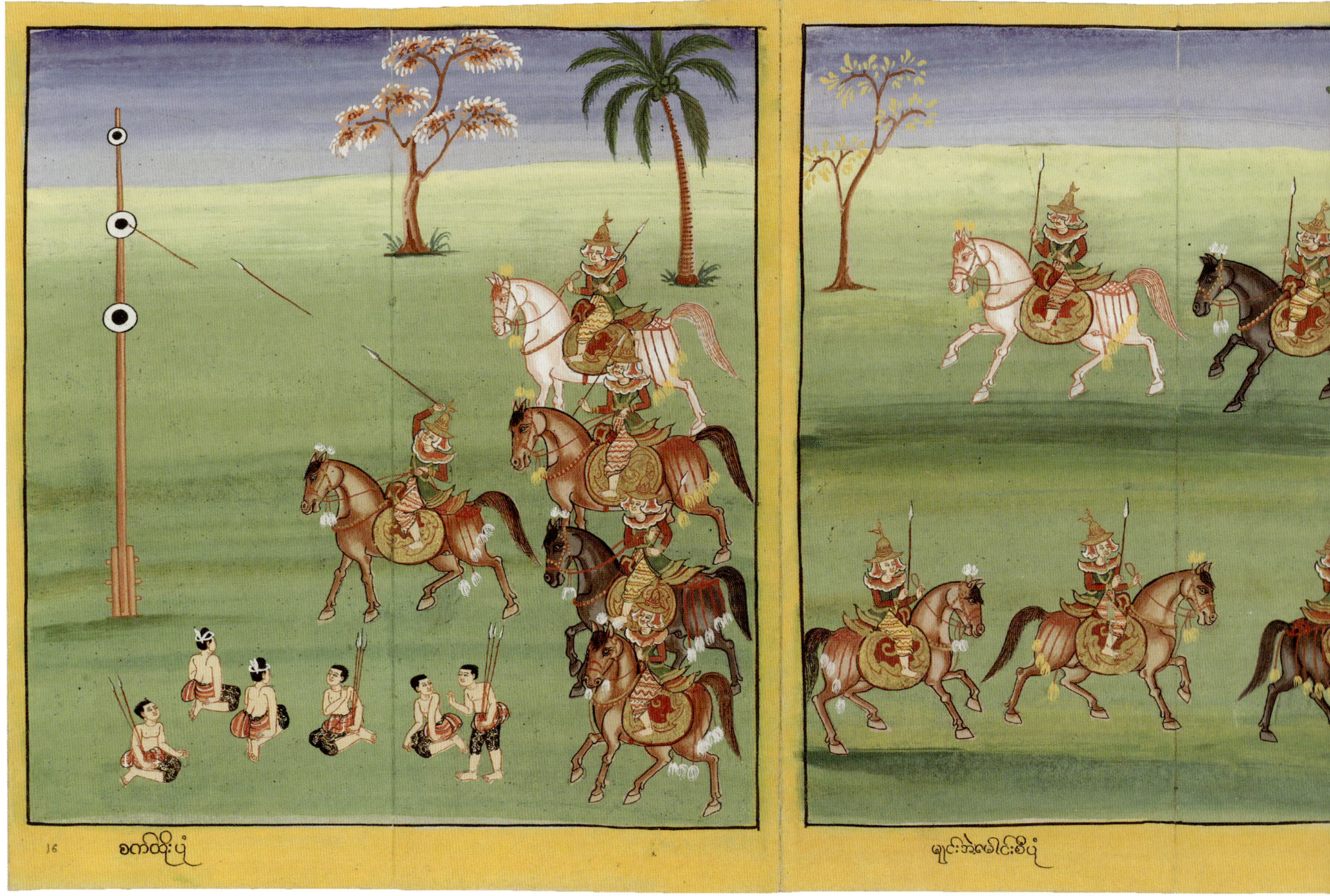

From left:

Figure 41. Archers practicing.

Figure 42. Cavalry training with javelins.

Figure 43. Soldiers going to fetch water for an allegiance-swearing ceremony.

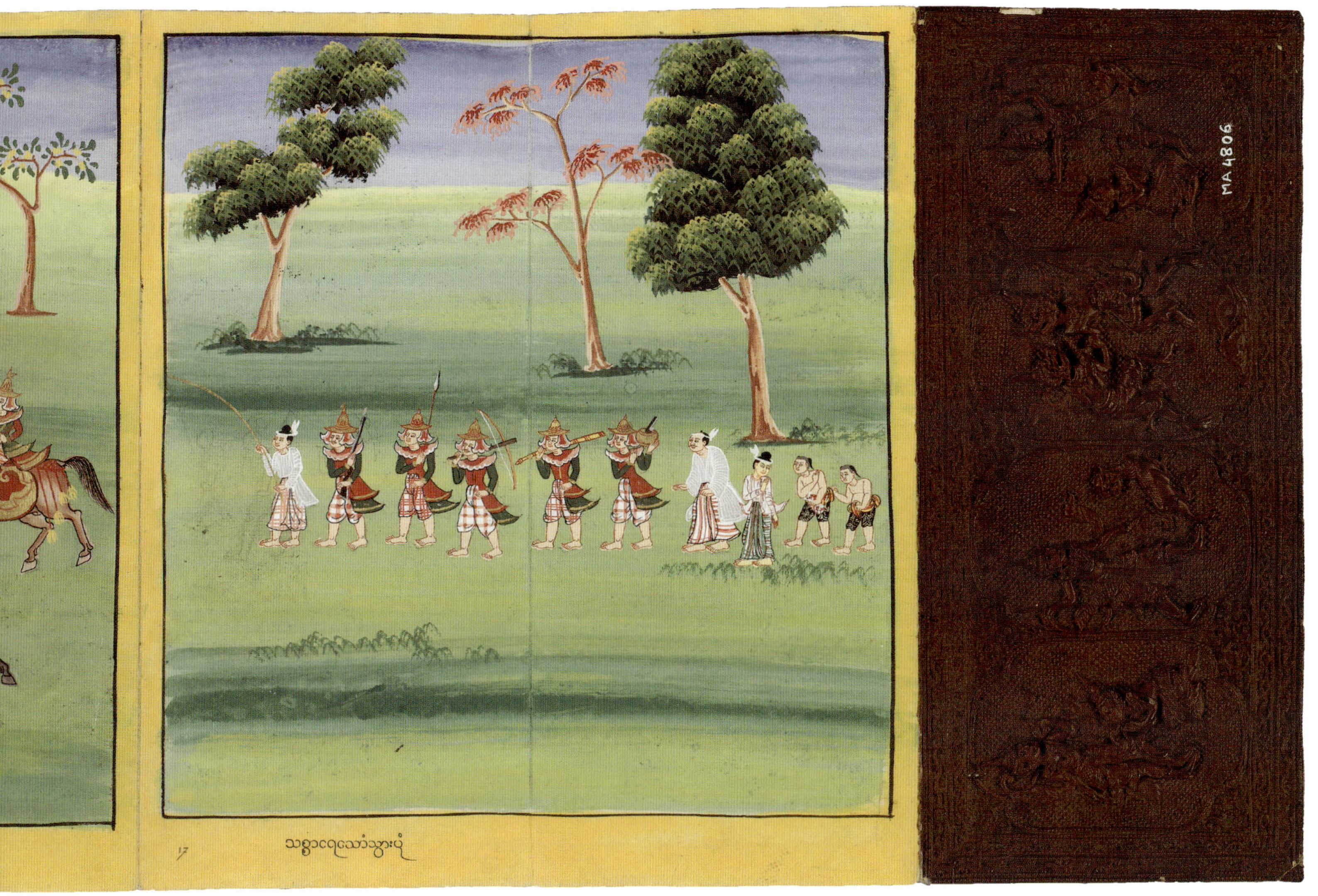
MA 4806
17
သစ္စာရေသောံသွားပုံ

Similar scenes are found in the second *parabaik* in the Bonvillain collection (MA 4807), though the manuscript is arranged a little differently. There is no text to help us identify the scenes, and it is not as large or as richly produced as the other *parabaiks*, but it is of great interest nonetheless. Other aspects of court life are depicted in its nine scenes. The royal monastery shown in the first scene (fig. 45) is reminiscent of the ones that were built at the end of the dynasty by Princess Salin, who had the Salin Kyaung built in 1876, and above all Queen Su-hpaya-lat, who had the Mya-taung Kyaung built in 1881. This last monument stands out because of the extensive gilding that covers the entire surface of the sculpted wood, just as can be seen in the *parabaik*. On the terrace, monks are bent over their palm-leaf manuscripts, attentively listening to the instructions of the teachers (*acariya*). All around the monastery are depicted the day-to-day activities of a large monastery: novices are tending to the grounds, helped more or less efficiently by active boys, furious that they cannot take part in the games of the other boys. A pious layman approaches the monastery with his offering in his hands.

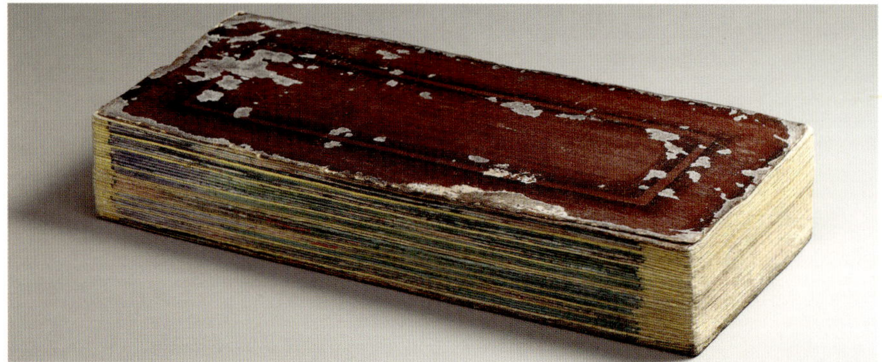

Figure 44. (Right) *Parabaik* MA 4807, folded.
Figure 45. Royal monastery.

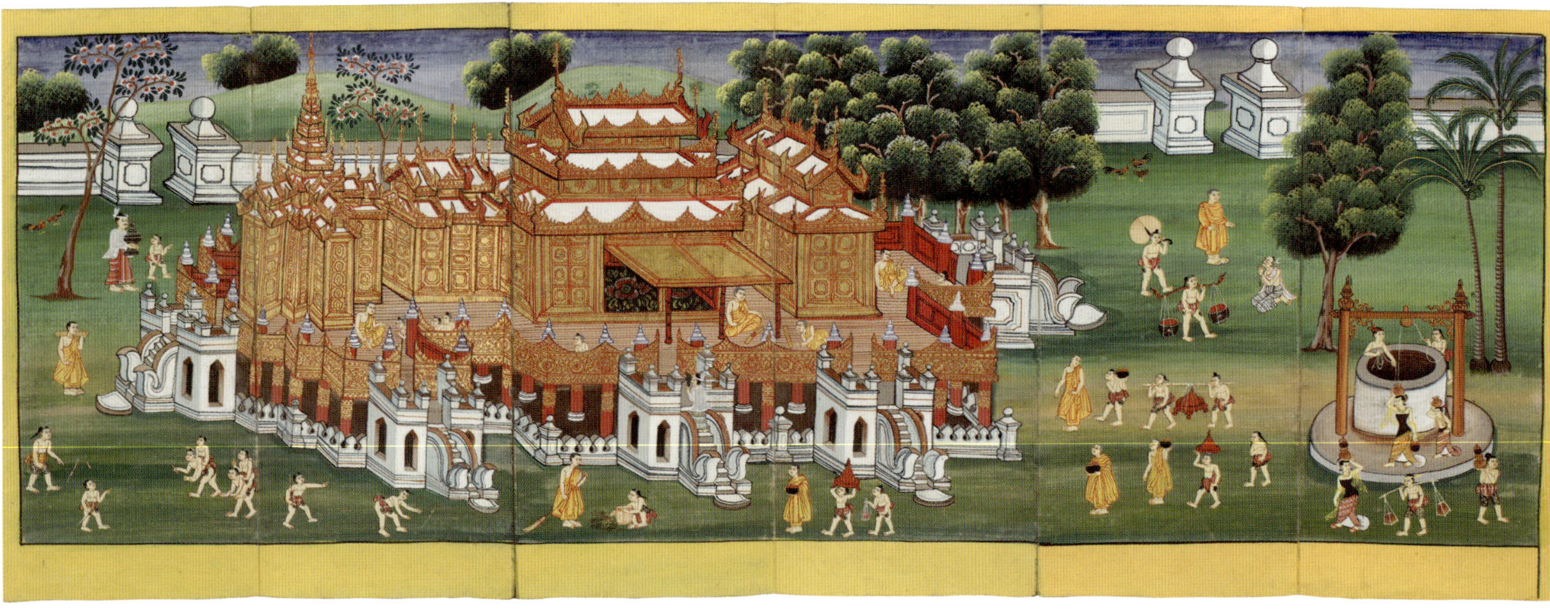

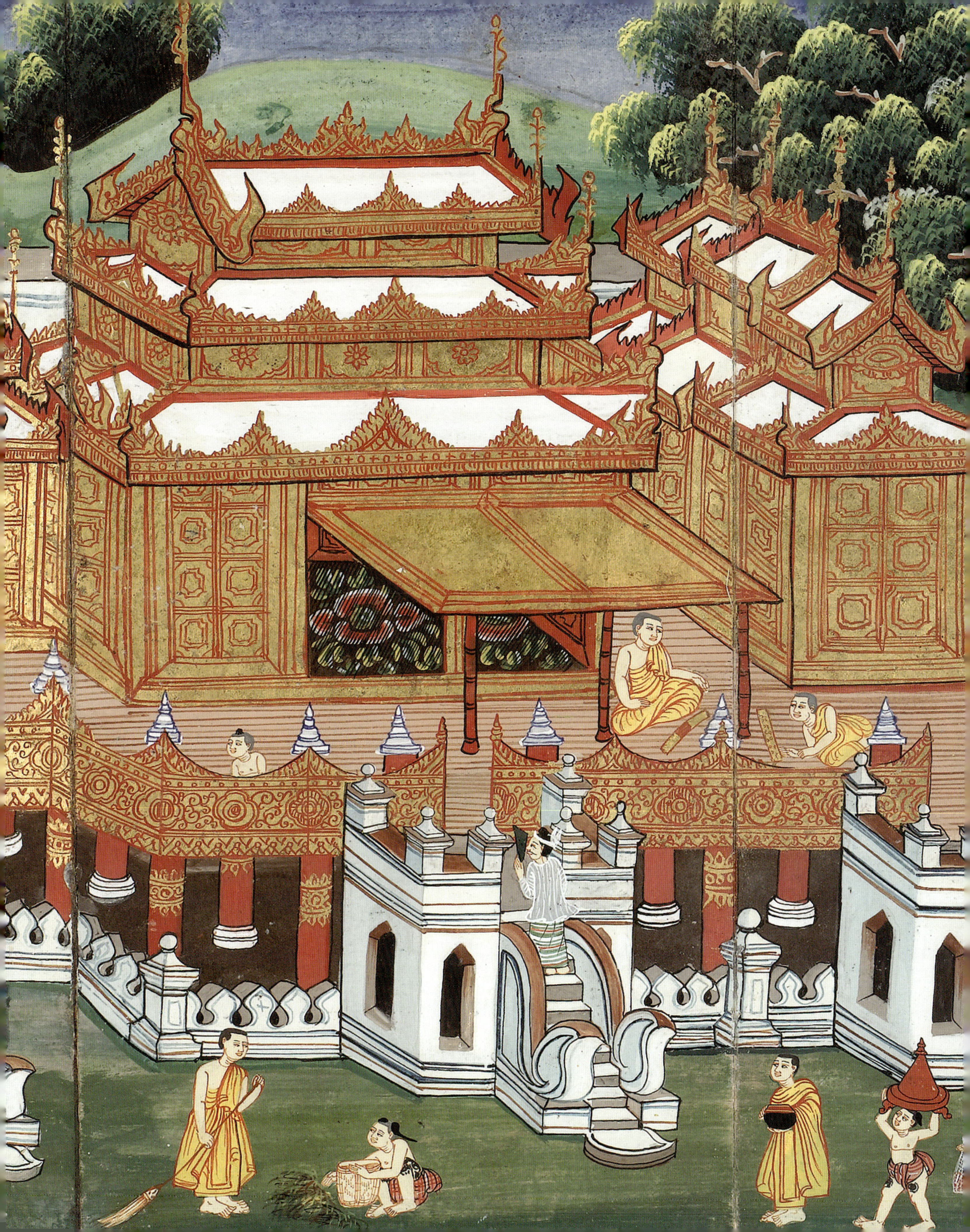

Various processions are the subject of the next three scenes, offering an excuse to show off the royal splendor. In figure 46, there are three princes dressed like ministers perched on elephants in harness and accompanied by a large following. Next (fig. 47) comes a general with his troops of artillerymen, who are armed with Western guns and a type of portable mortar. Then (fig. 48) comes the group of the Chinese embassy, recognizable by the banners with invented letters resembling Chinese writing and especially by the hairstyles that are characteristic of the Qing dynasty (1644–1911). Surrounded by the Burmese army, the imperial officials wear the plait mandated by the Manchu sovereigns along with the long blue robes of administrators. Perhaps they are going to Mandalay to negotiate a treaty that would allow the Chinese to trade along the Gulf of Martaban.

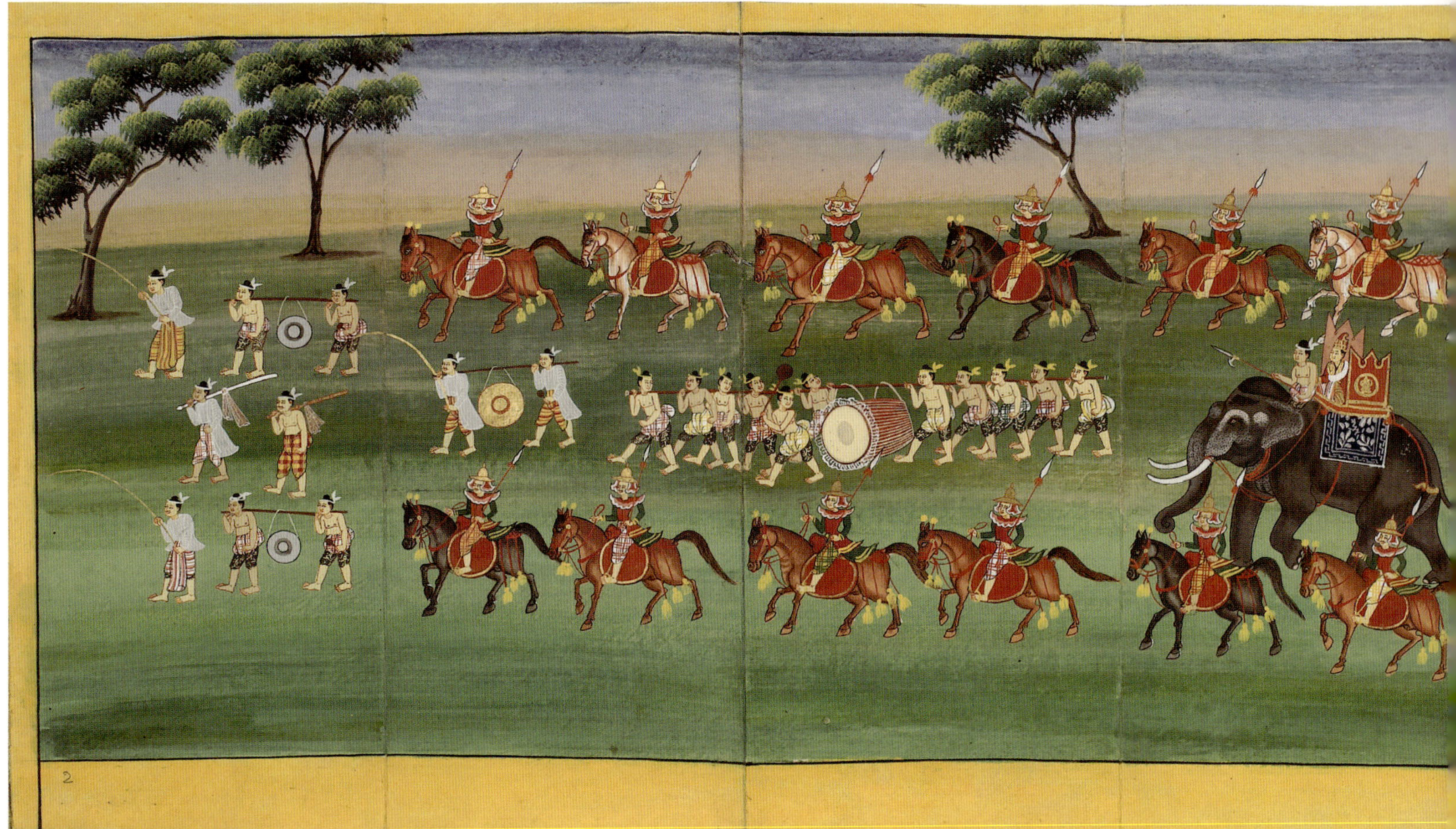

Figure 46. Three princes in procession.

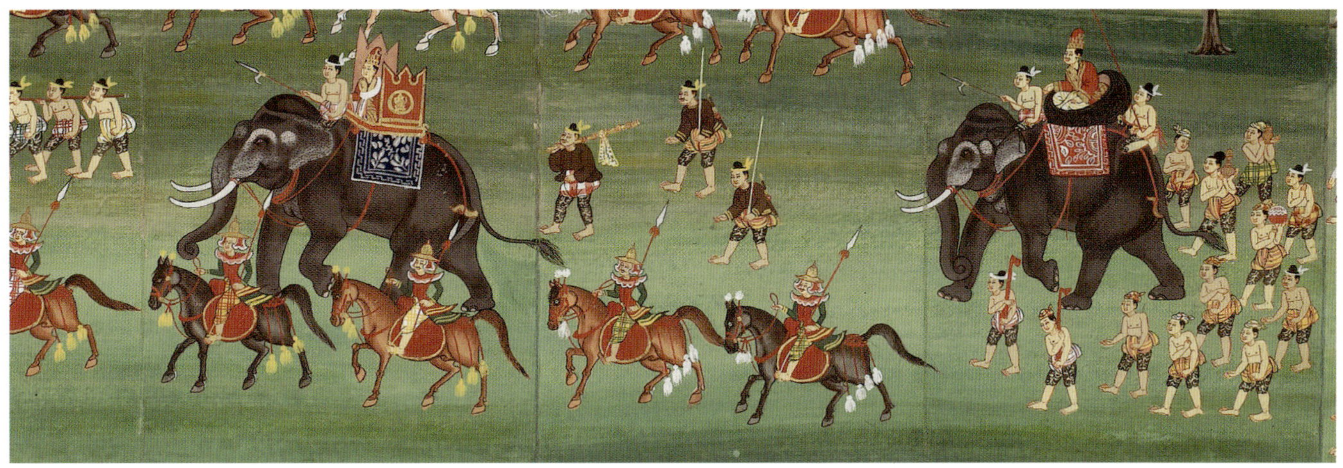

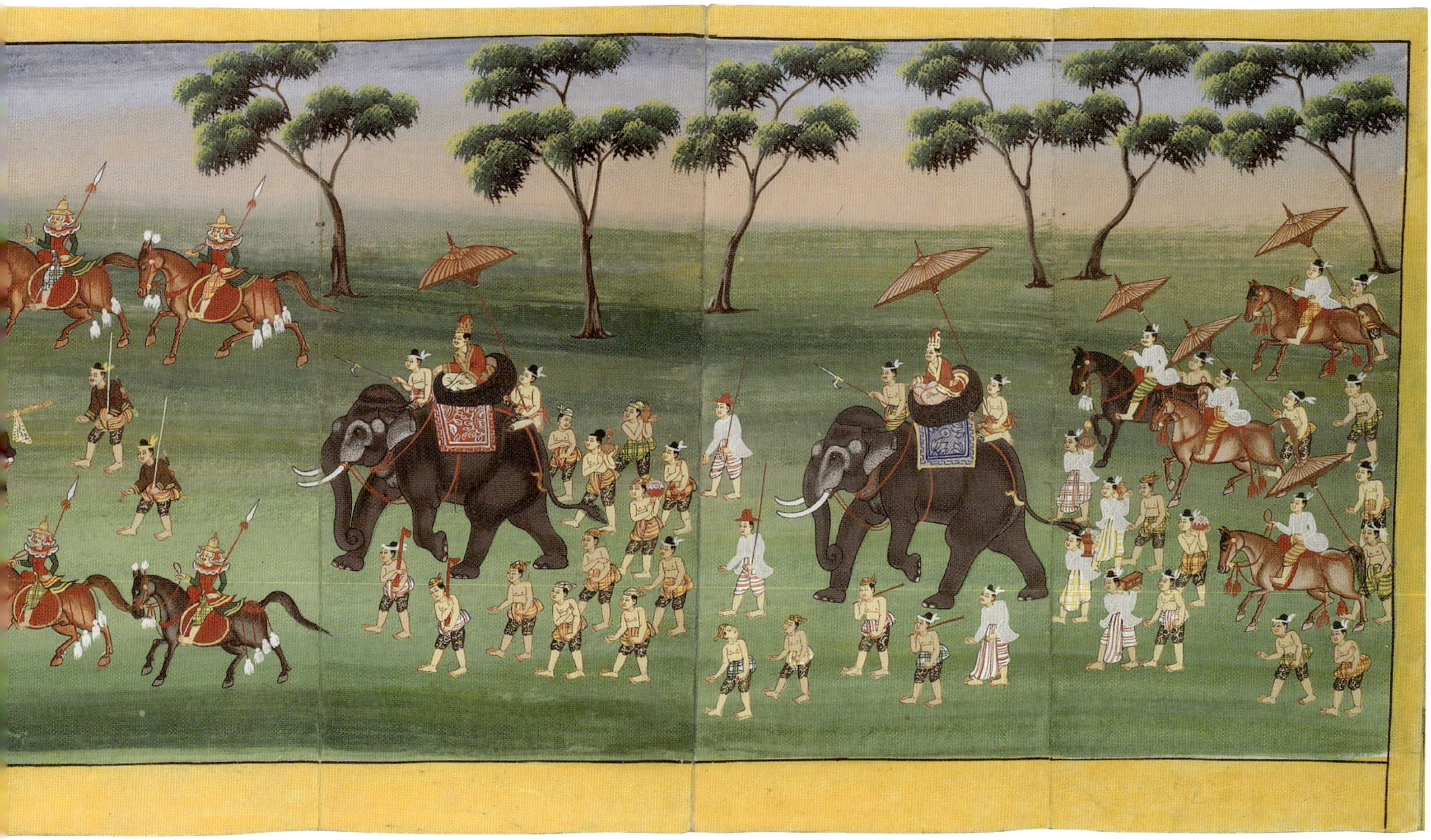

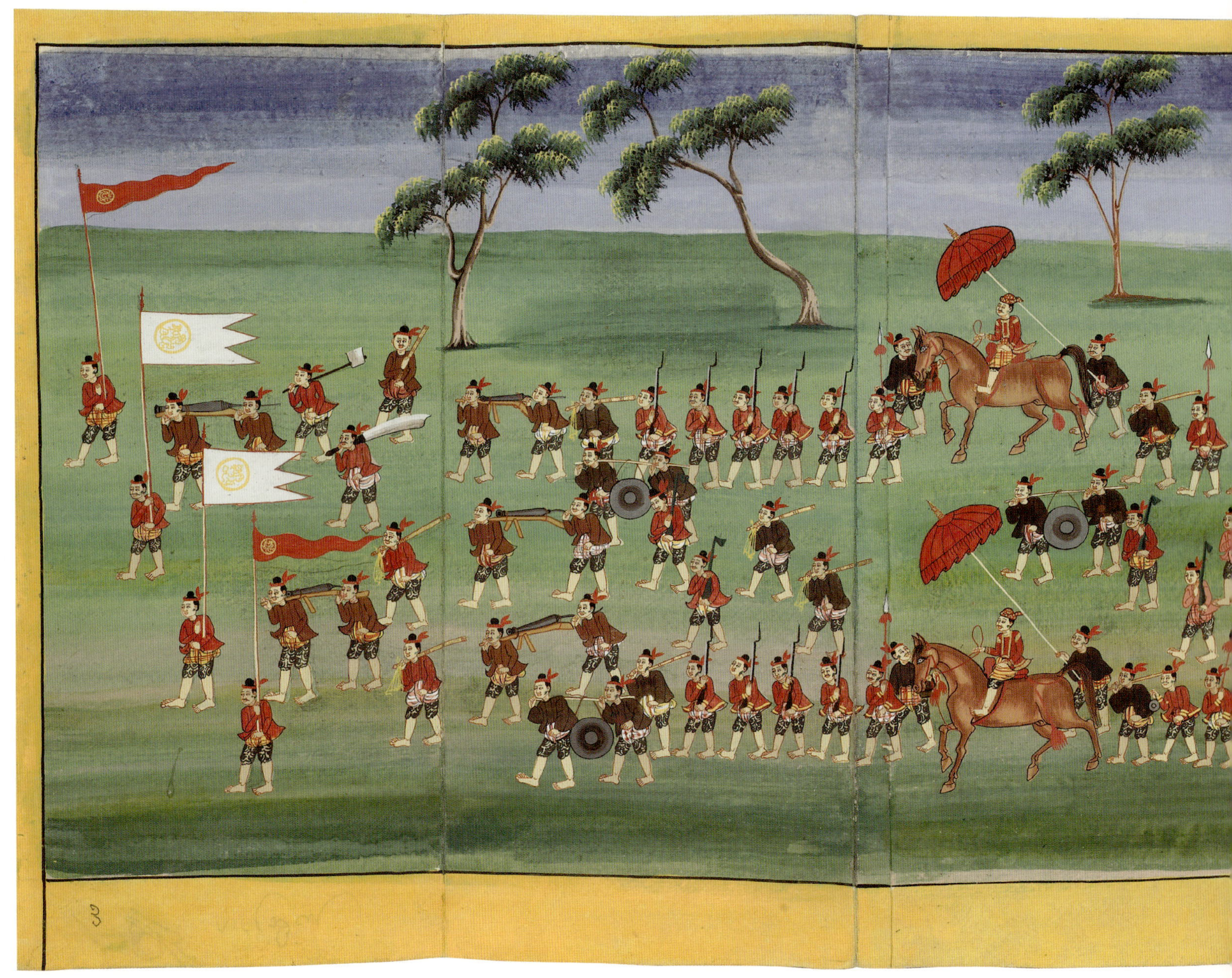

Figure 47. A general and his artillery.

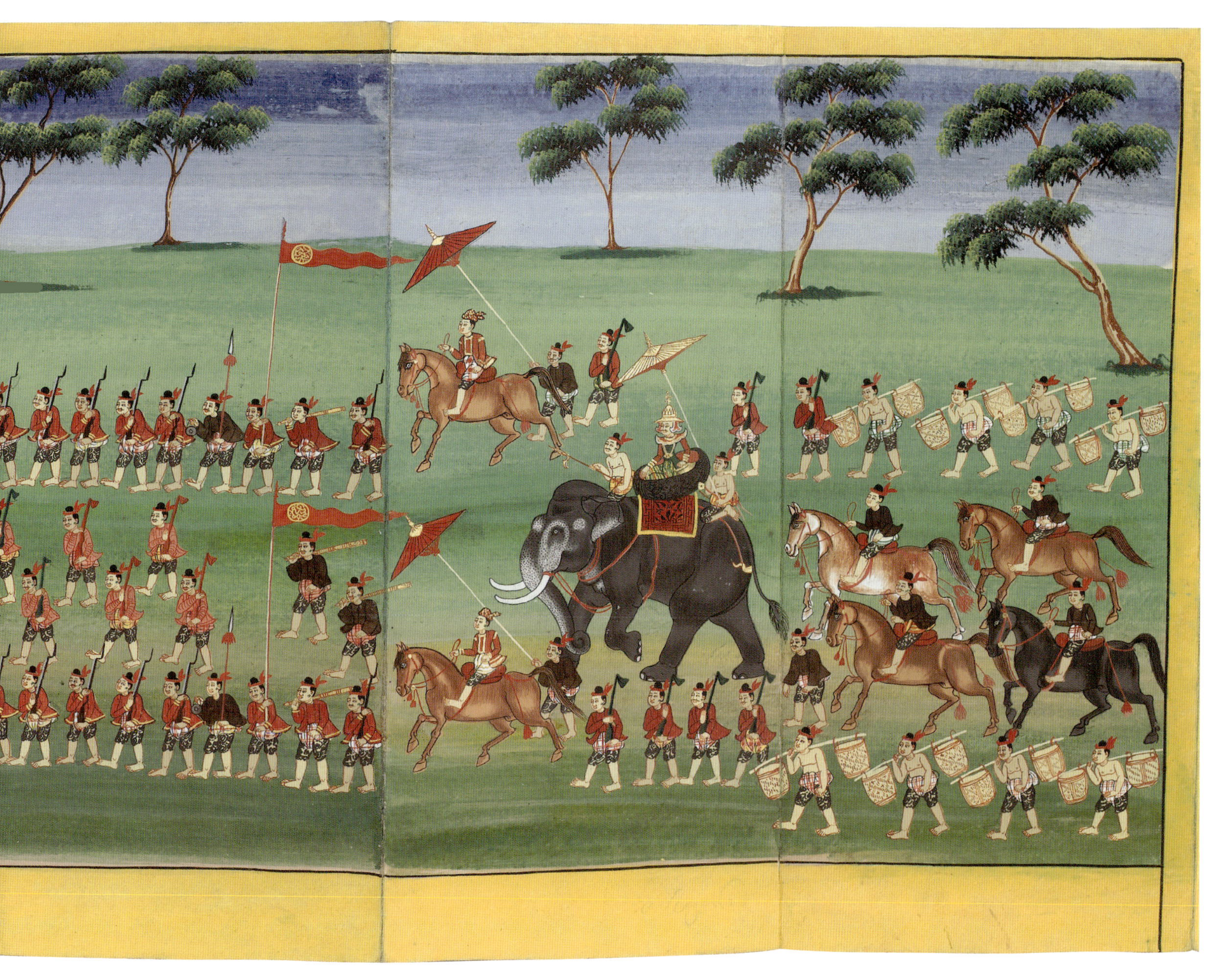

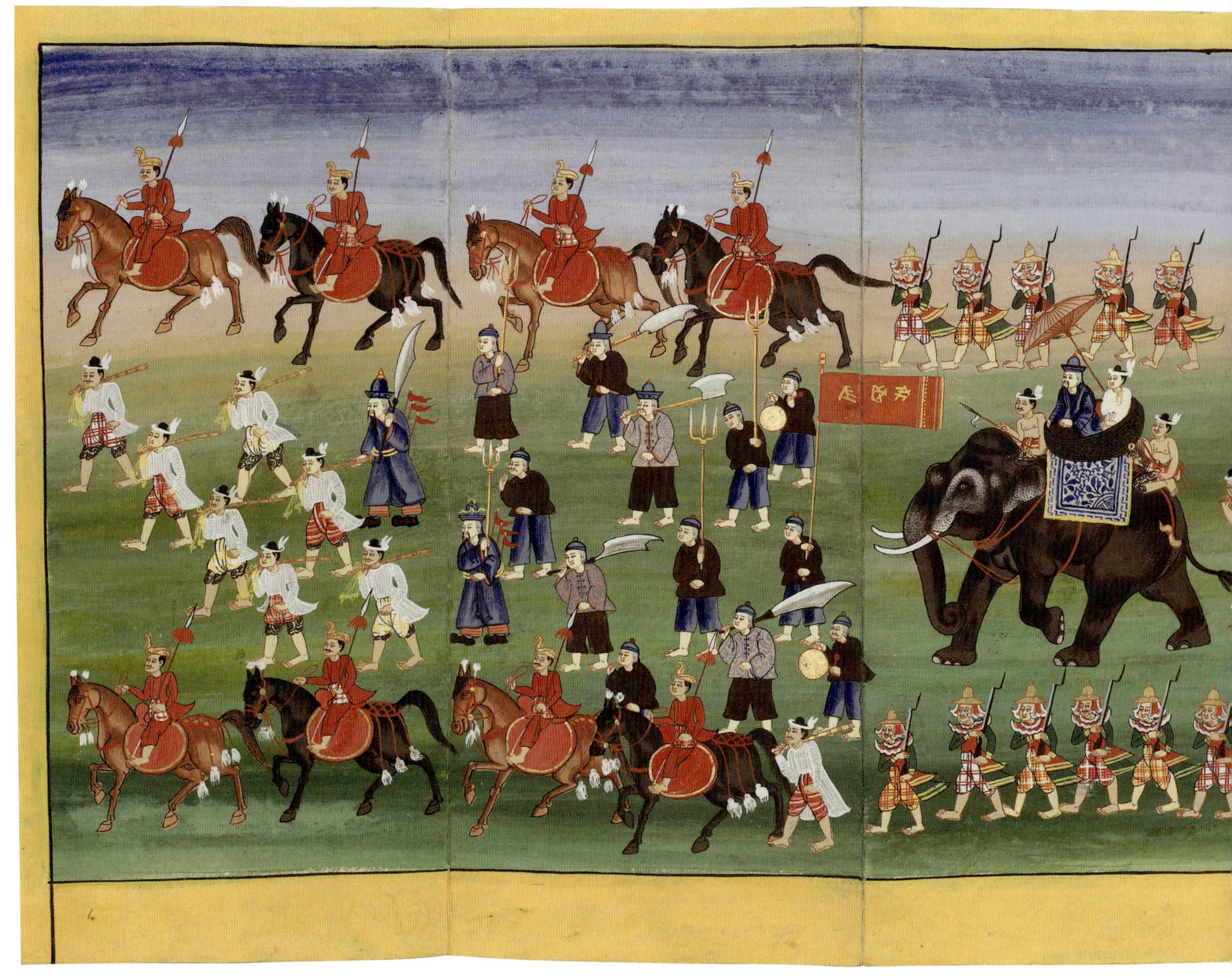

Figure 48. A Chinese embassy.

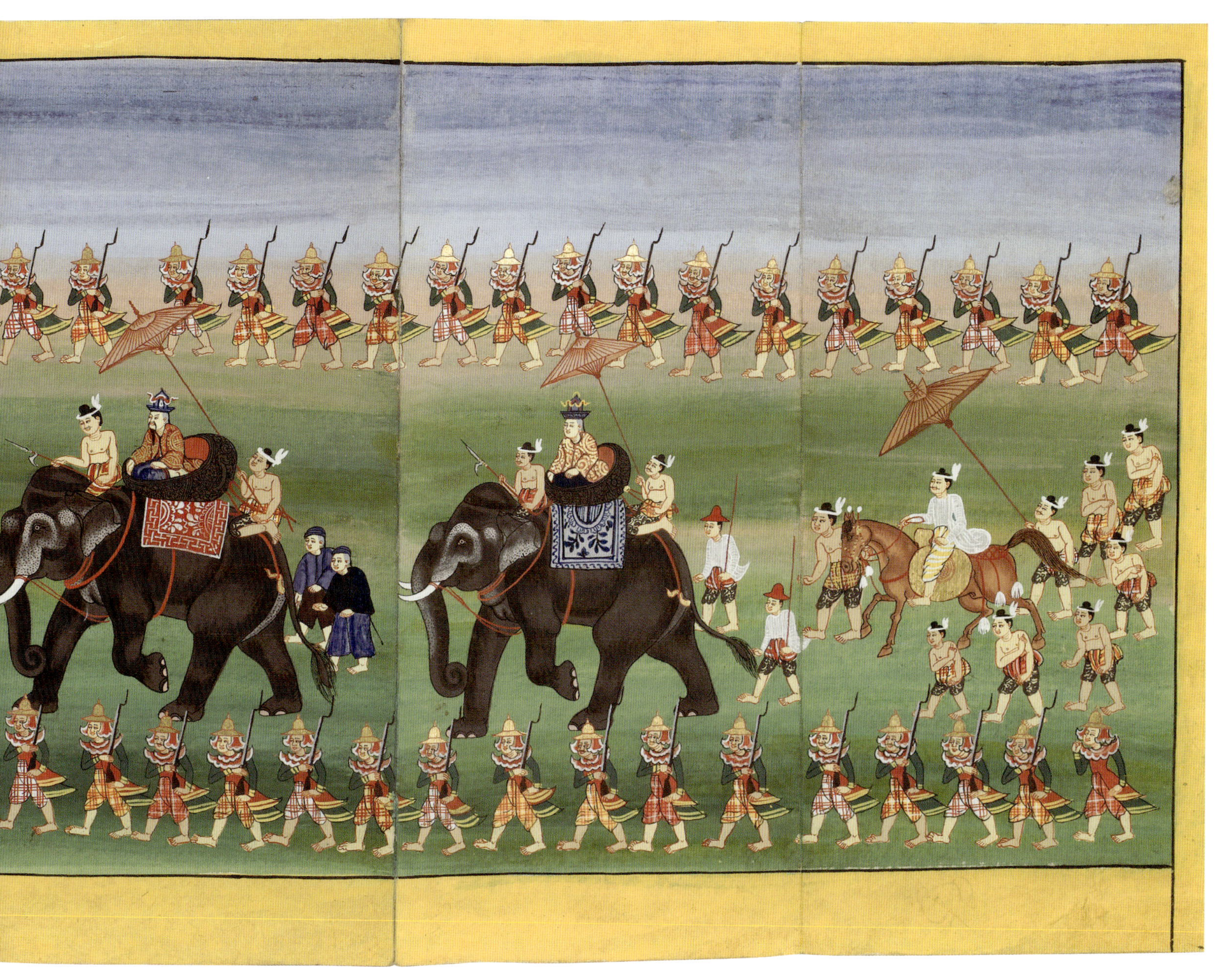

The following two scenes are of a very important event: the procession of a white elephant, whose capture is shown in the last scene of the manuscript. An albino elephant is considered to have a sacred significance in Indian traditions; one of the seven treasures of a universal monarch is a white elephant, the god Indra has a white elephant as his mount, and the mother of the future Buddha dreamed of a white elephant when Siddhattha was conceived. This explains how prestigious it was to discover and capture a white elephant. In figure 49, the animal is welcomed by troupes of male and female dancers dressed for the occasion and gathered under canopies. There is a large assembly of musicians and actors wearing masks for the drama *Yama Zatdaw*, the Burmese version of the *Rāmāyaṇa* that was extensively developed at court through the influence of classical Thai theater (*khon*) beginning at the end of the eighteenth century. The musicians playing the *gamelan* have trouble following the procession as they are surrounded by their heavy instruments, carried by their assistants. The orderly crowd is in fact accompanying a group of elephants who surround and protect a pale-skinned female elephant on a ceremonial dais. The procession in the second scene (fig. 50) is no less august than the first one, and it accompanies an adult white elephant being pulled on a platform with a three-tiered roof so that its feet will not touch the impure soil. The platform is pulled by twenty-three men, who are helped by various assistants bearing bars to facilitate transporting the elephant. The floor of the platform is strewn with colorful flowers. Princes on foot or on horseback, monks, and people carrying offerings surround the elephant, which is the center of attention.

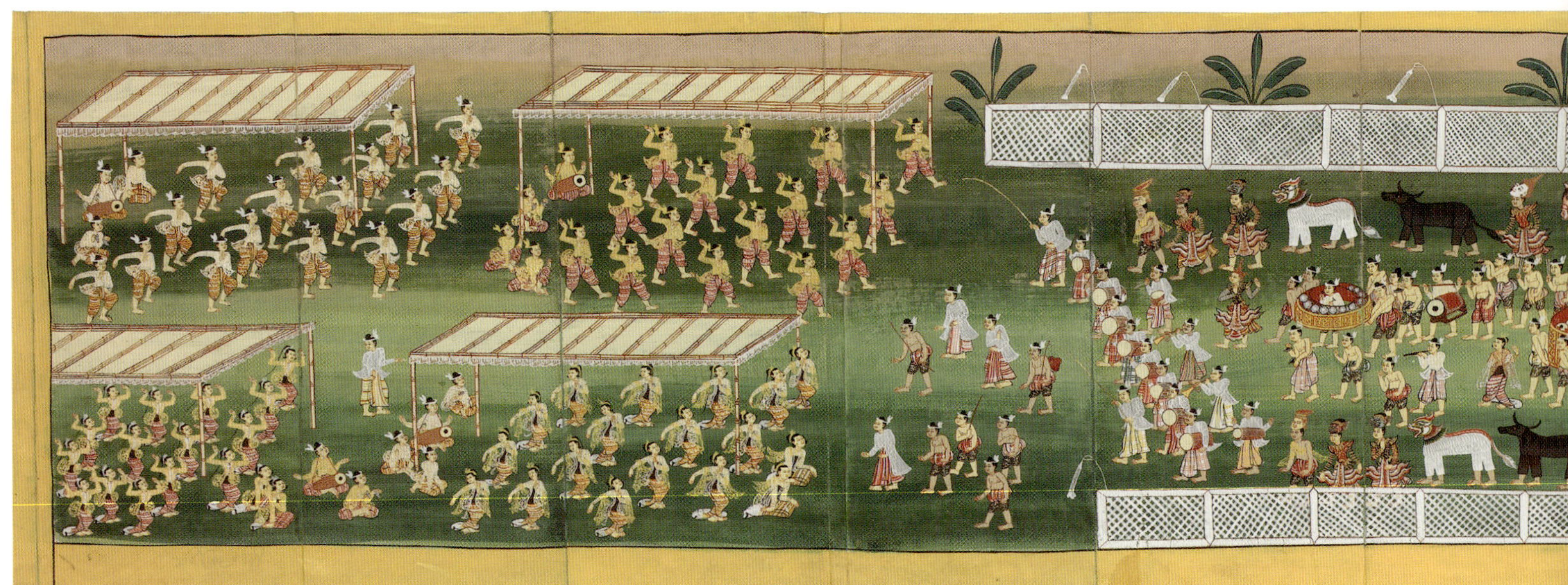

Figure 49. Yama Zatdaw performance in procession.

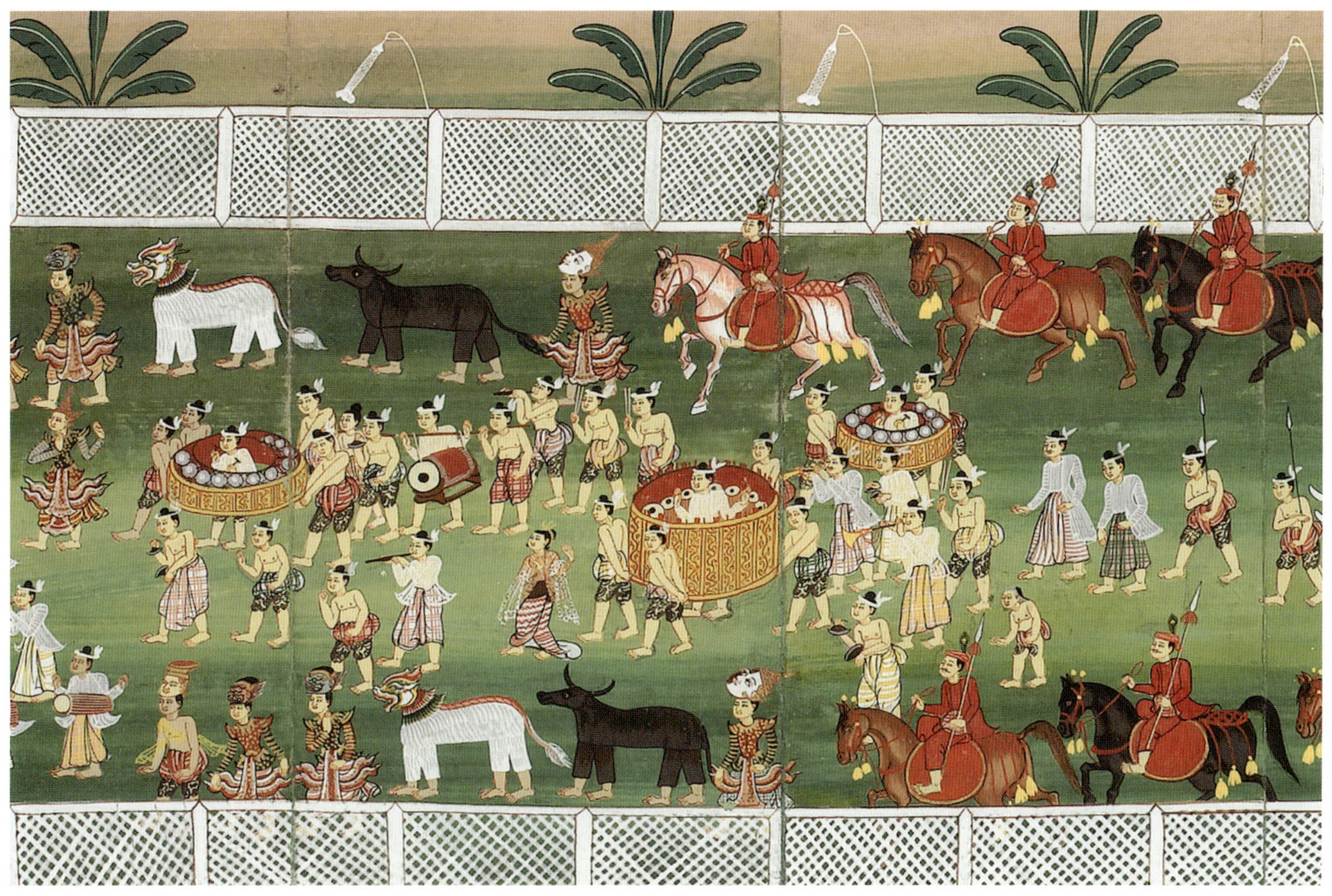

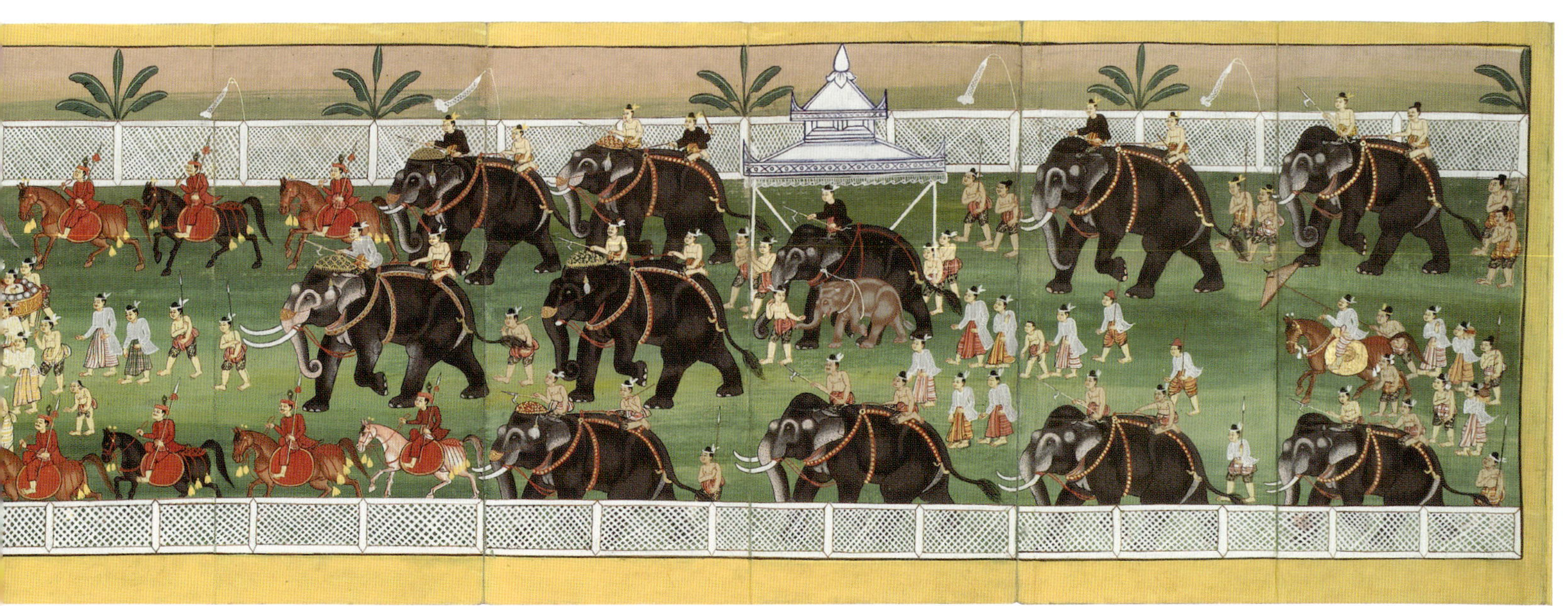

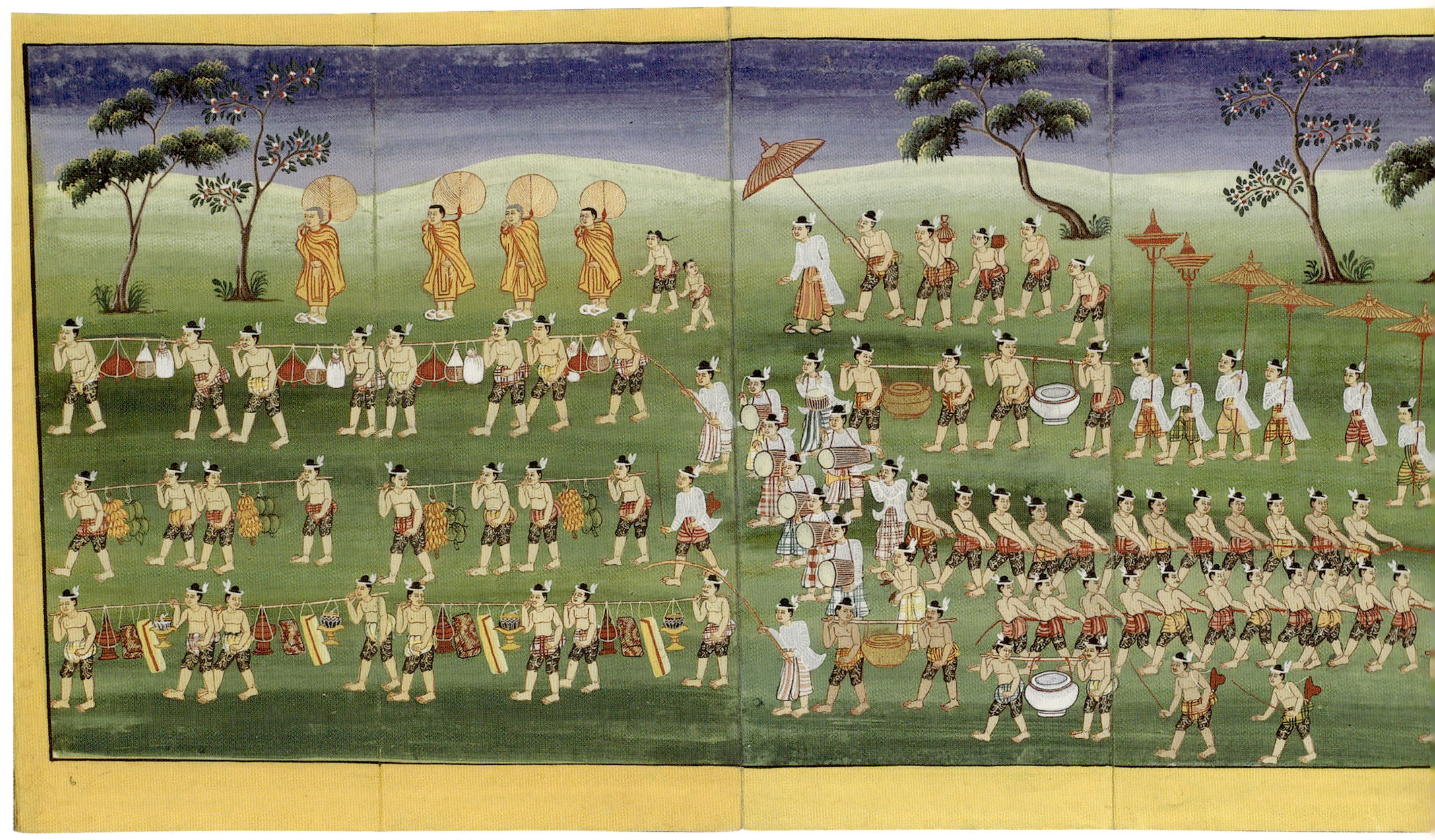

Figure 50. Parade of a white elephant.

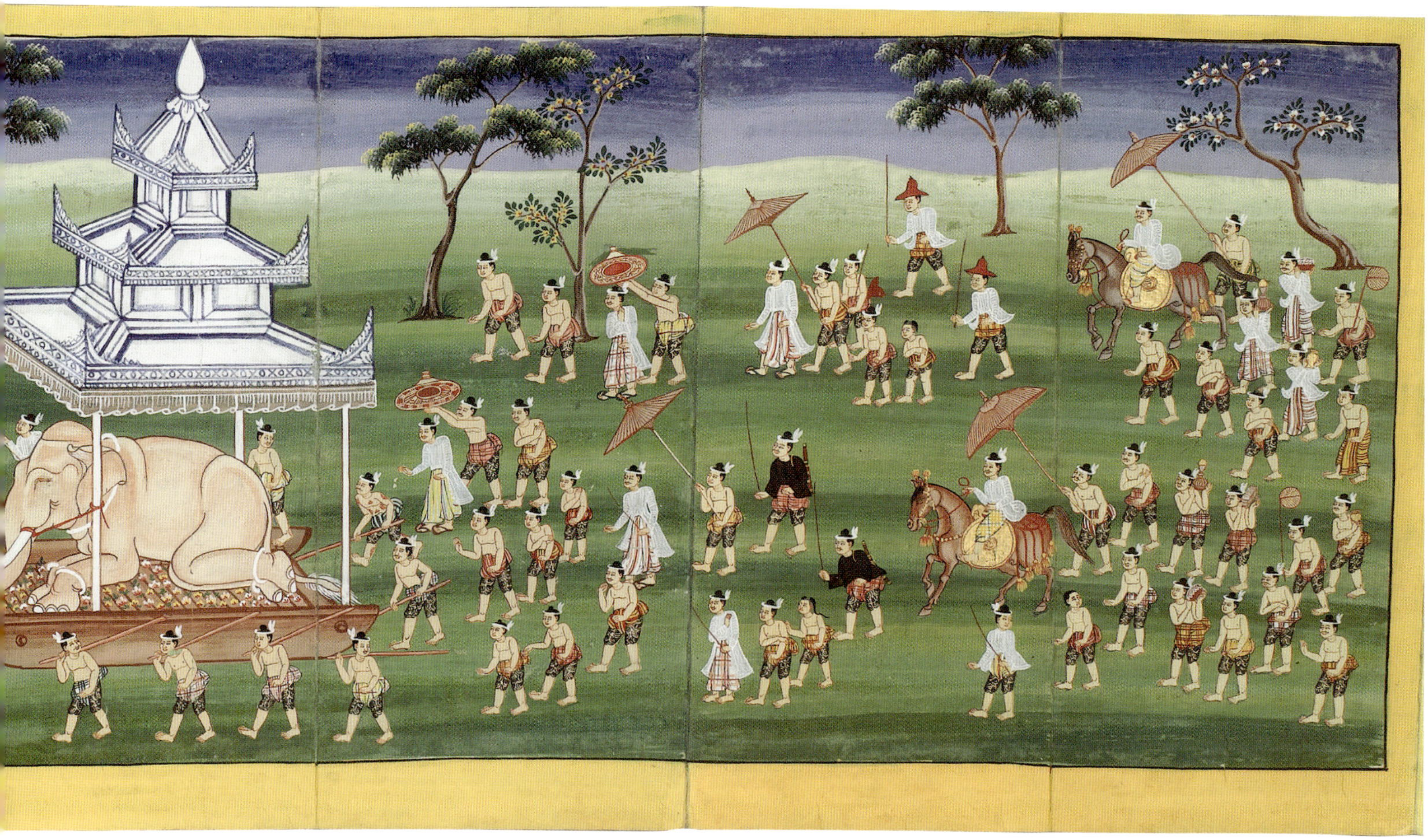

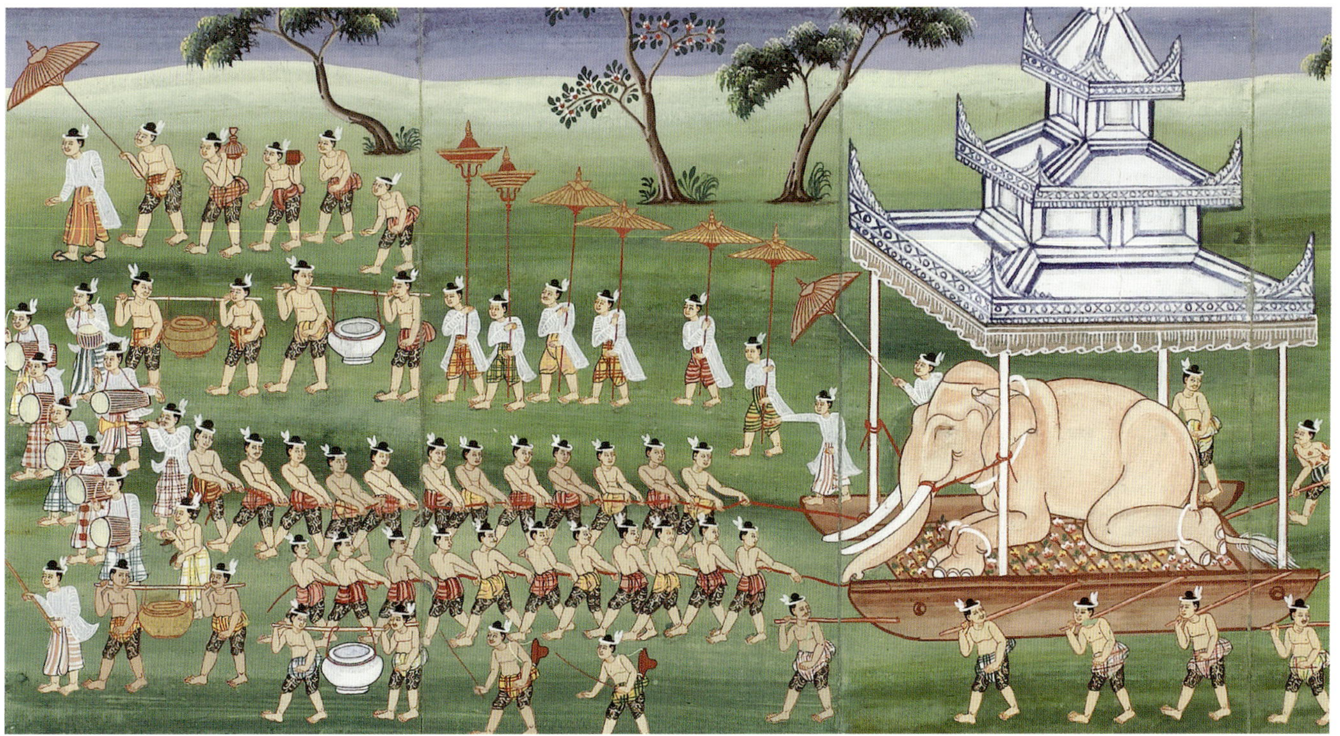

The next scene (fig. 51) is a spirit festival (*nat pwe*). It takes place in a monastery, and the number of peddlers, fortunetellers, mediums (*nat kadaw*), people with offerings, dancers, and courtesans shows how popular it is. It may be possible to identify where this is; it could well be Yadanagu in Amarapura, which is not far from Mandalay. An important festival was held there every year in honor of Popa Medaw—mother of Mount Popa, an extinct volcano—and her two sons, the lords Taungbyone Min Nyinaung. The statuettes on the altars that have been erected would suggest this is the festival in the illustration. It is not unusual to find the presence of *nat* worship in Buddhist monasteries in Burma, a phenomenon found all over Asia, showing a syncretism that can surprise Westerners.

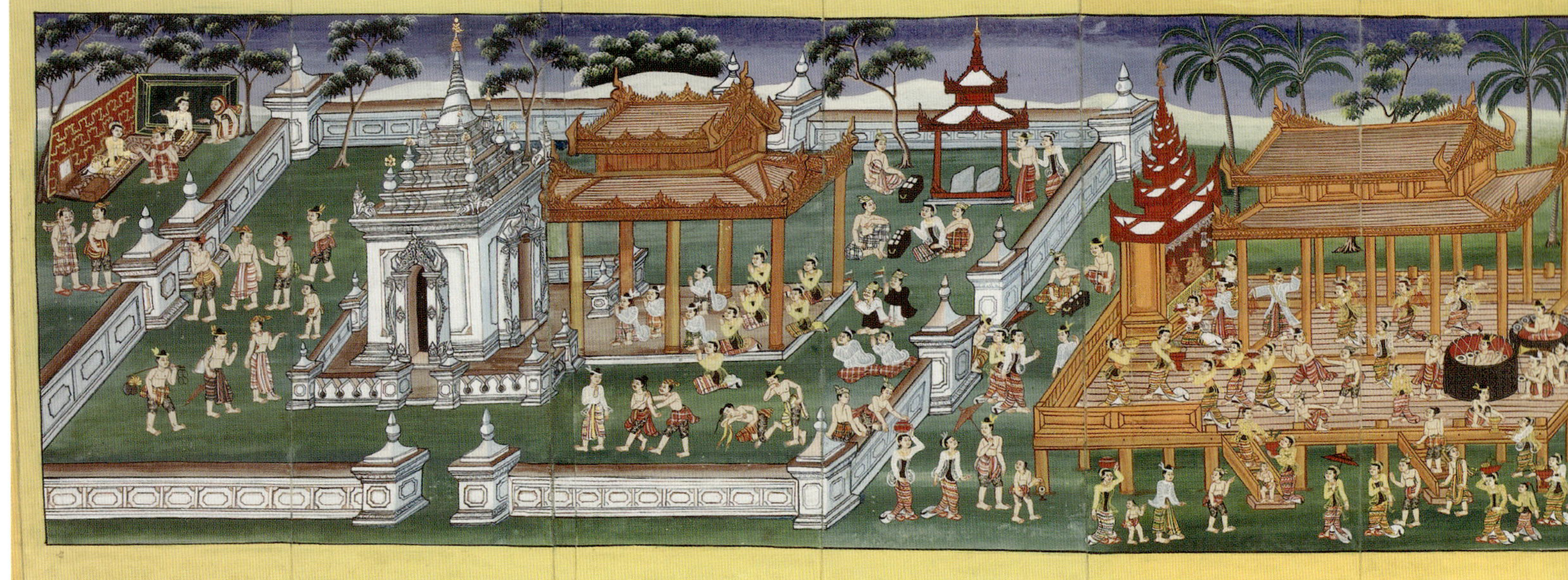

Figure 51. *Nat* festival.

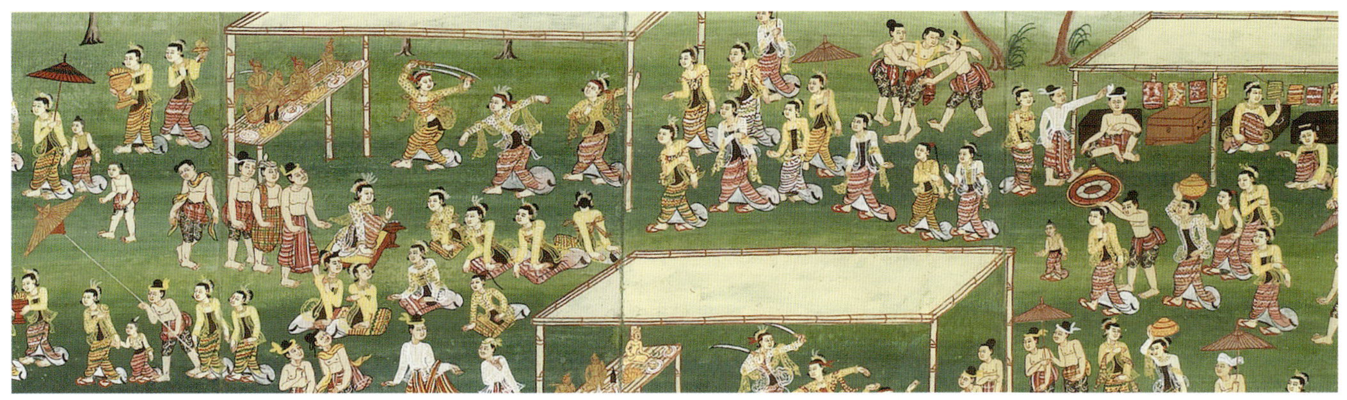

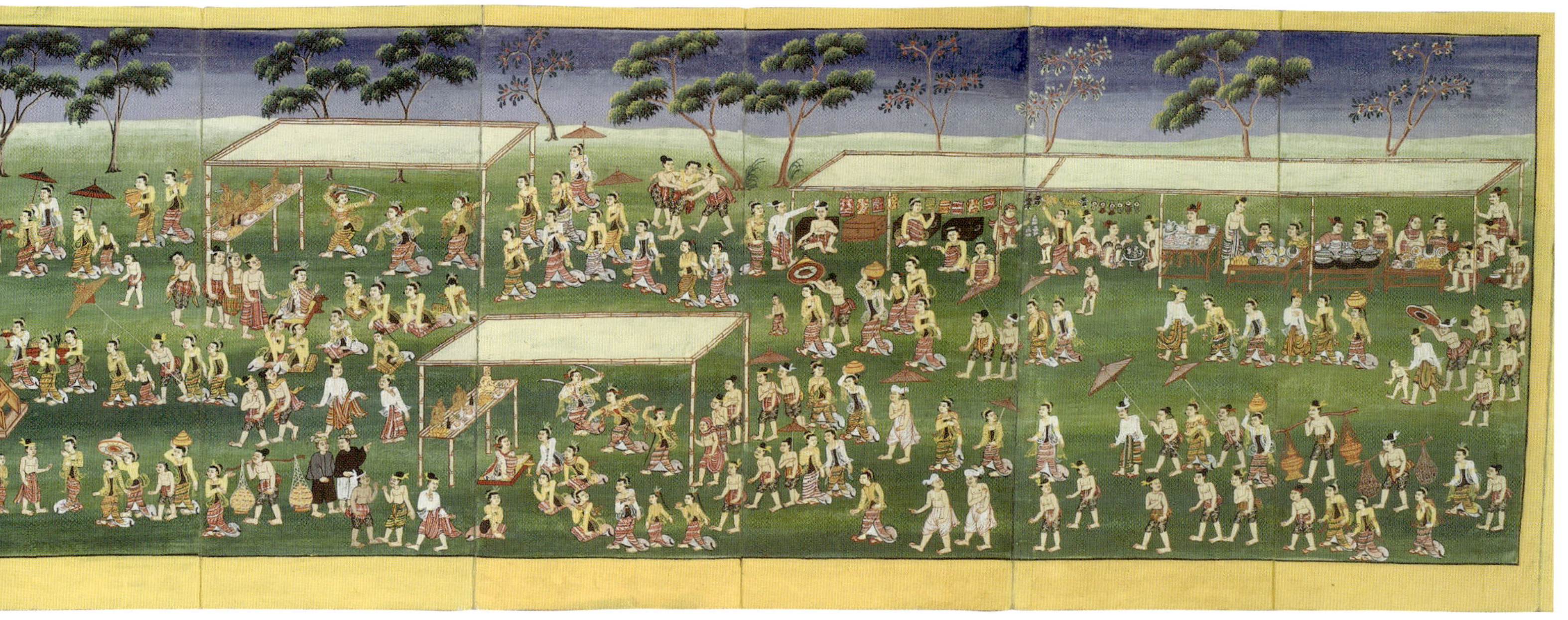

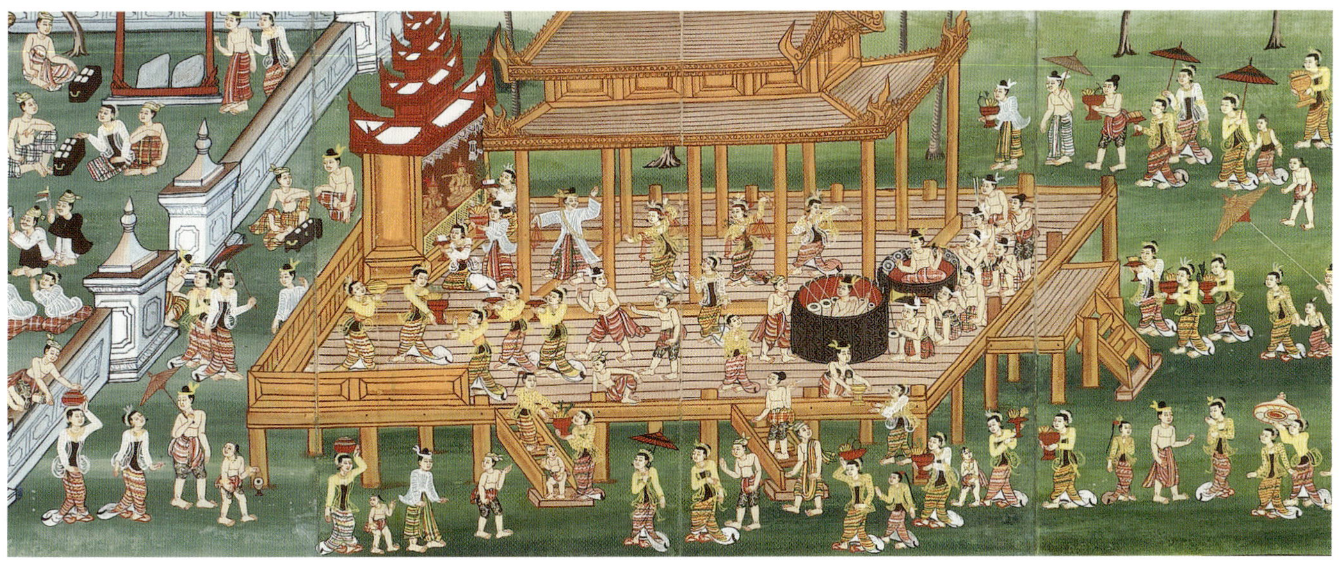

The next scene (fig. 52) shows a pilgrimage site, Shwe Hset Taw, where the Buddha is said to have left two footprints (*Buddhapāda*). One is down by the river and the other up on the hill with a covered staircase leading to it. It is still an important place of pilgrimage today. In addition to the Burmese making offerings to the monks, there are couples whose attire marks them as coming from other ethnic groups, such as the Mon or Shan. The last scene (fig. 53) shows a bird's eye view of a bucolic landscape with valleys and forests that are more or less dense. It depicts what was required to capture a troop of elephants. Among the troop there is a young white elephant. This scene follows a pictorial tradition that the Burmese inherited from China as well as Thailand. It uses broad strokes and a varied palette.

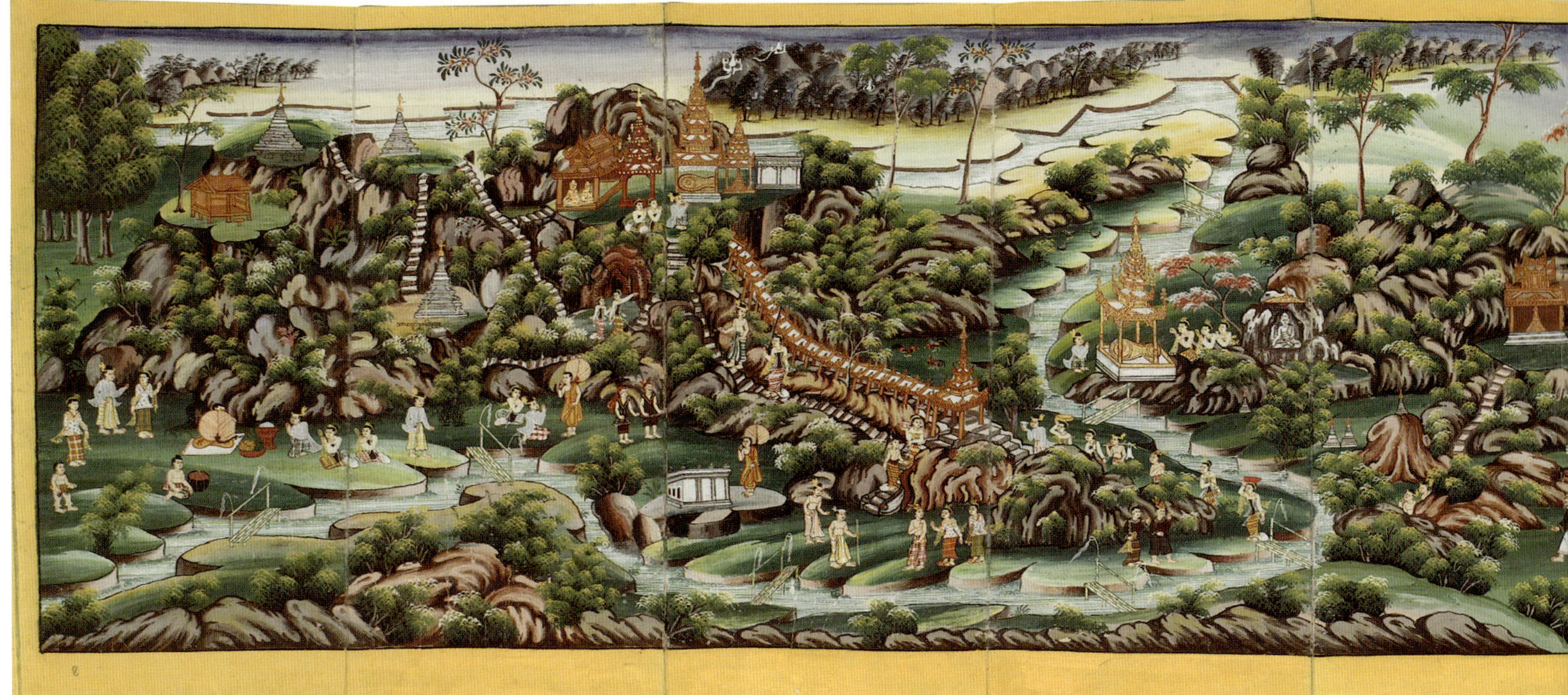

Figure 52. Shwe Hset Taw pilgrimage site.

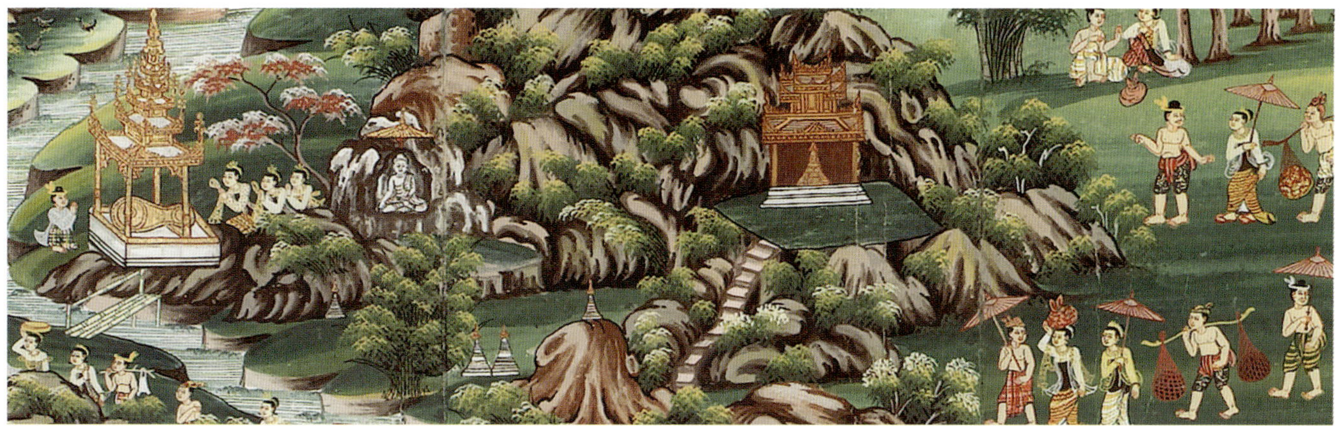

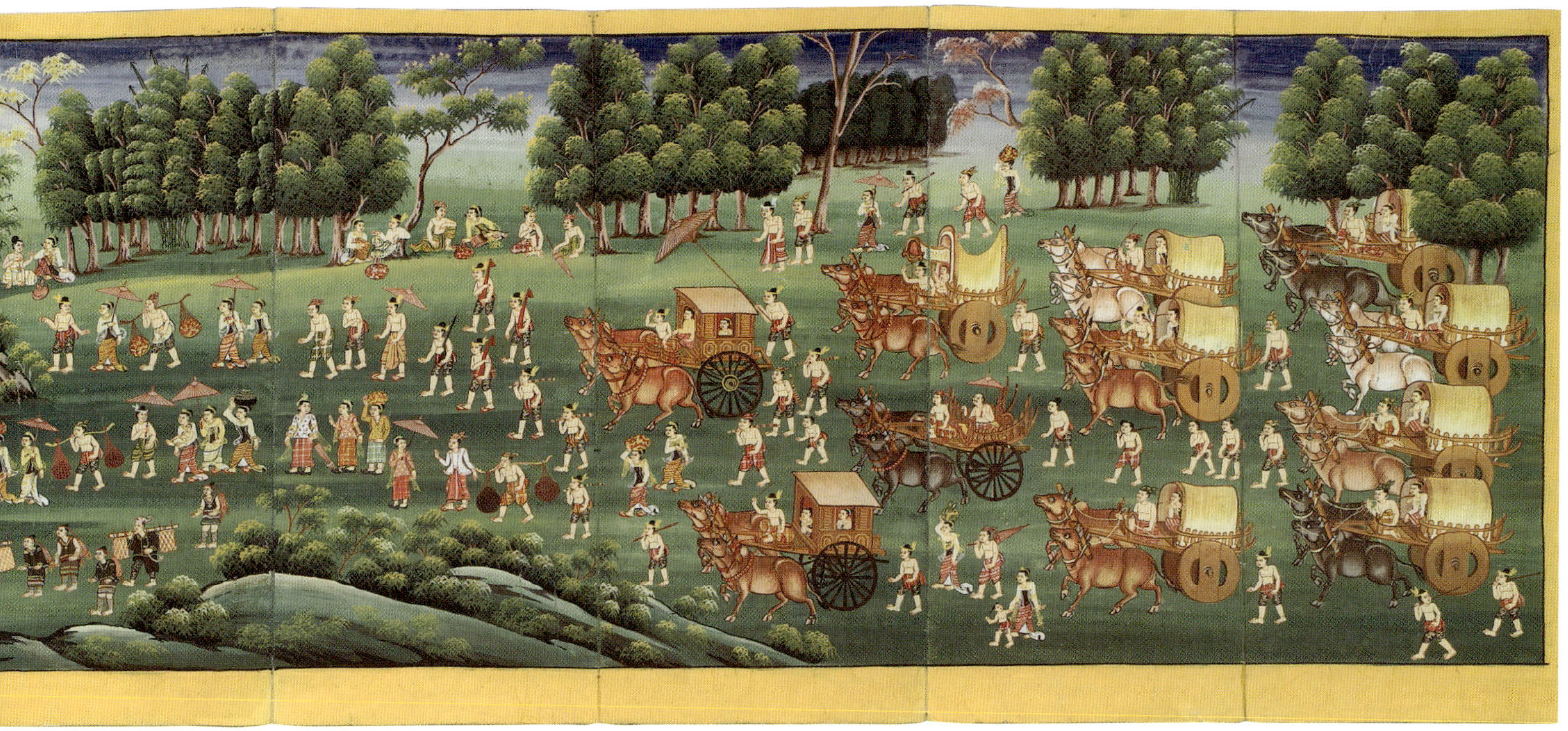

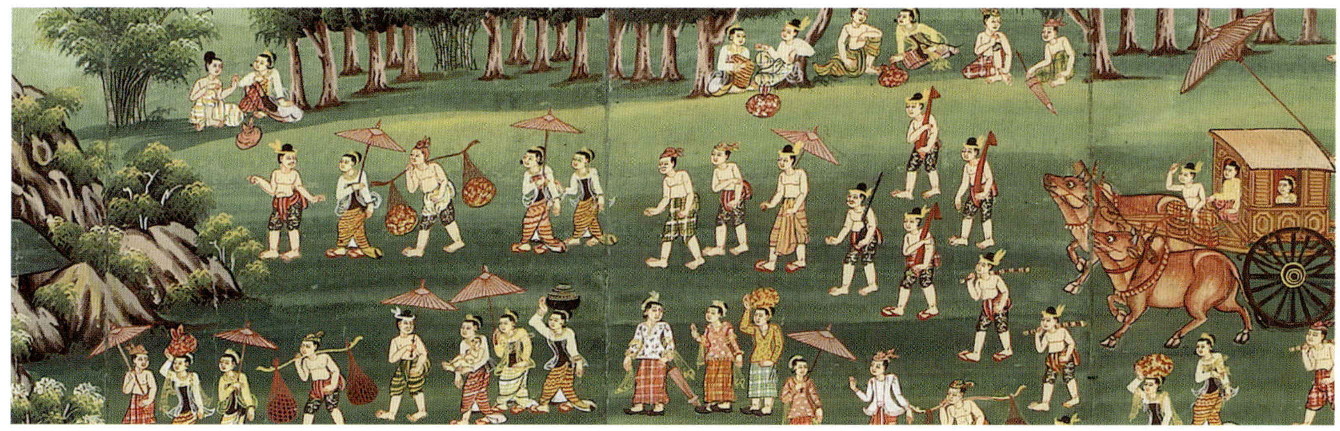

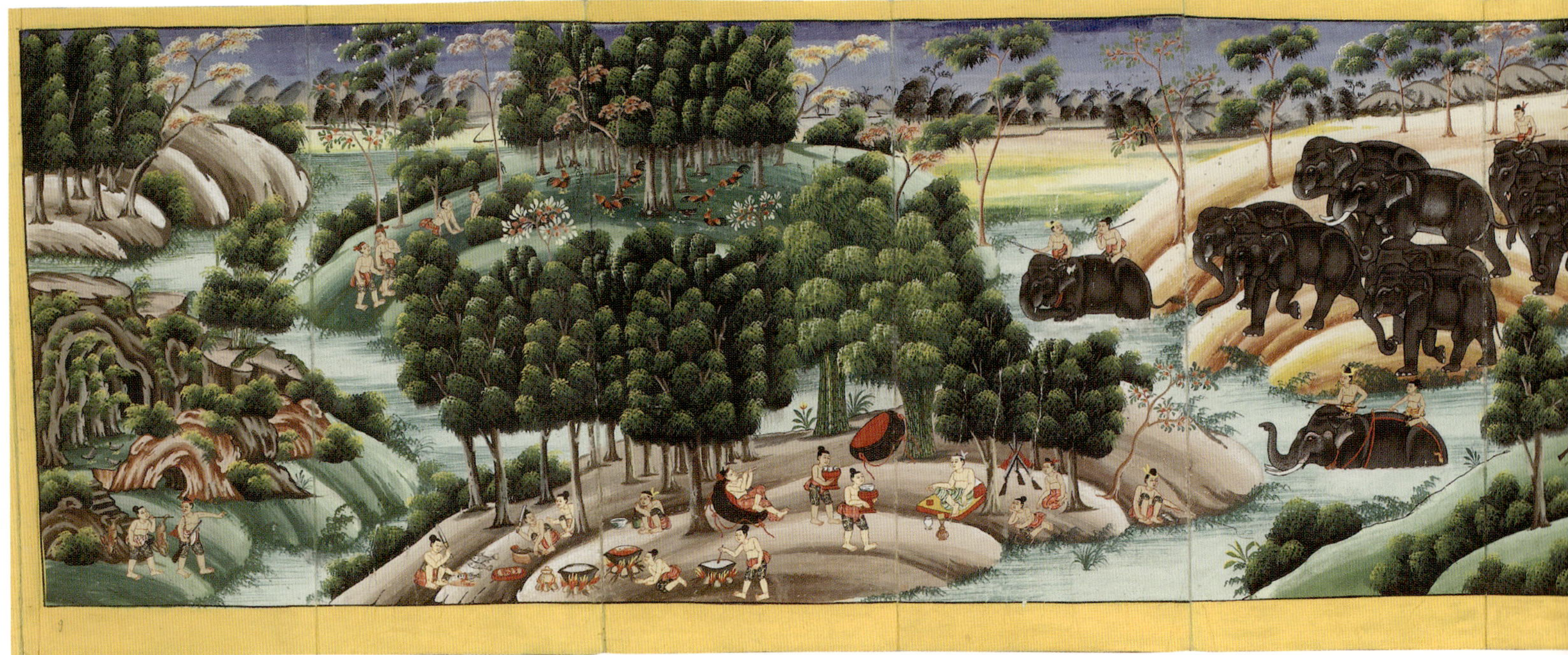

Figure 53. Capture of elephants.

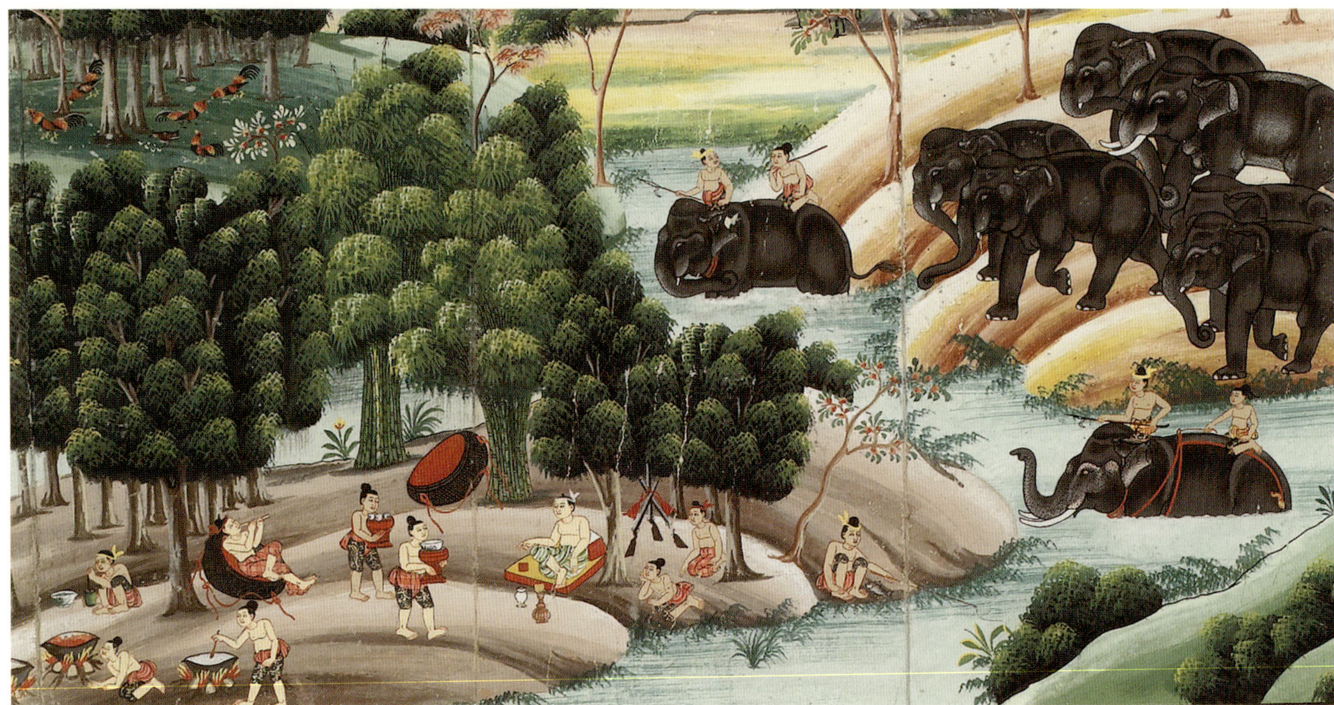

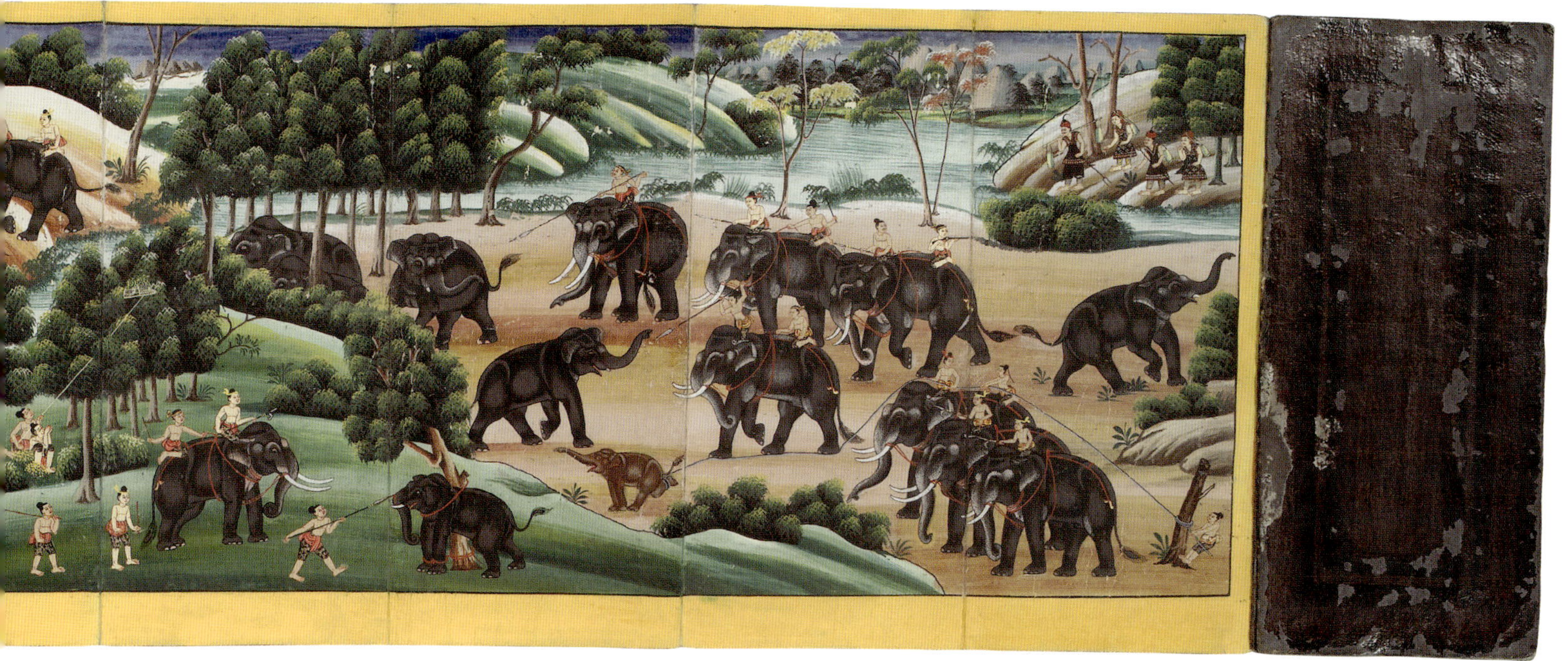

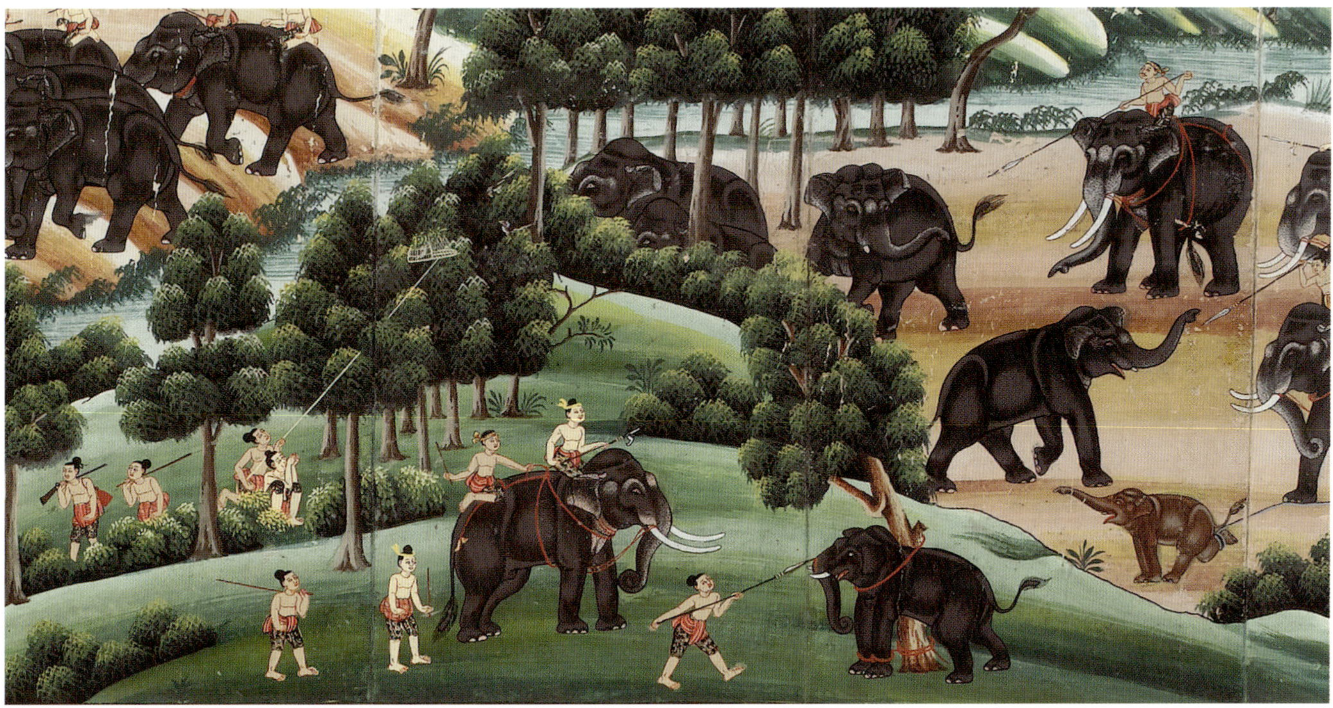

The last *parabaik* (MA 1661) was acquired by the museum in 1955 and was studied by Marguerite-Marie Deneck, who worked at the Guimet Museum at that time. She was able to connect this impressive manuscript with another Burmese manuscript in the museum that relates a former life of the Buddha, the Nimi Jātaka (MA 565)—a manuscript with the artist's name, Saya Ko Kya Niun, and dated 1869. The impressive manuscript has carved wooden covers (fig. 54) that are lacquered and feature four *devatā* in relief who are shown flying and armed with batons. Colored glass is inlaid in the ornamental borders. Four carved ivory buttons in the corners protect the covers when laid flat so that the decorative elements are not crushed when the miniatures are viewed.

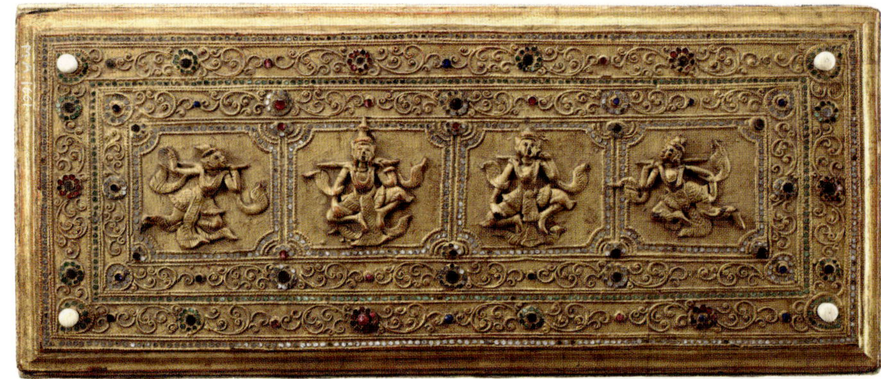

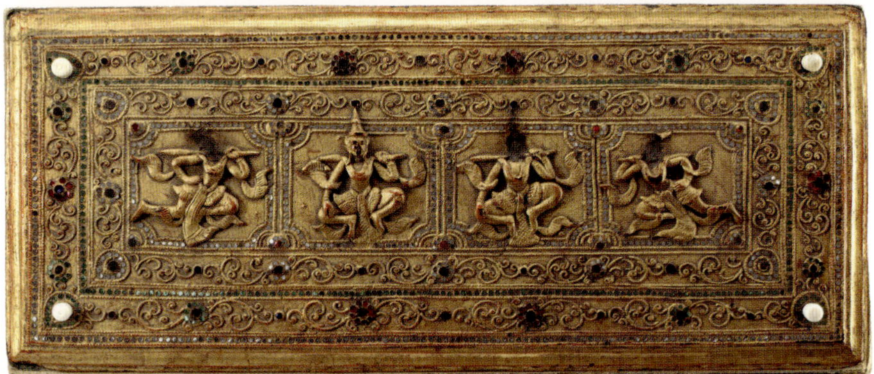

Figure 54. Lacquered wooden covers of *parabaik* MA 1661.

Figure 55. (*Below*) Audience hall at the Mandalay royal palace.

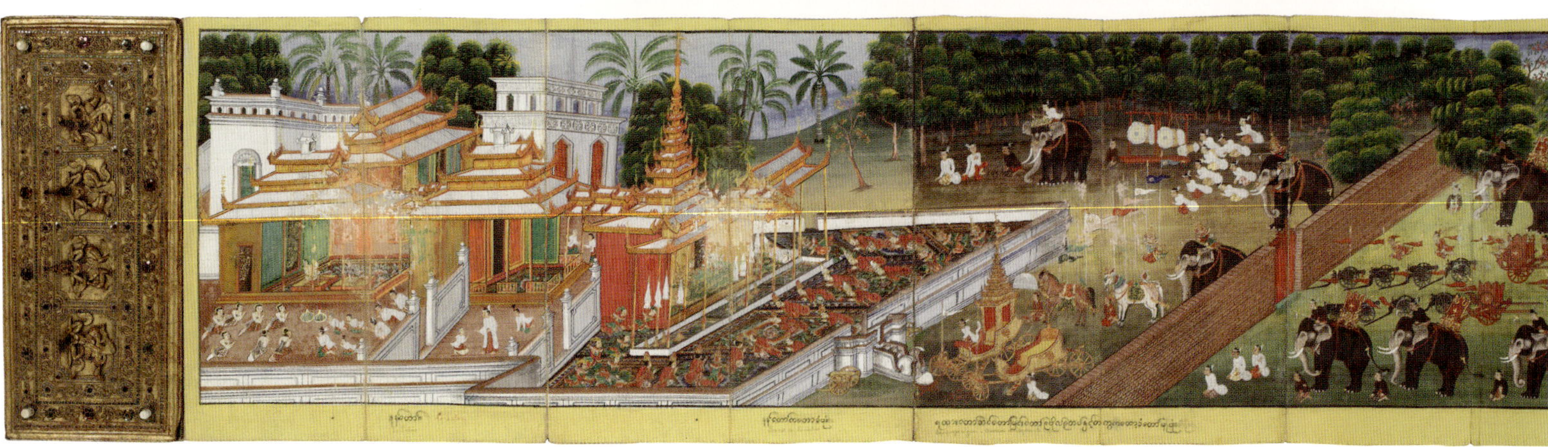

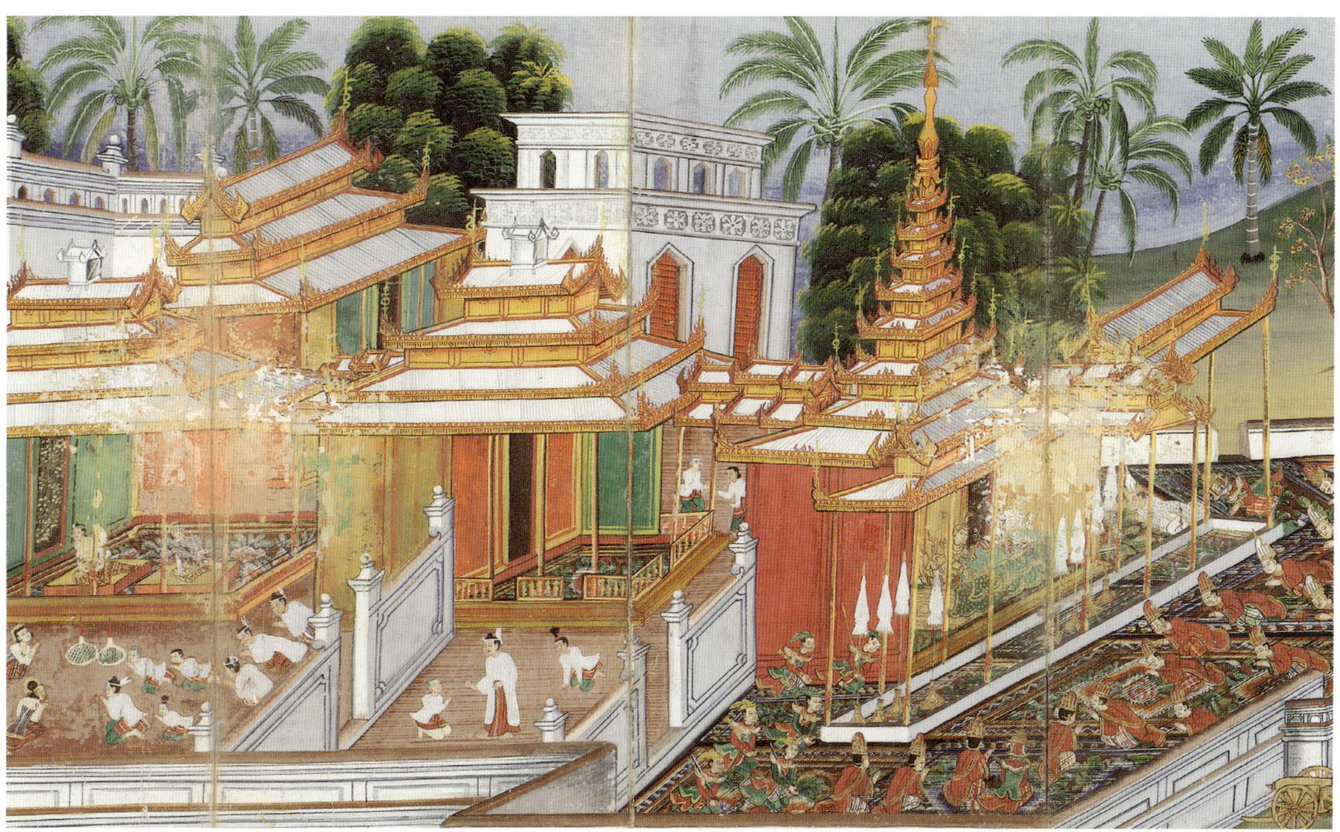

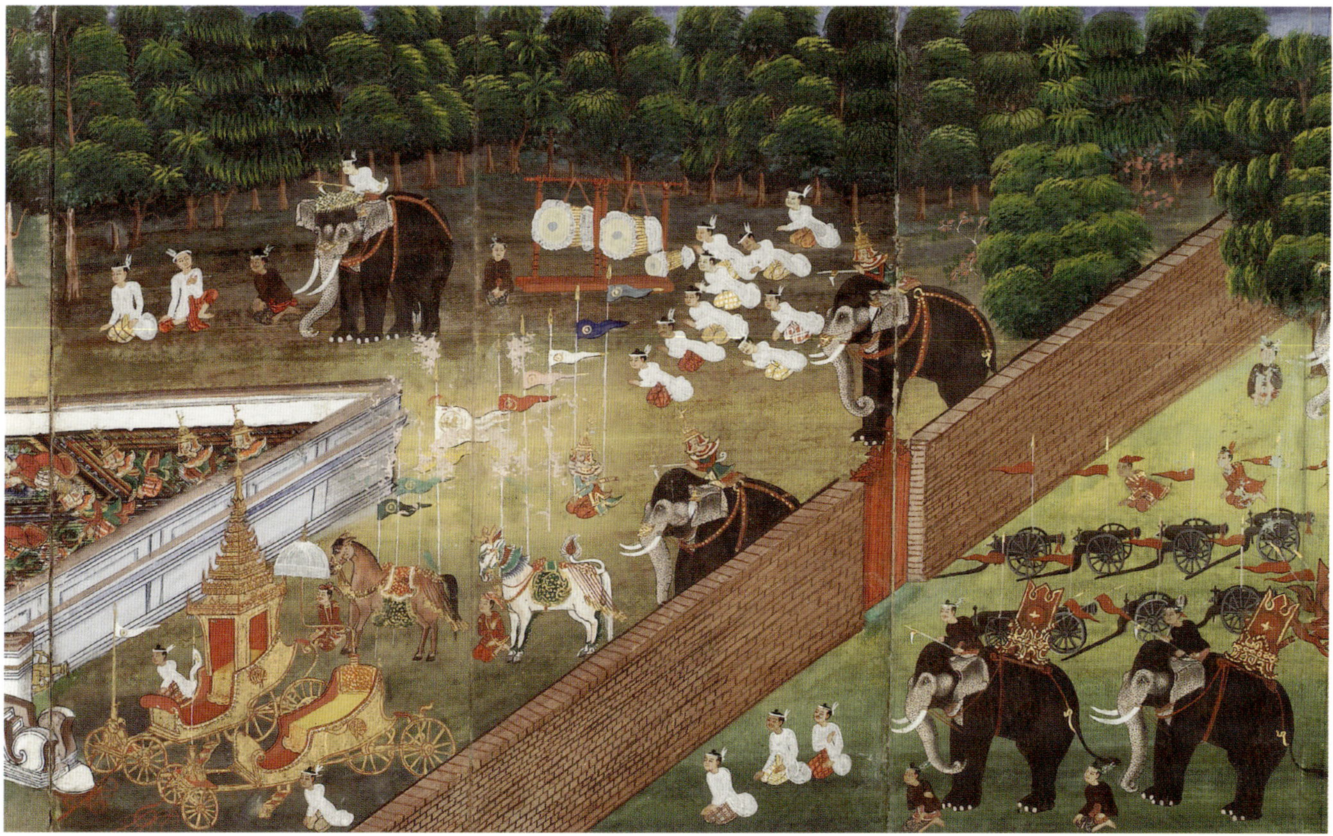

Inside, the scenes mark the court festivals held throughout the year following an original approach. The first part (fig. 55) shows in more detail the great audience hall of the Mandalay royal palace where "ministers and nine officers present the soldiers of their regiments," whose arrival can be seen.[1] This scene is followed in figure 56 by the "entry of the Sawbwas (Shan princes) tributary to the king, and ministers and nobles." Their palanquins are stationed by the palace walls and they get ready to enter the palace on foot. A little further away (fig. 57), some of them are still on the road, surrounded by their escorts, having just entered the

Figure 56. Arrival of Shan tributary princes at the royal palace.

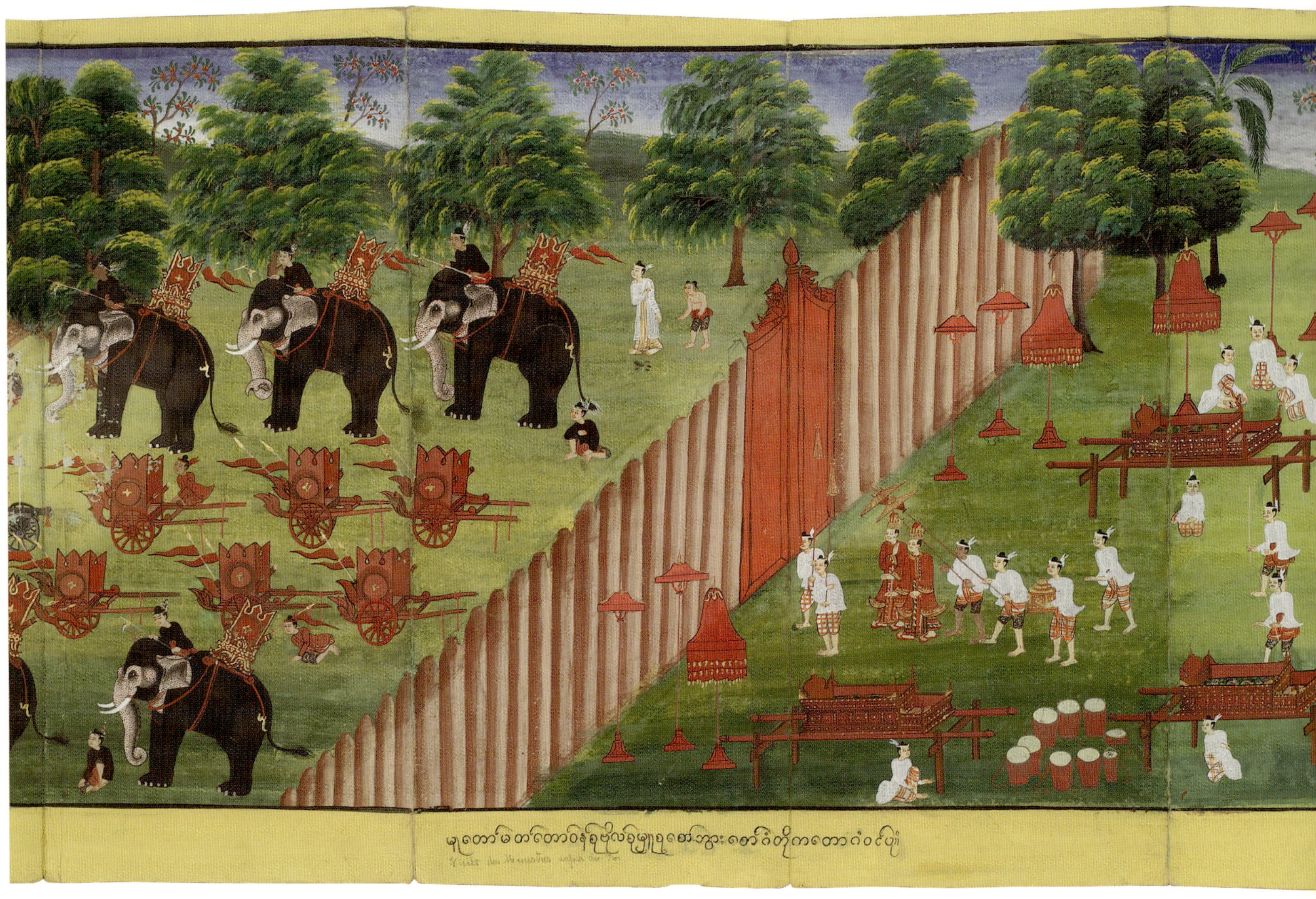

gates of the city. The ramparts and moat serve to make a transition to the next scene (figs. 57–58), which, in contrast, shows a royal excursion. A sophisticated protocol means there are many retinues surrounding the royal couple in their covered chariot, which is pulled by four soldiers. Standard bearers, men with fans or offerings, foot soldiers, mahouts, and even artillerymen, all arranged in perfect symmetry, are part of the slow procession. They are perhaps going to the royal pavilion in the following scene (fig. 59), which is next to a royal monastery that is painted with the same attention to detail.

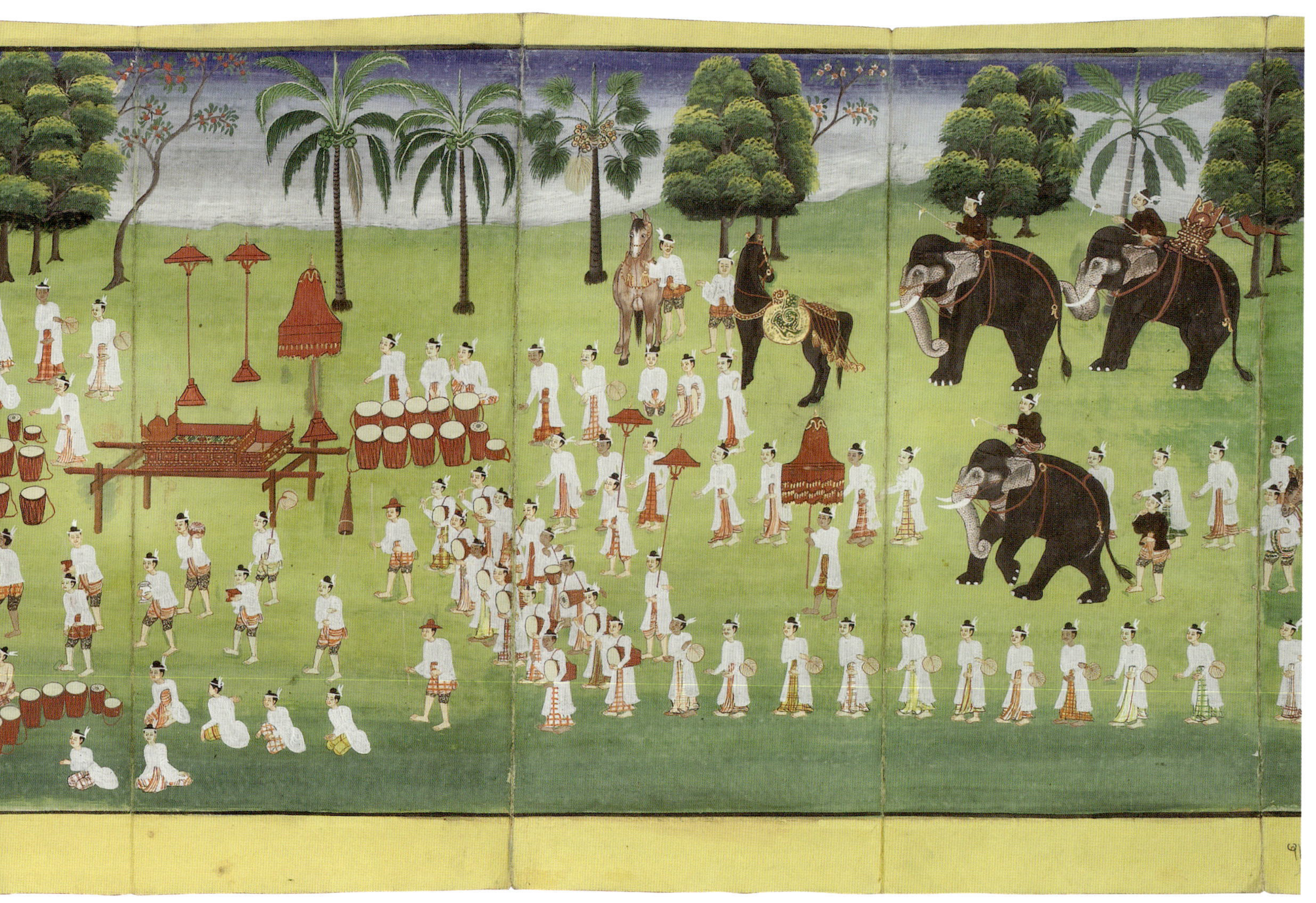

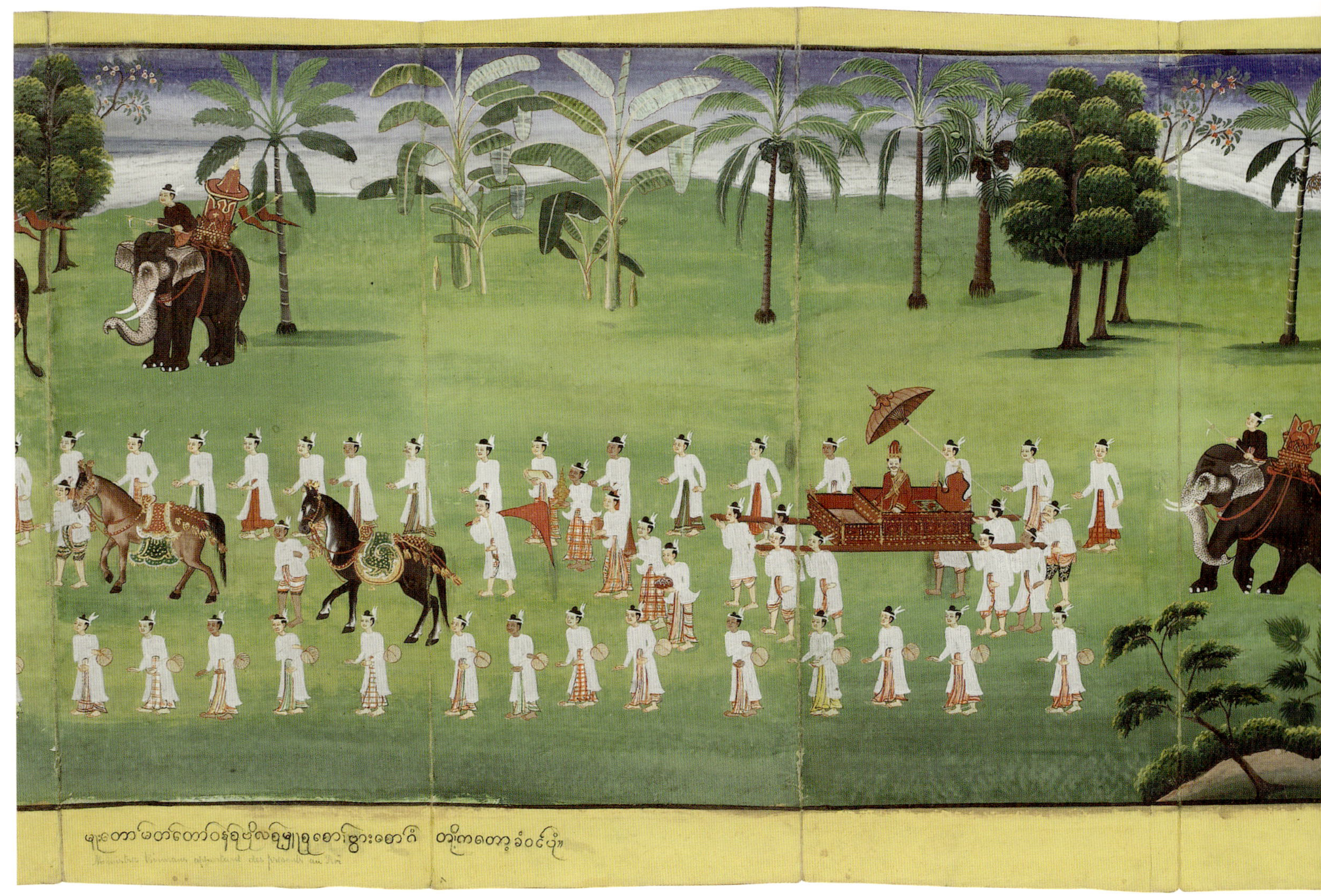

Figure 57. Entry of Shan princes into the city.

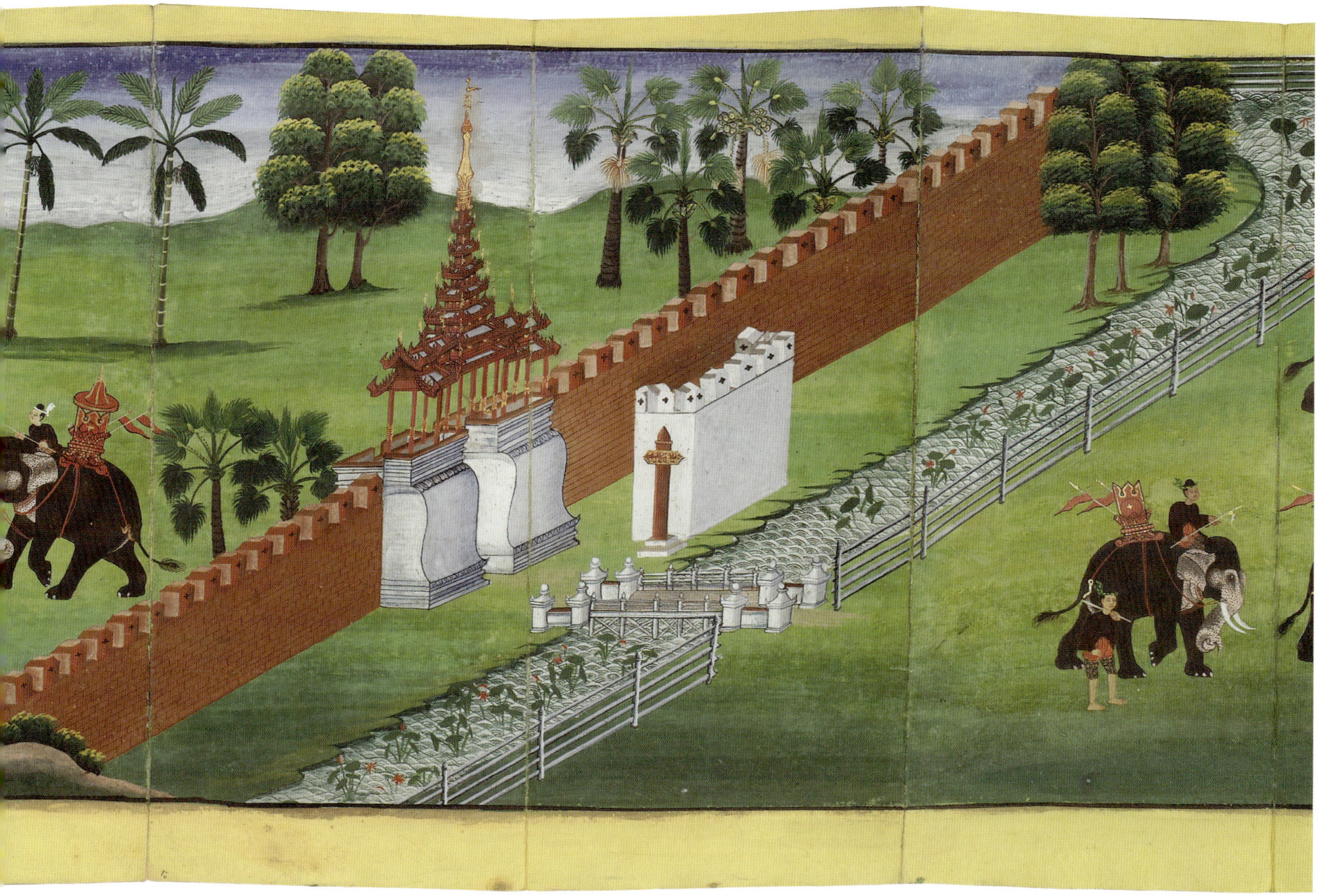

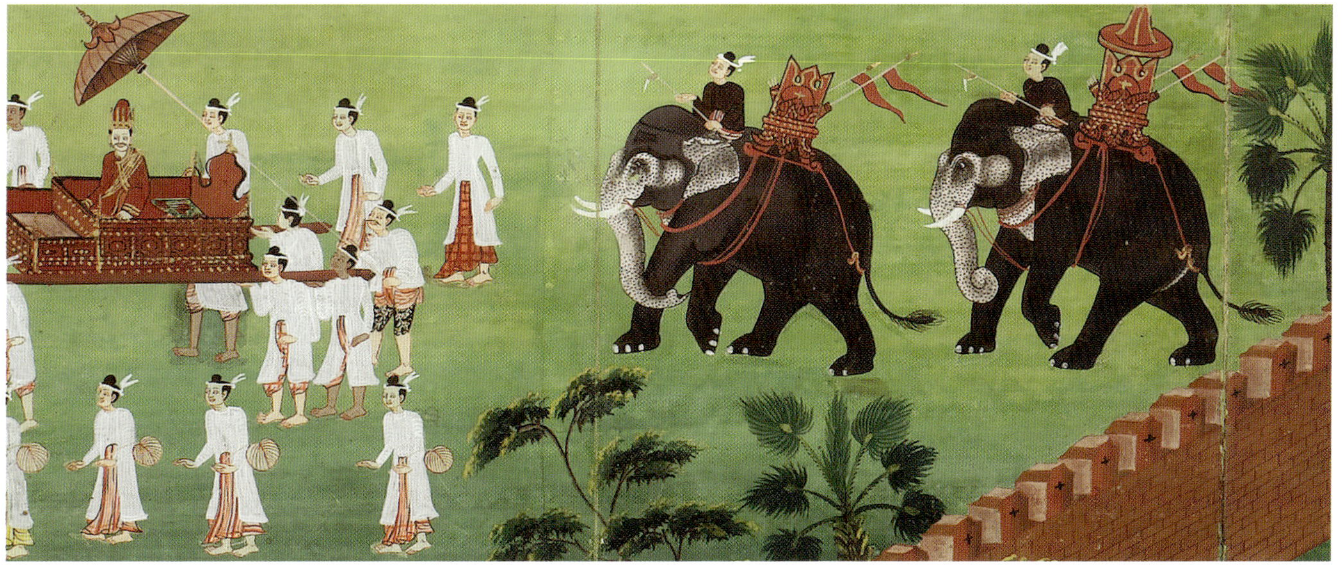

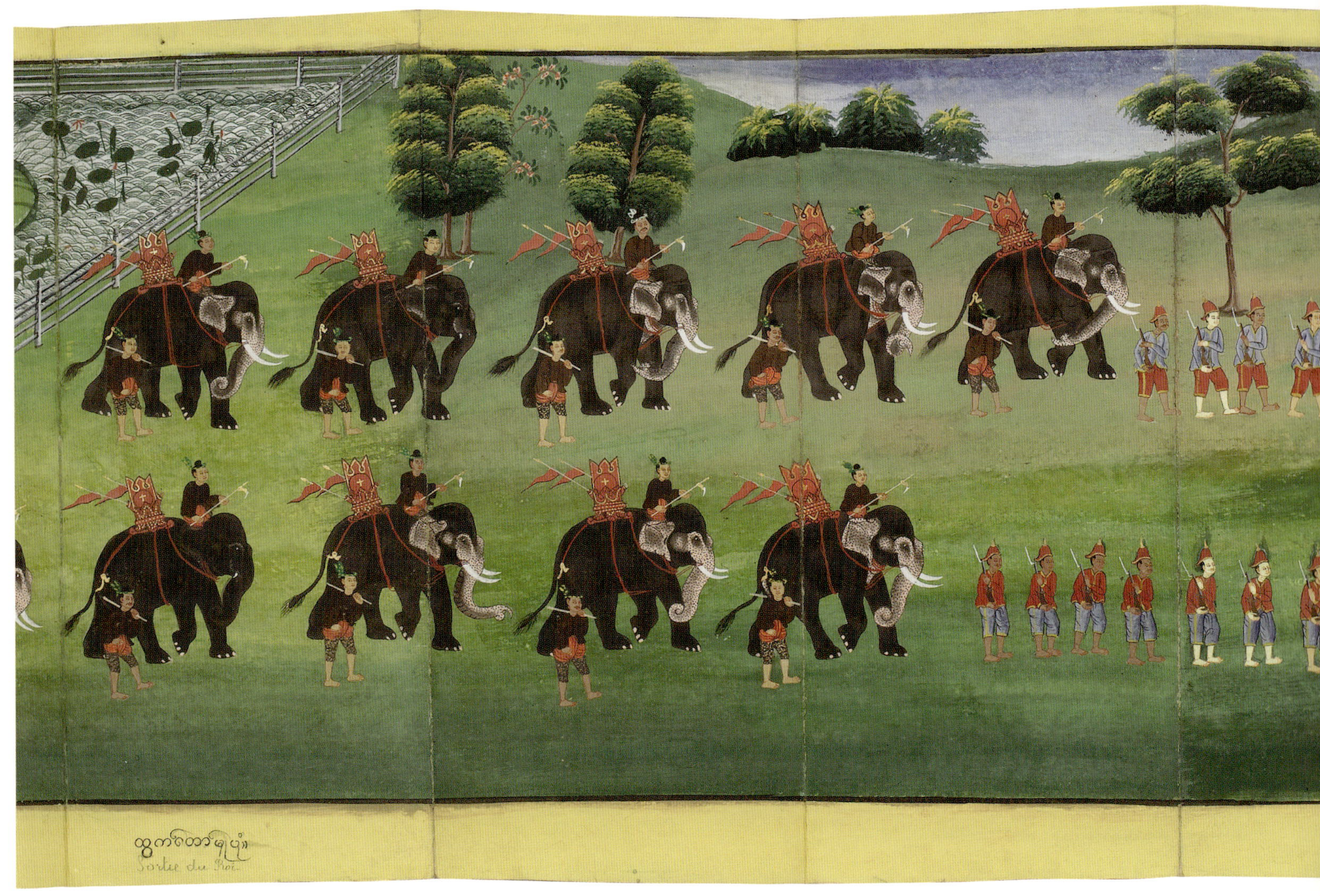

Figure 58. A royal excursion.

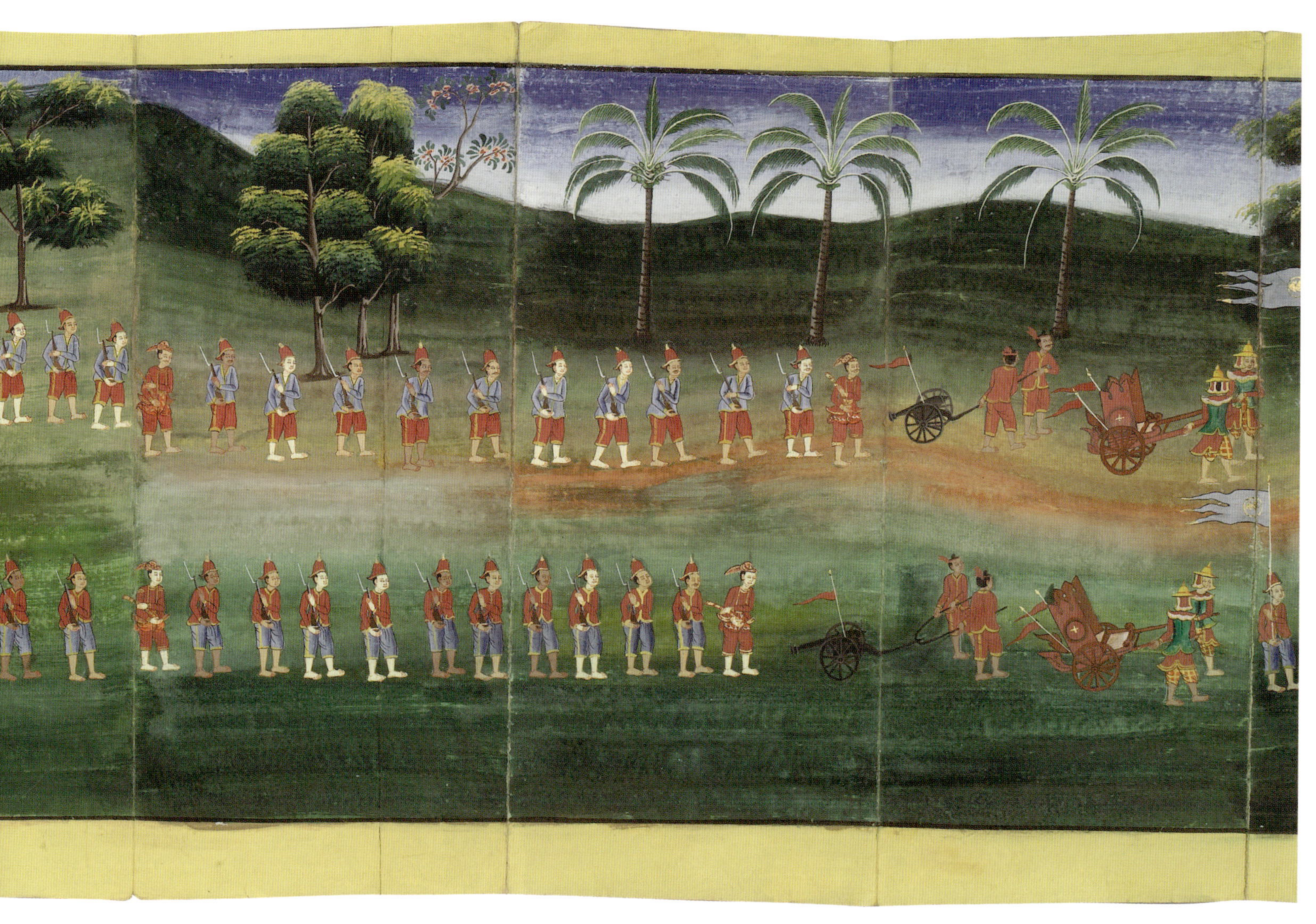

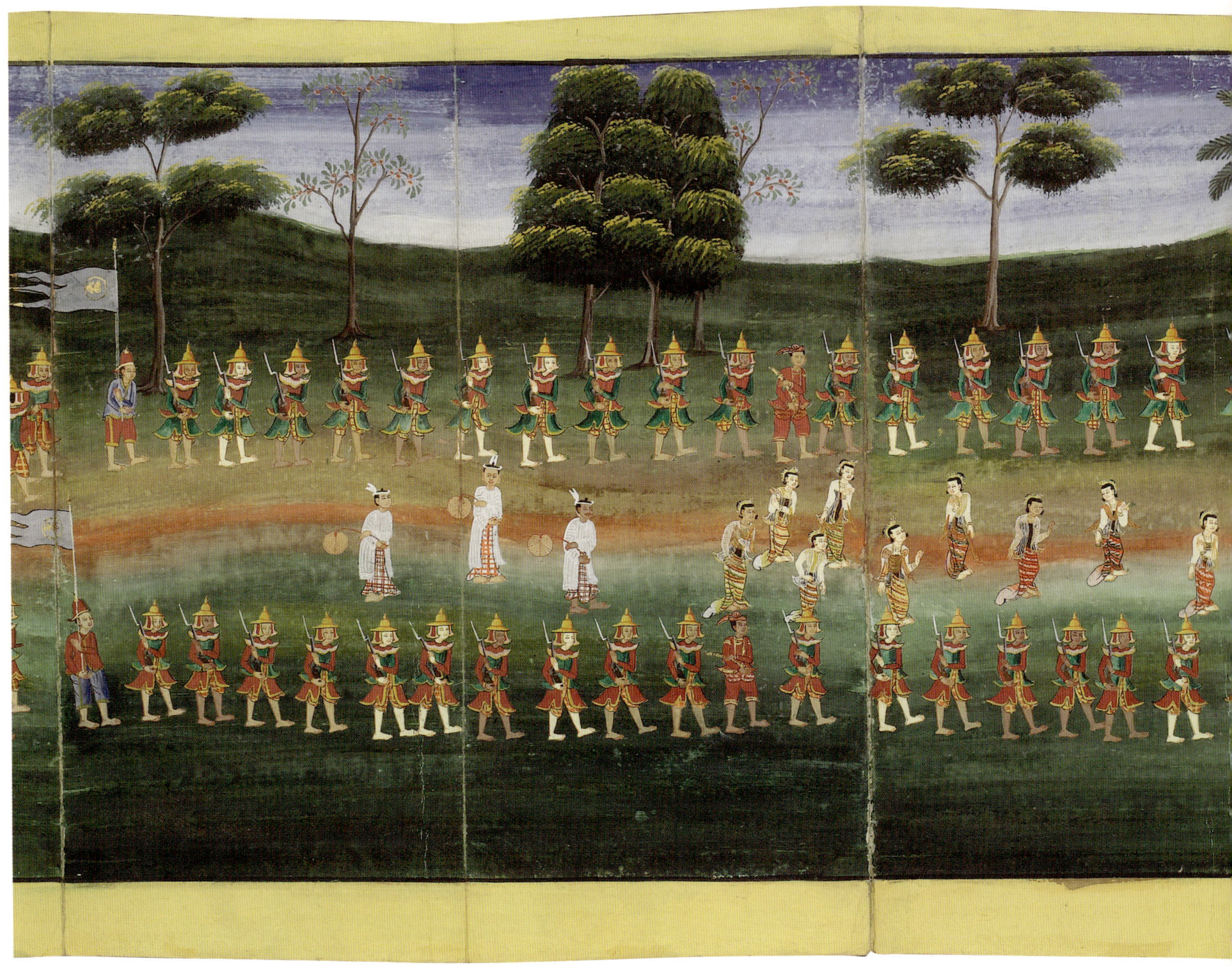

Figure 58. (continued)

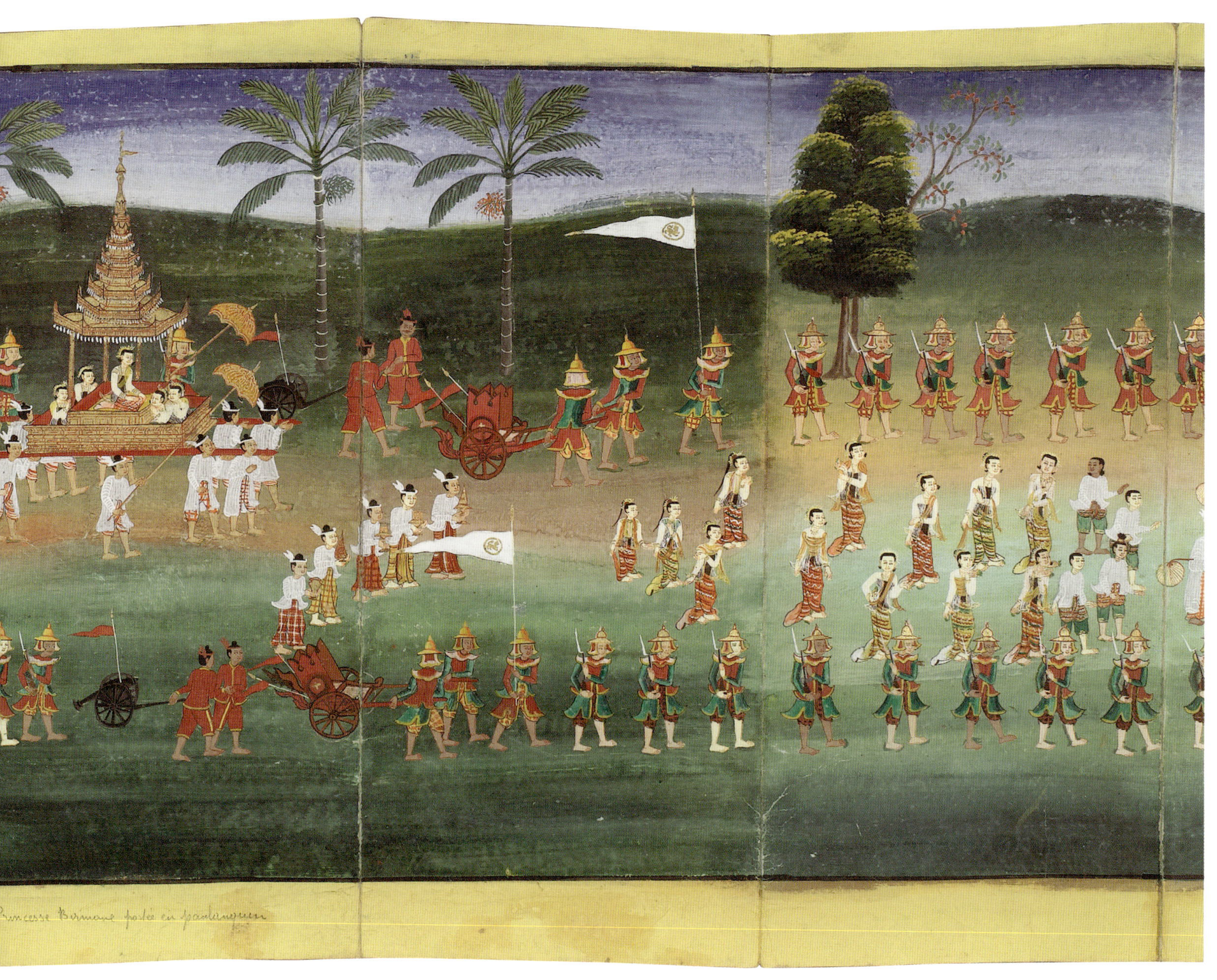
Princesse Birmane portée en palanquin

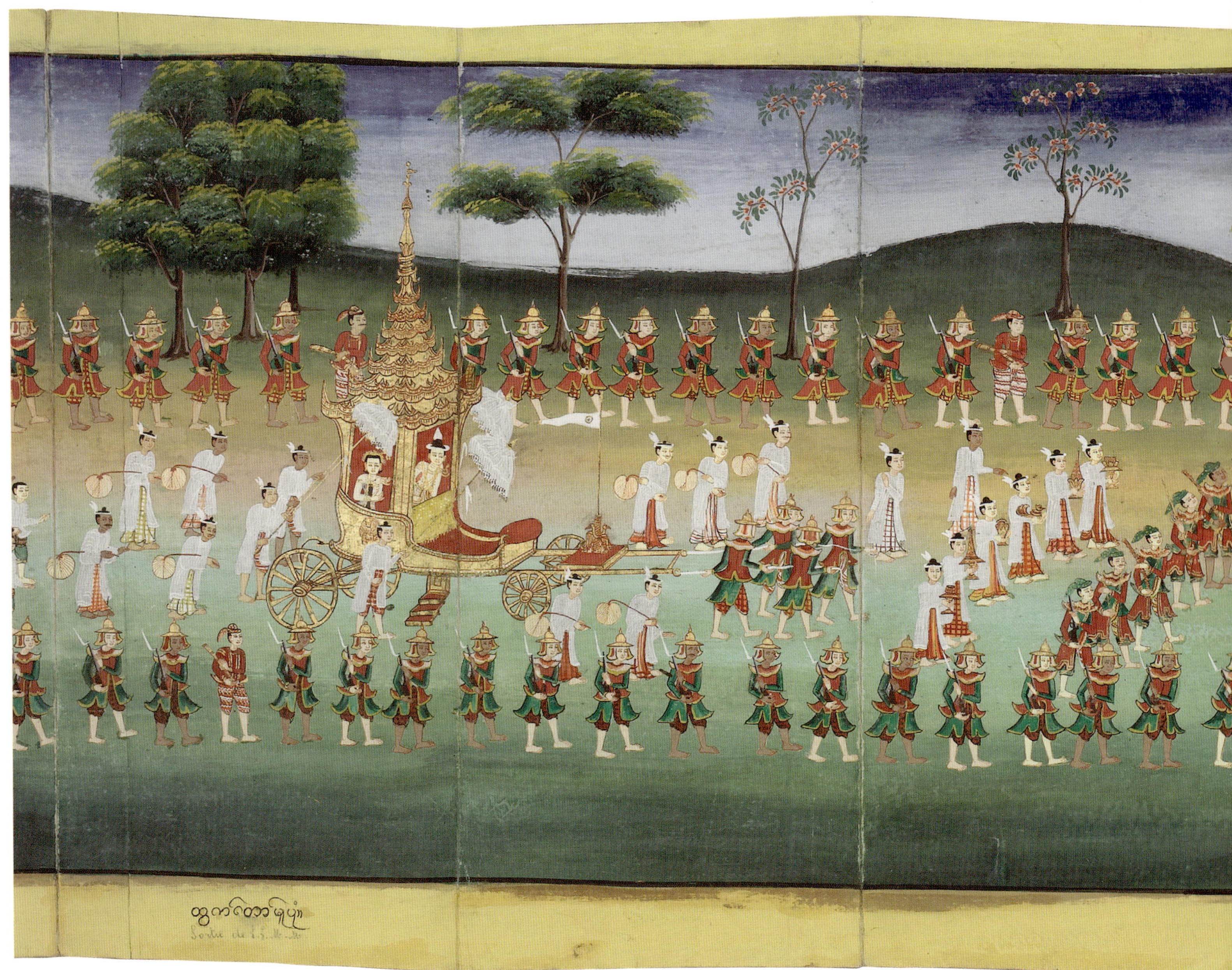

Figure 58. (continued)

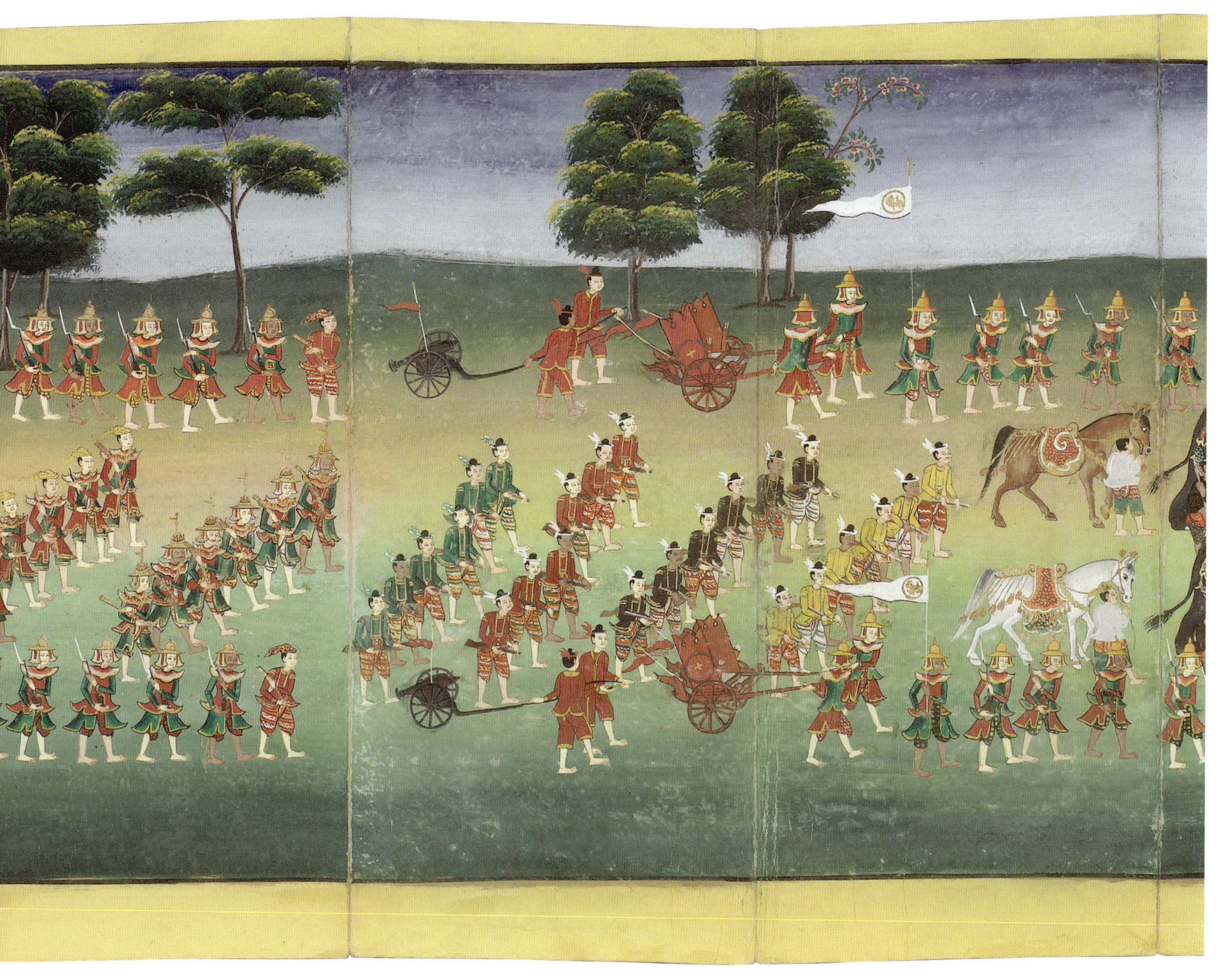

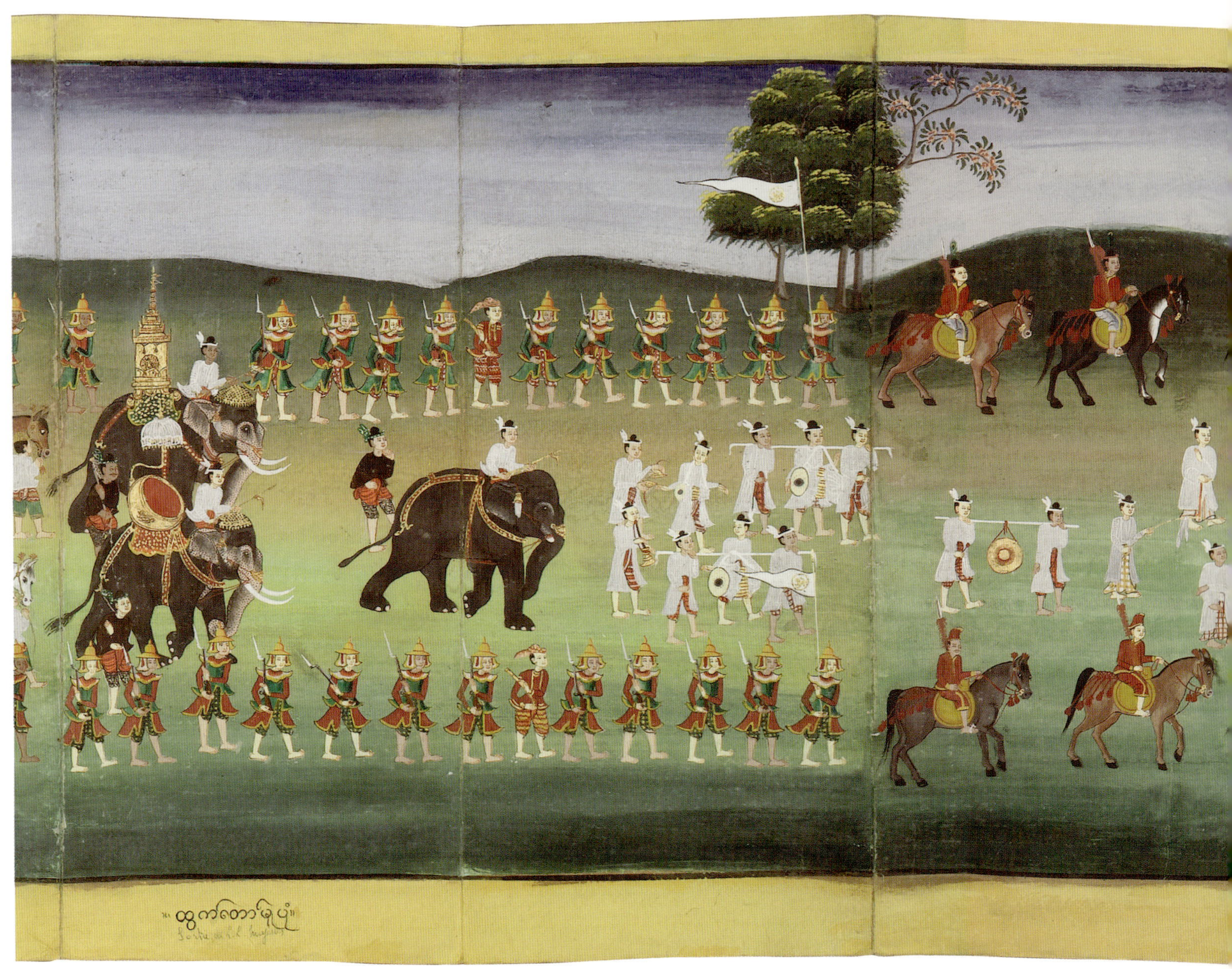

Figure 58. (continued)

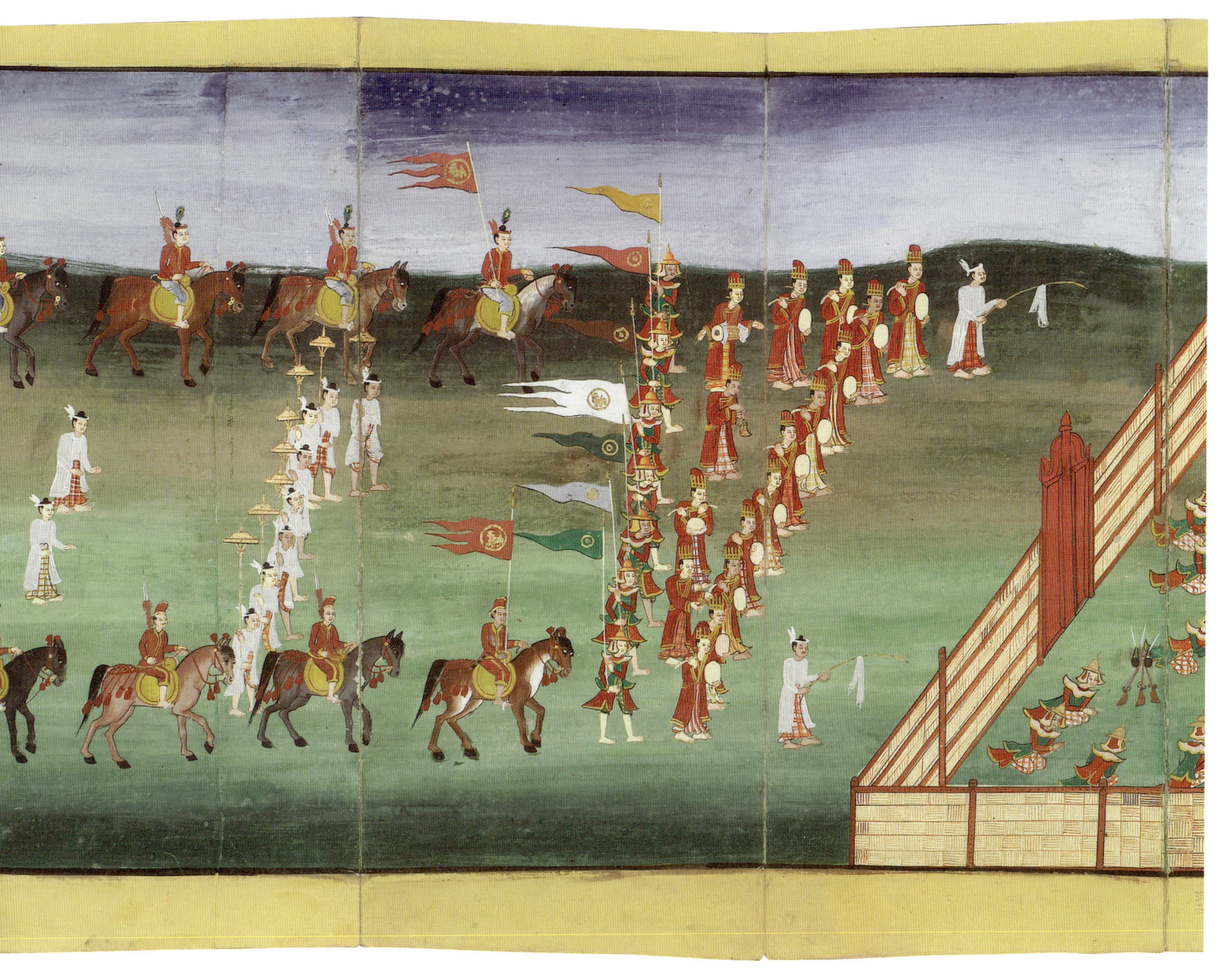

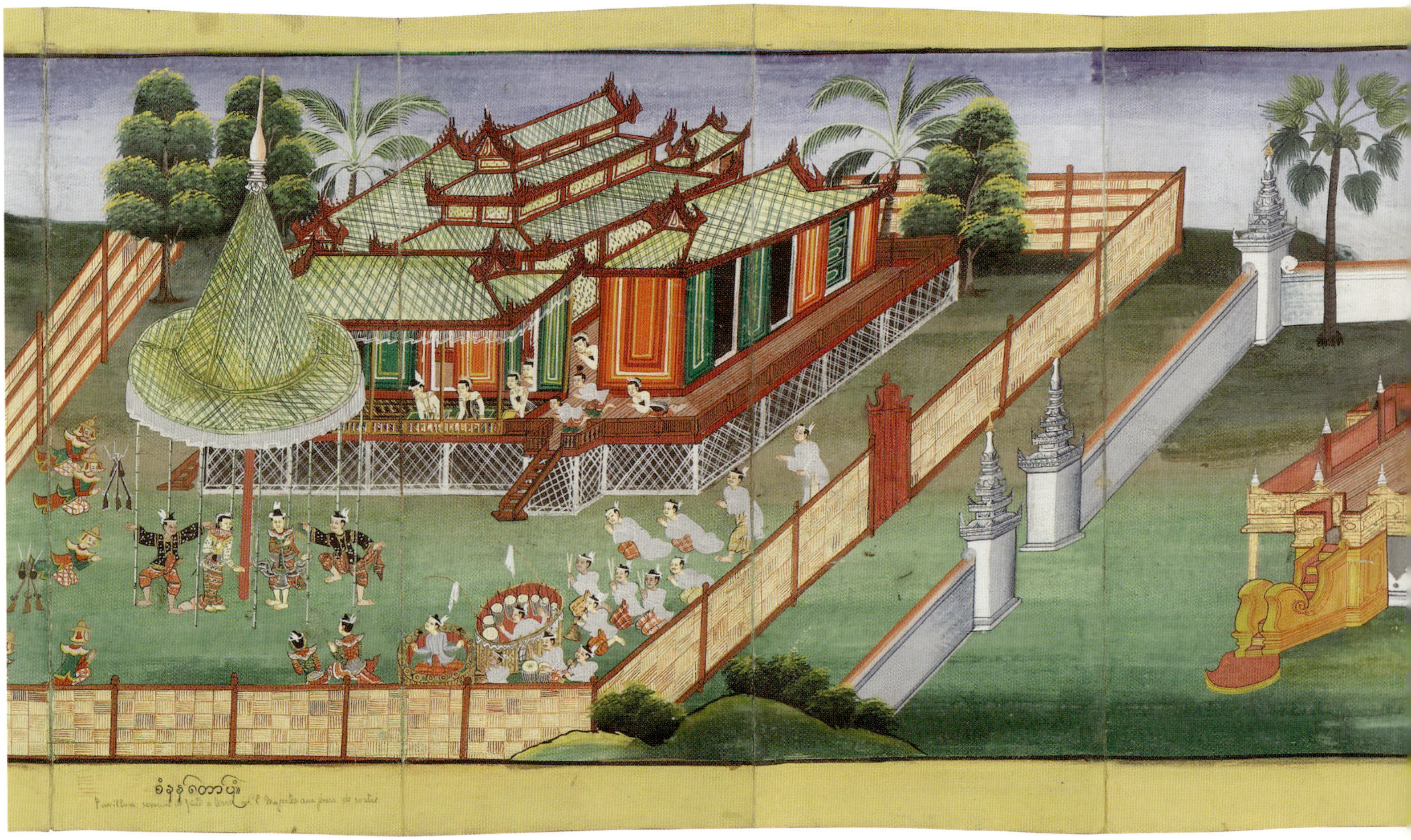

Figure 59. Royal pavilion next to a royal monastery.

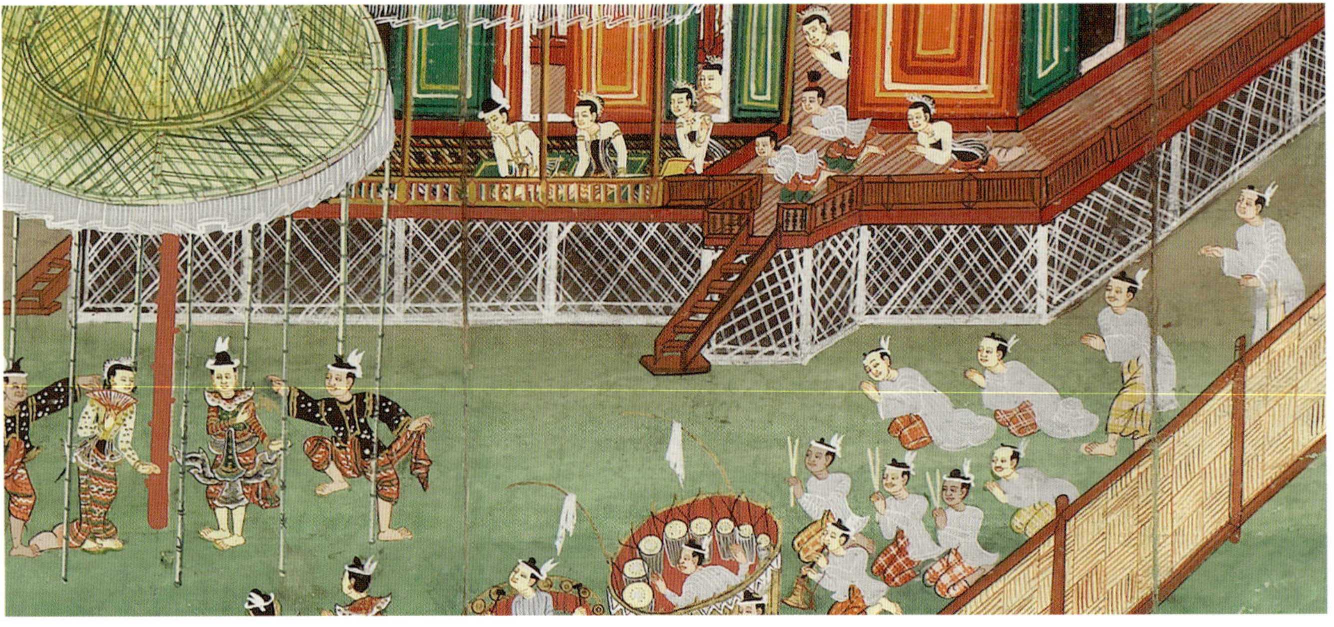

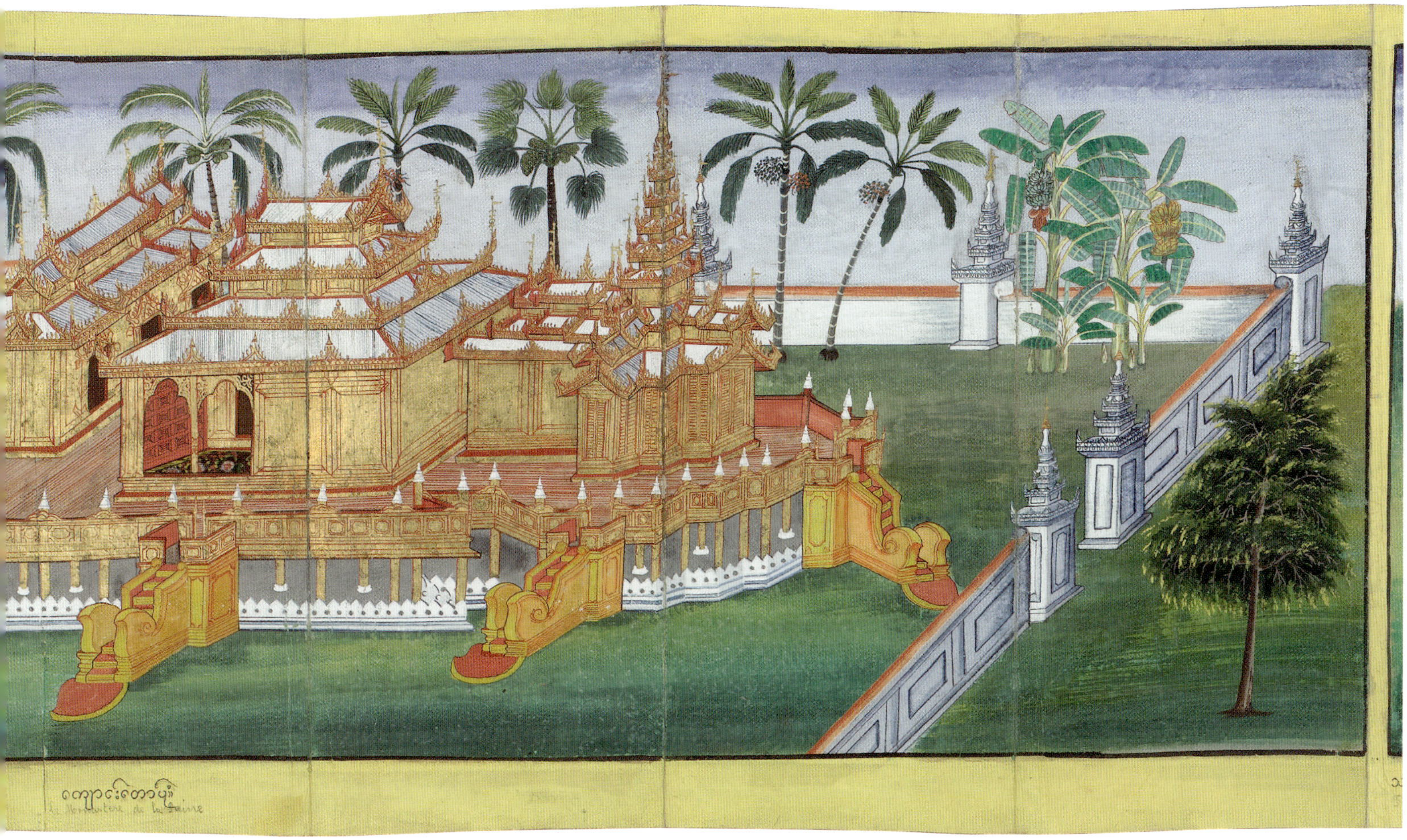

ကျောင်းတော်ပုံ။
Le Monastère de la Reine

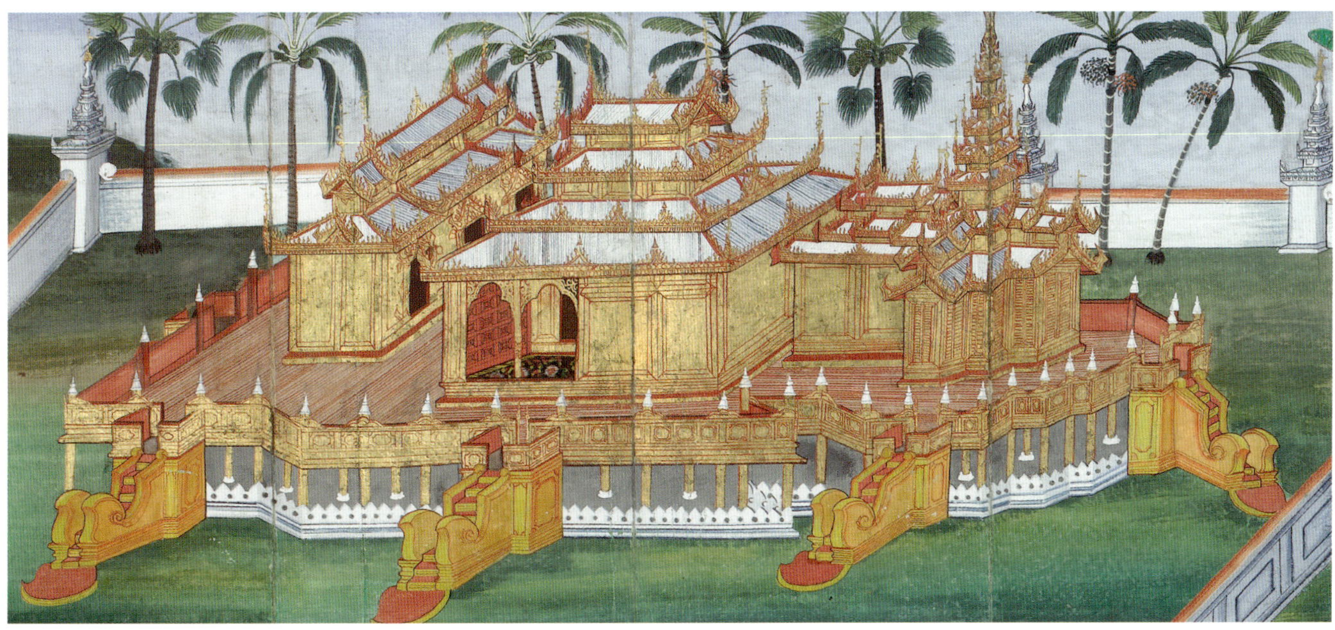

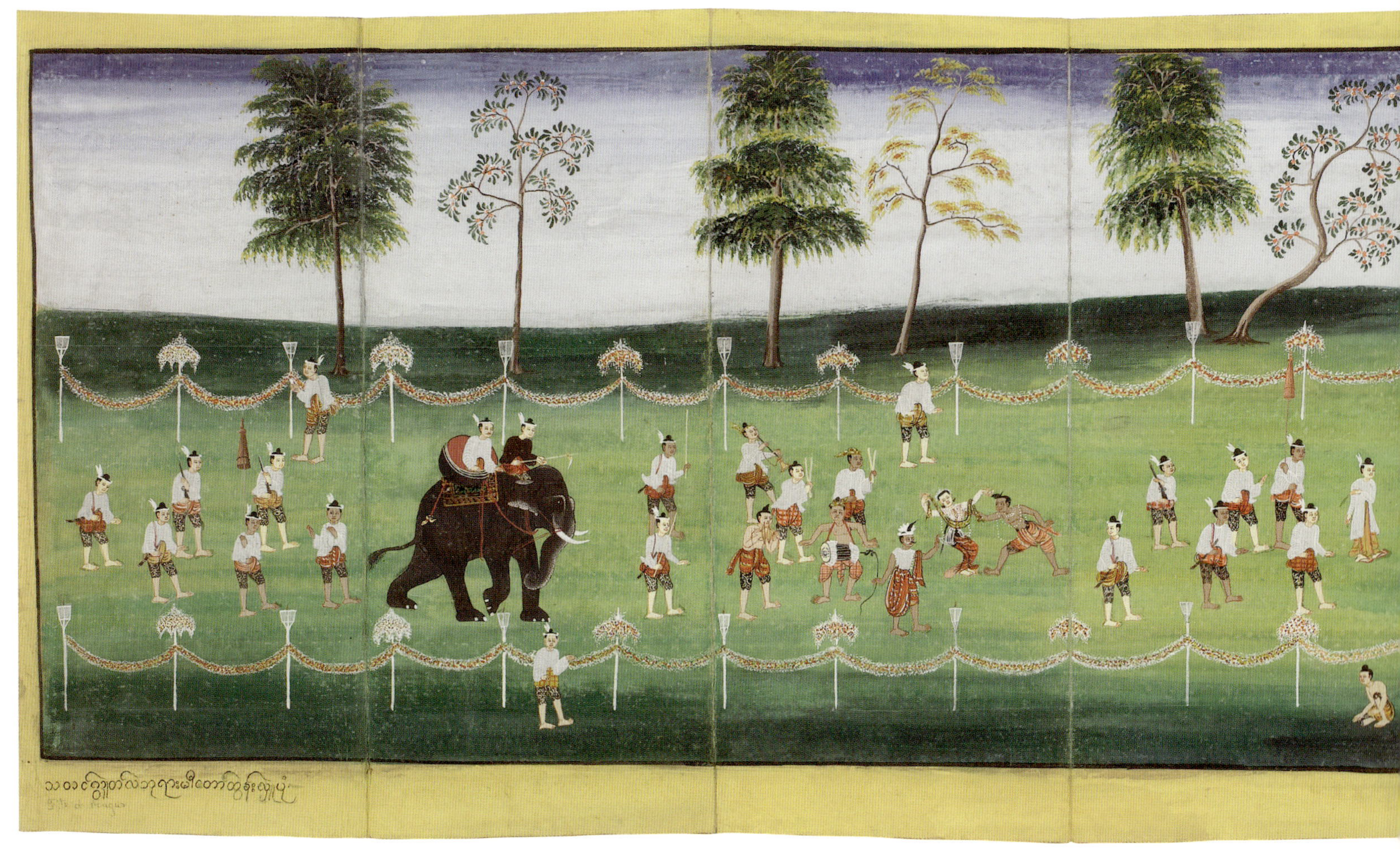

Figure 60. Thadingyut သီတင်းကျွတ် (September–October).
Making offerings at the shining pagoda.

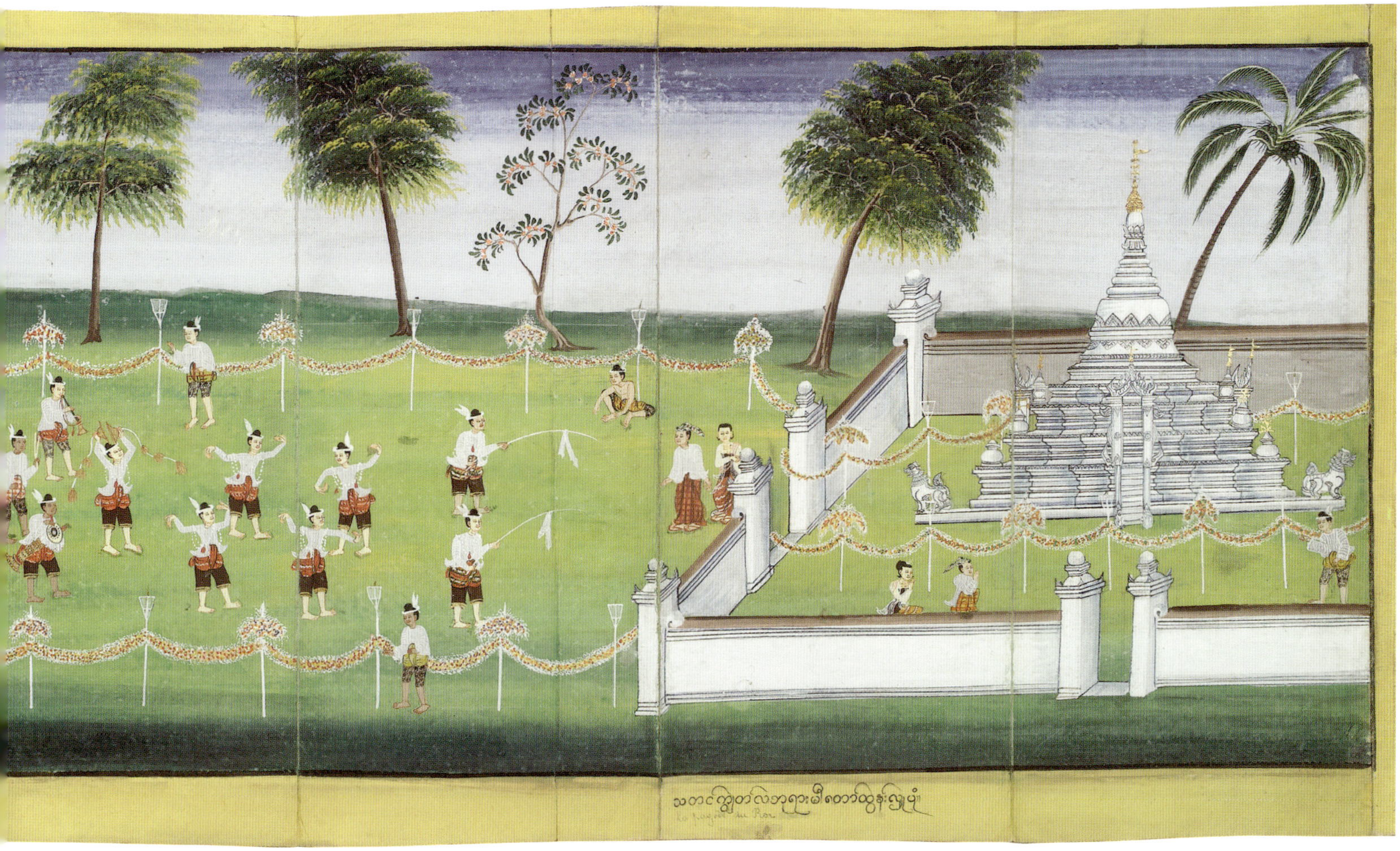

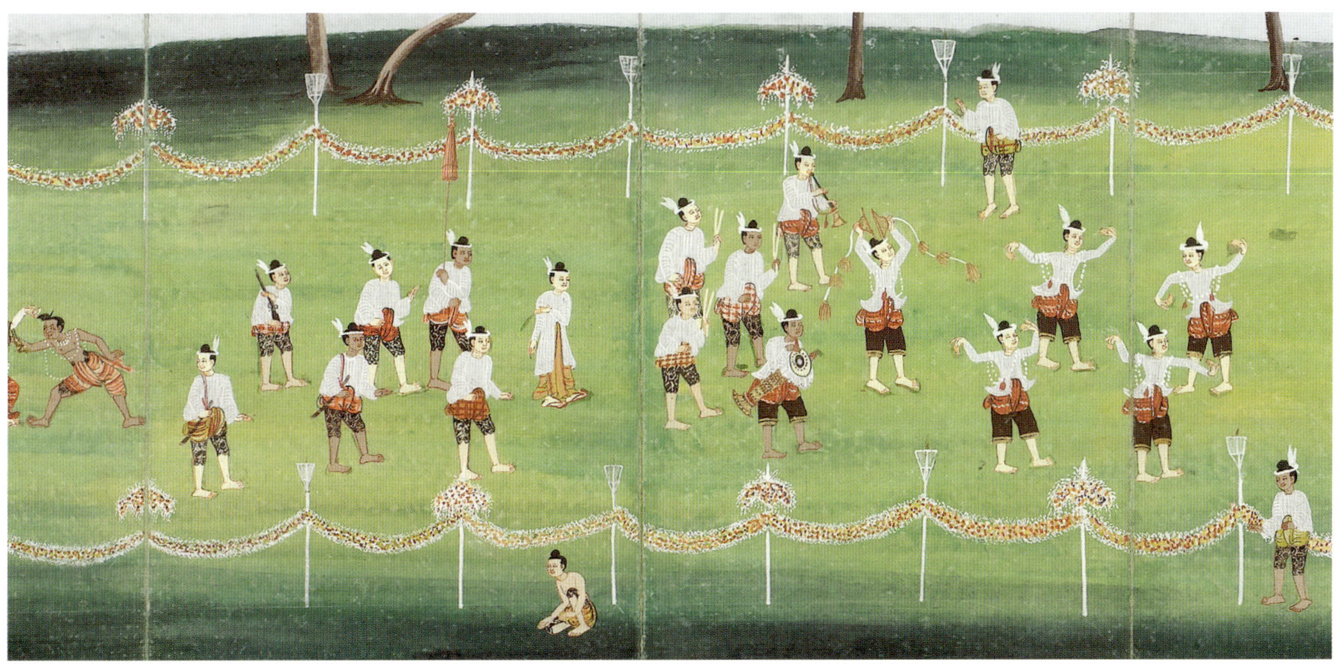

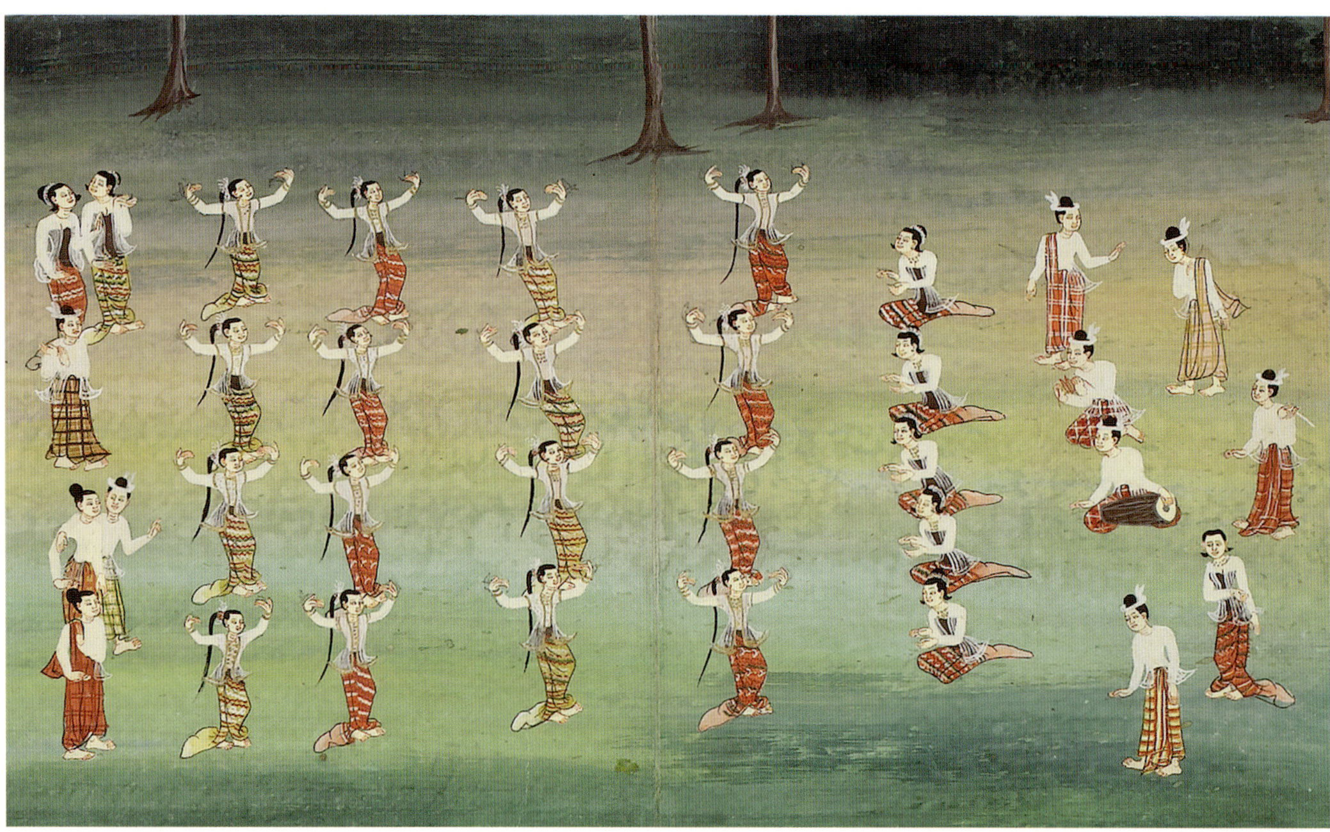

Figure 61. The dance for the entry of the white elephant.

The second part of the manuscript shows the festivals of the twelve months, whose names are given under each scene. During Thadingyut (the seventh month, September–October), which is pictured in figure 60, there are pagoda festivals with full illuminations. Musicians, dancers, and actors add to the festivities leading up to the stupas decorated with garlands of flowers. This is followed by an interpolating scene of dancers welcoming the entry of a royal white elephant (fig. 61) and the entry of the elephant itself (fig. 62). For the new year, in Tagu (the first month, March–April), the royal water festival is held (fig. 63). This is the moment to purify and pay respects to Buddha statues placed on top of artificial mounds. Women and men offer flowers and water. This full-moon day is a time for dance, pantomimes, and water battles. The second month (fig. 64), Kason (April–May), is the period of the court festival when "the Bodhi tree is watered with shrine water." The manuscript then shows a royal procession (fig. 65) led by musicians and Yama Zatdaw actors as mentioned above. Waso (the fourth month, June–July), is the occasion for giving alms to monks, assigning the alms by drawing lots. The next extended scene is of a royal regatta, which is organized during the sixth month, Tawthalin (August–September). Among the boats in the flotilla painted here (fig. 66), the gilded royal barge with two figureheads of nagas and yakkhas is conspicuous. This impressive panorama is preceded in the manuscript by a vignette from the Nat festival in Wagaung, or August (fig. 67). Thadingyut (September–October), as mentioned earlier, is the occasion of monastery festivals. The scene here (fig. 68) shows a procession with models being offered. For the eighth and ninth months, Tazaungmon and Nadaw (October–November and November–December, respectively), more impressive chariots made of papier-mâché carry the offerings for pagodas (fig. 69). Elephant battles are organized for the tenth month, Pyatho (December–January), shown in figure 70, while more recreational festivities are shown in figure 71. For the eleventh month (fig. 72), Tabodwe (January–February), men playing tambours take offerings to the Buddha, while the twelfth month (fig. 73), Tabaung (February–March), is again a month for a pagoda festival during which there is a puppet show.

This last tableau is especially lively, with its theatrical spectacle that serves as a scene within a scene, echoing the first illustration in the manuscript; here, puppets on strings mimic the receiving of ministers at an audience in the palace. Like the *parabaiks*, these theater plays in miniature, still shown today, evoke with nostalgia the splendor of a court where all was show and celebration.

Notes

The author would like to thank the museum librarian, Dr. Cao Thi Liêu, for translating the captions in the manuscripts. Without her help, this article could not have been prepared in its present form.

1. See George W. Bird, Wanderings in Burma, pp. 254ff. for a detailed description of the royal palace, which became Fort Dufferin under British rule.

Bibliography

Bird, George W. *Wanderings in Burma*. London: F. J. Bright & Son, 1897.

Thant Myint-U. *The Making of Modern Burma*. Cambridge: Cambridge University Press, 2001.

Pollak, Oliver B. "Dynasticism and Revolt: Crisis of Kingship in Burma, 1837–1851." *Journal of Southeast Asian Studies* 7 (1976): 187–96.

Deneck, Marguerite-Marie. "Un manuscript birman au Musée Guiment: le Nimi Jataka." *Bulletin de la Société des études indochinoises* 32, no. 1 (1952): 63–78.

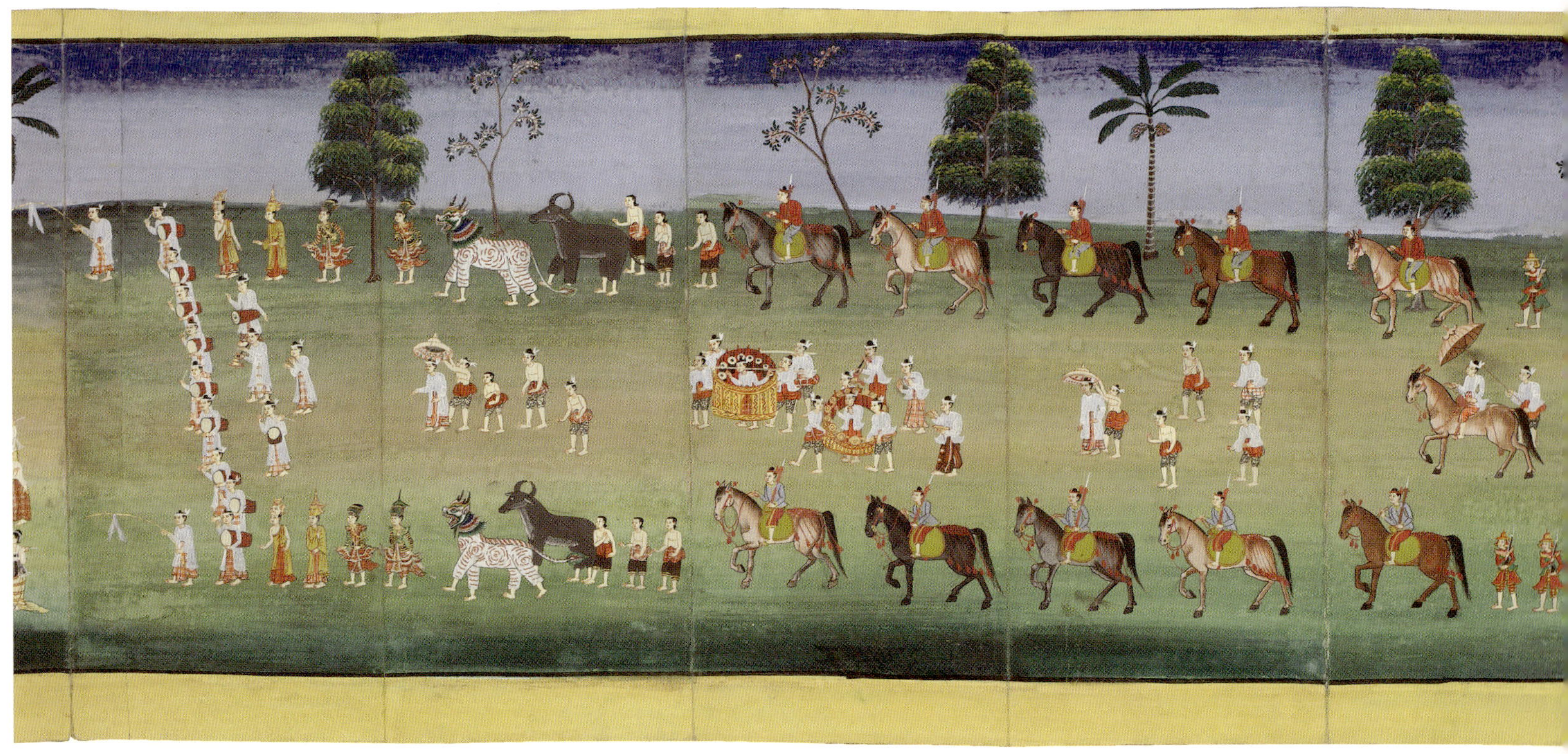

Figure 62. Entry of the royal white elephant.

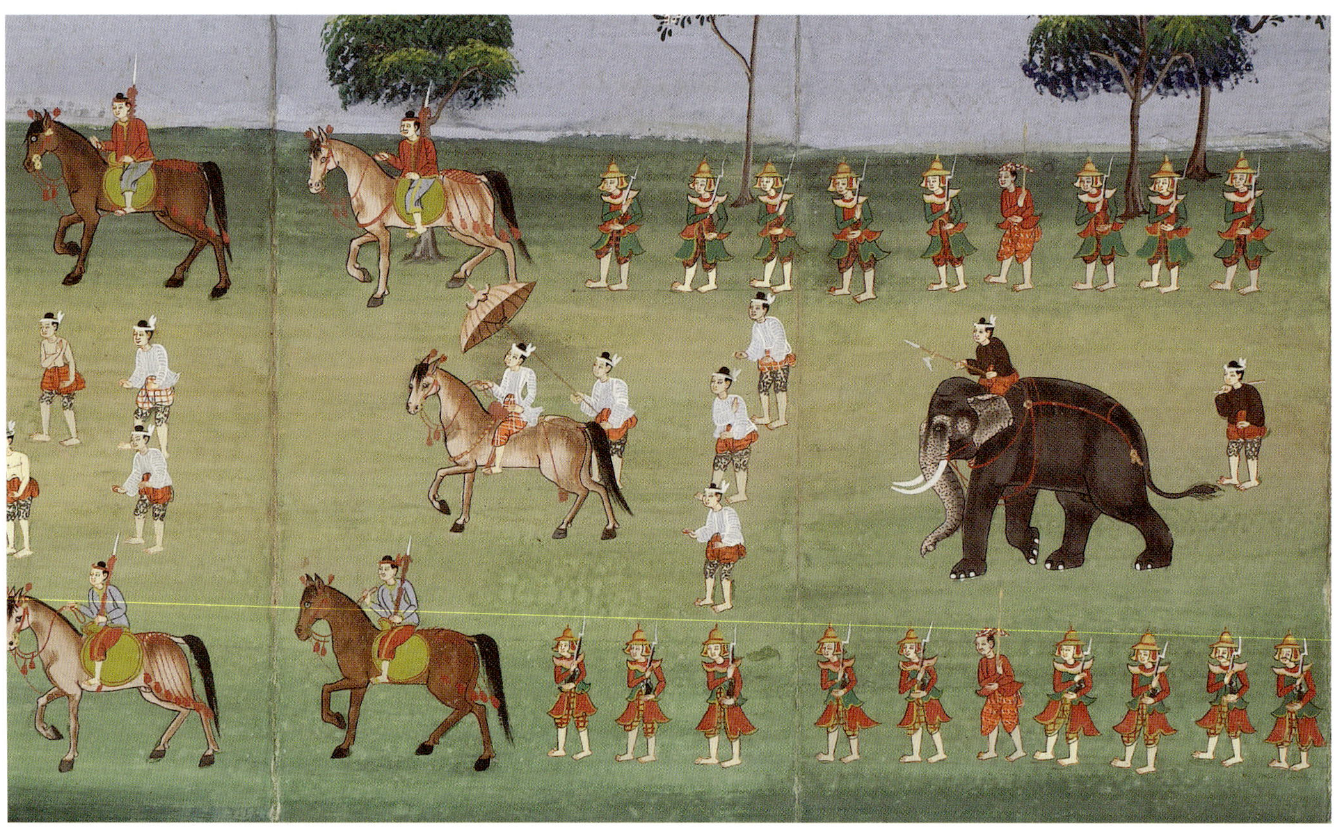

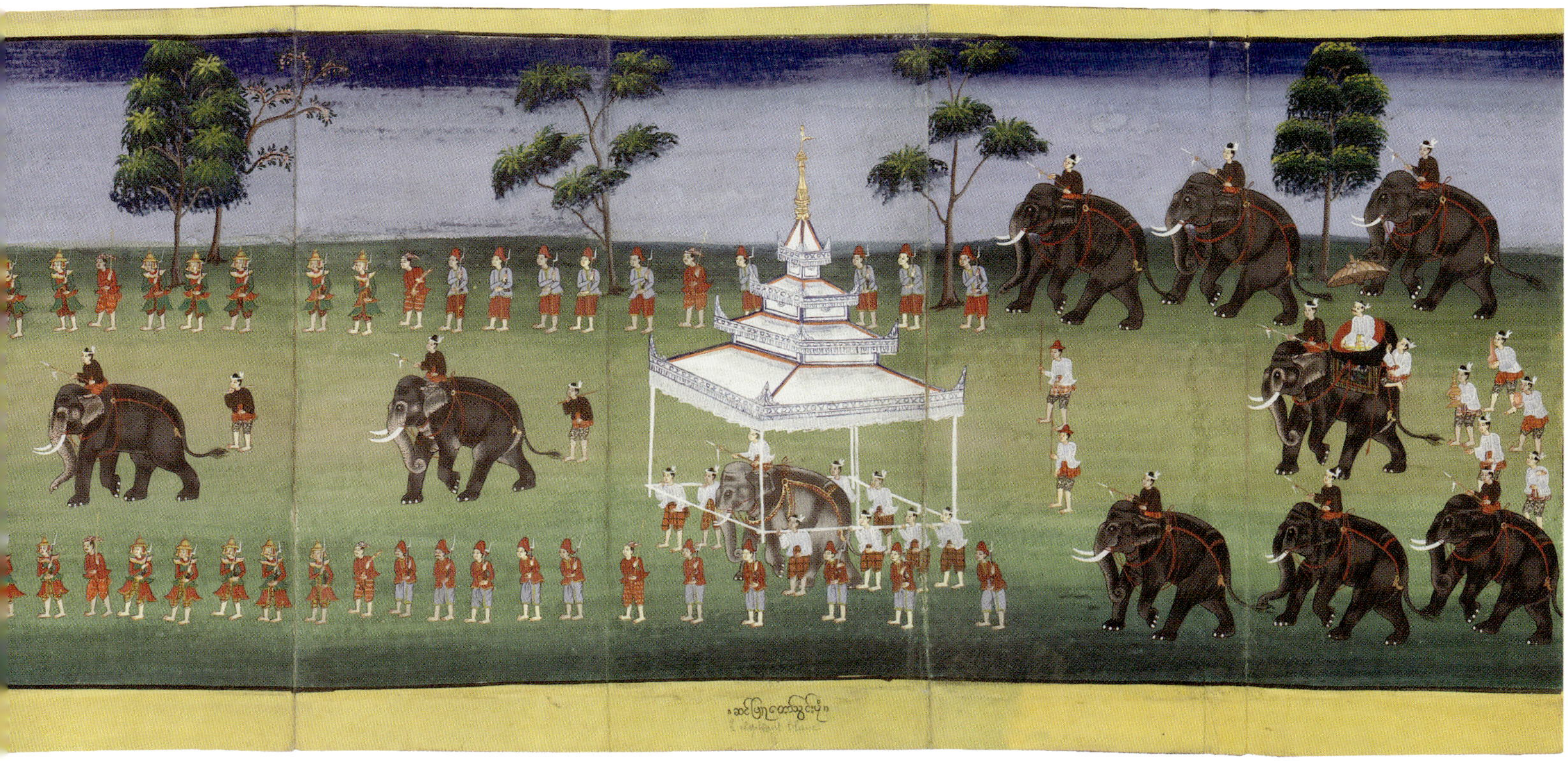

॥ ဆင်ဖြူတော်သွင်းပုံ ॥

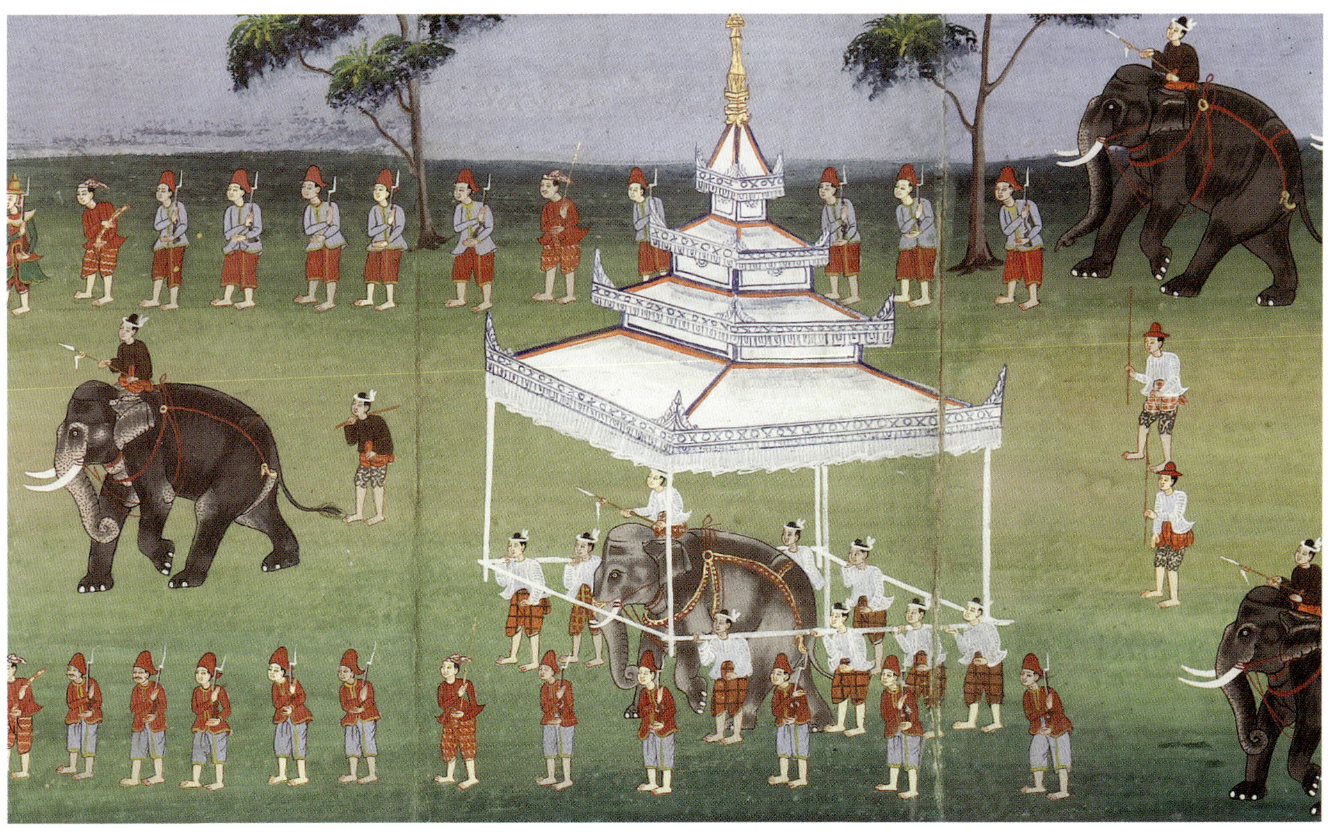

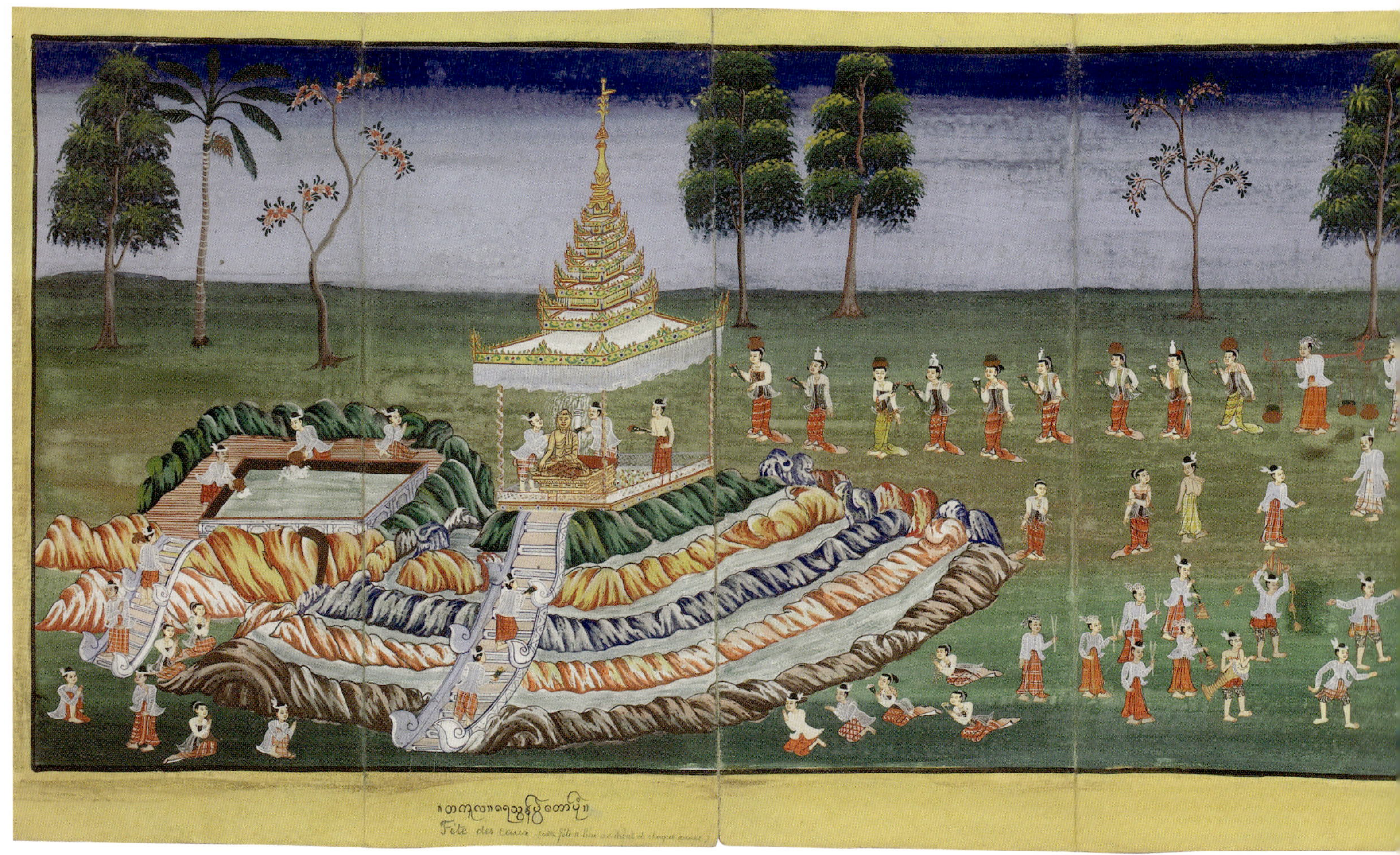

Figure 63. Tagu တဂူ (March–April). New year; water festival with an artificial mound representing Mount Meru with four rivers flowing down.

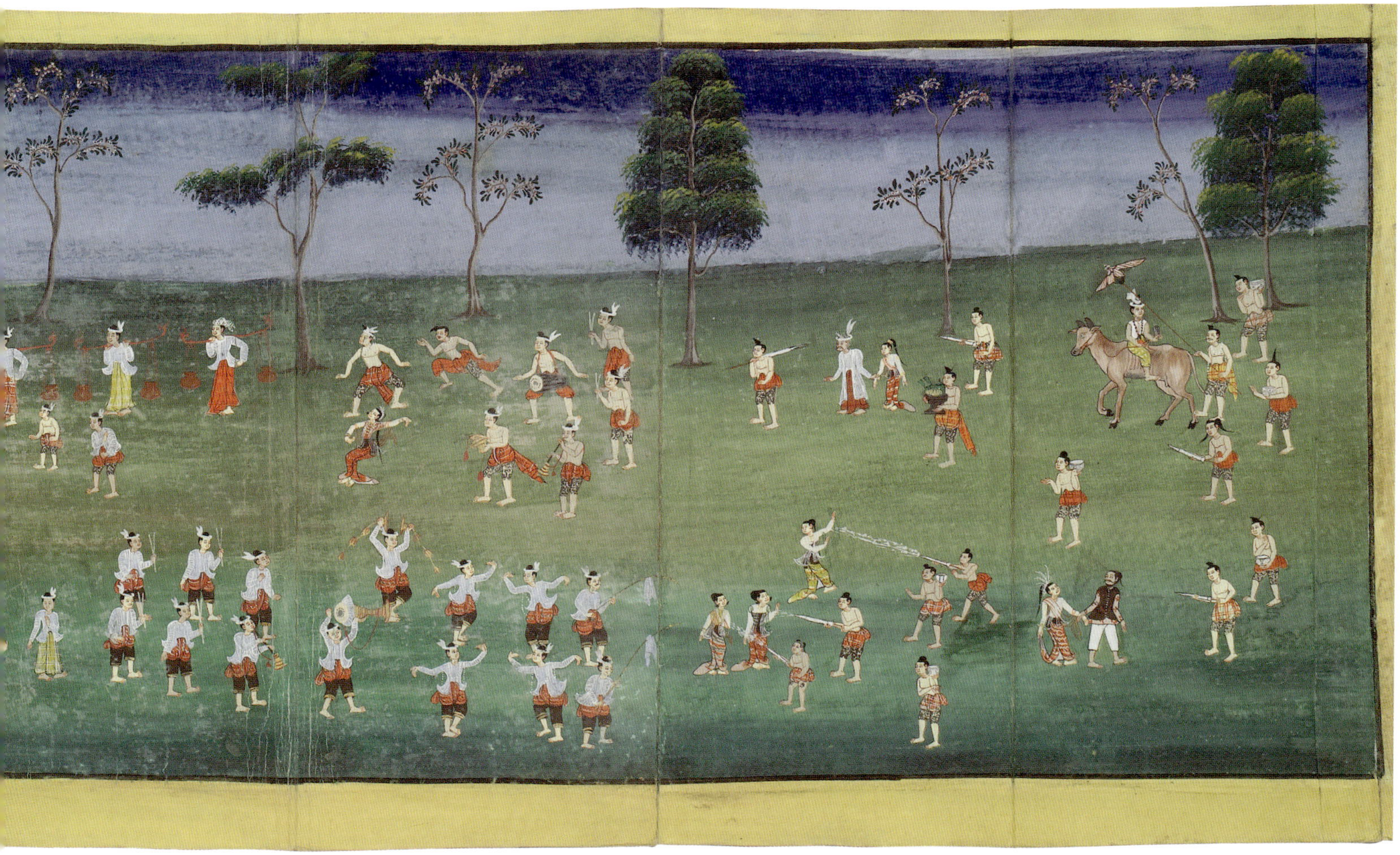

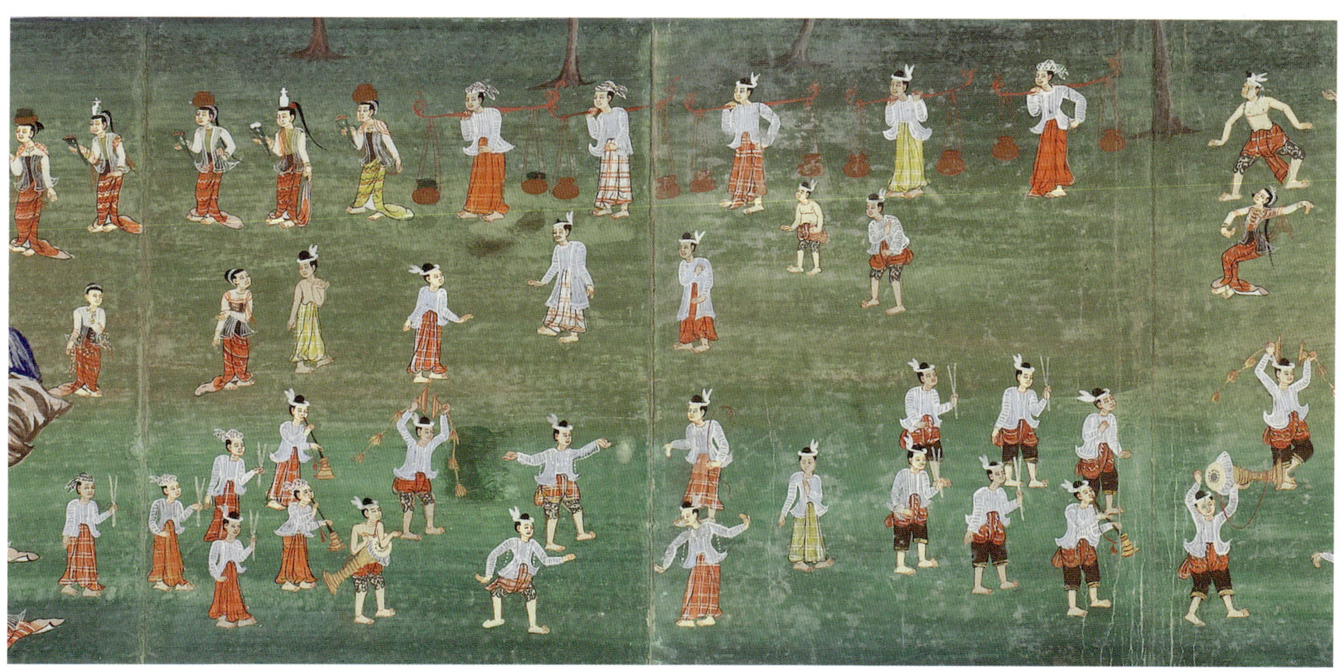

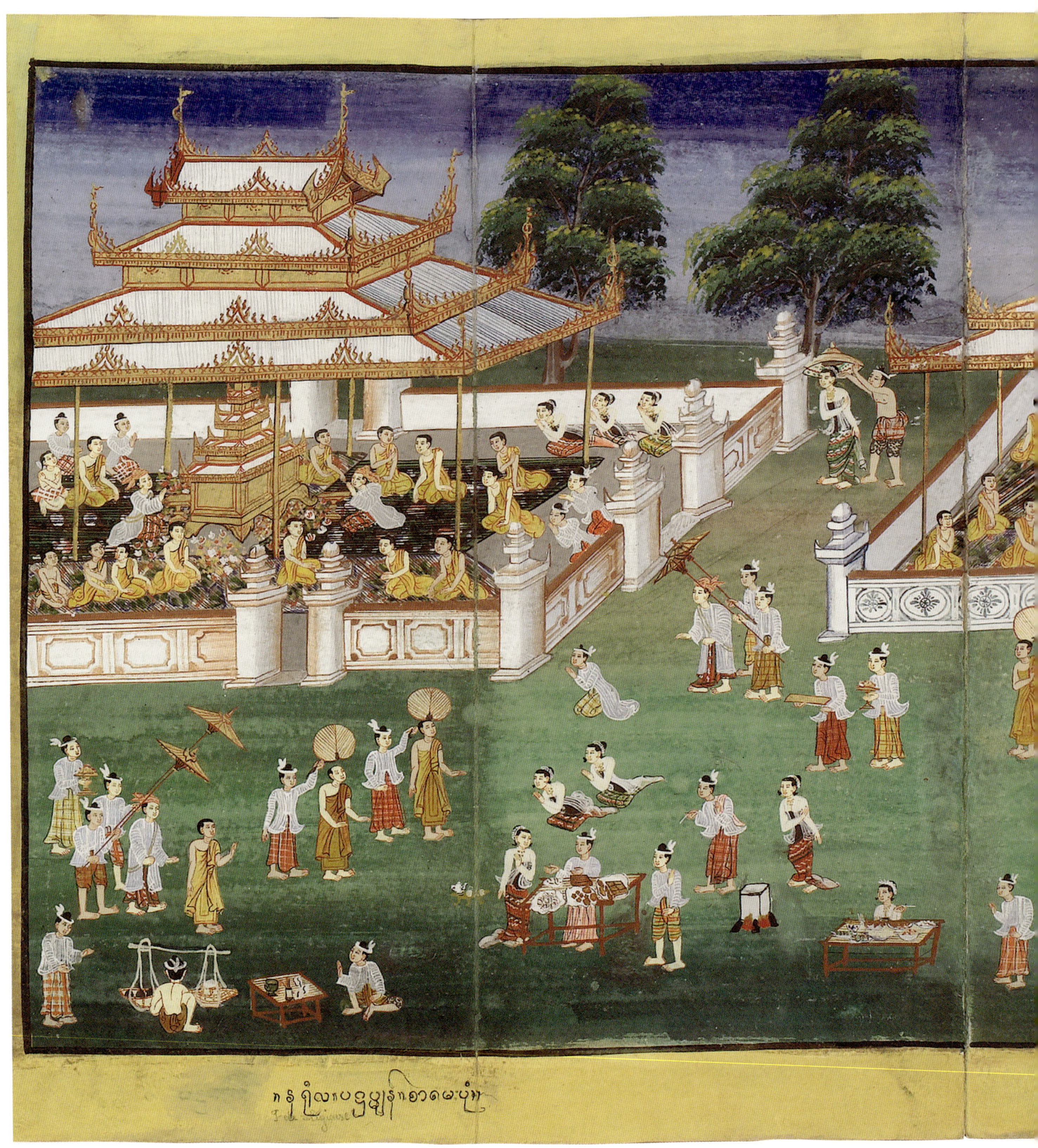

Figure 64. Kason ကဆုန် (April–May). Bodhi tree watering festival.

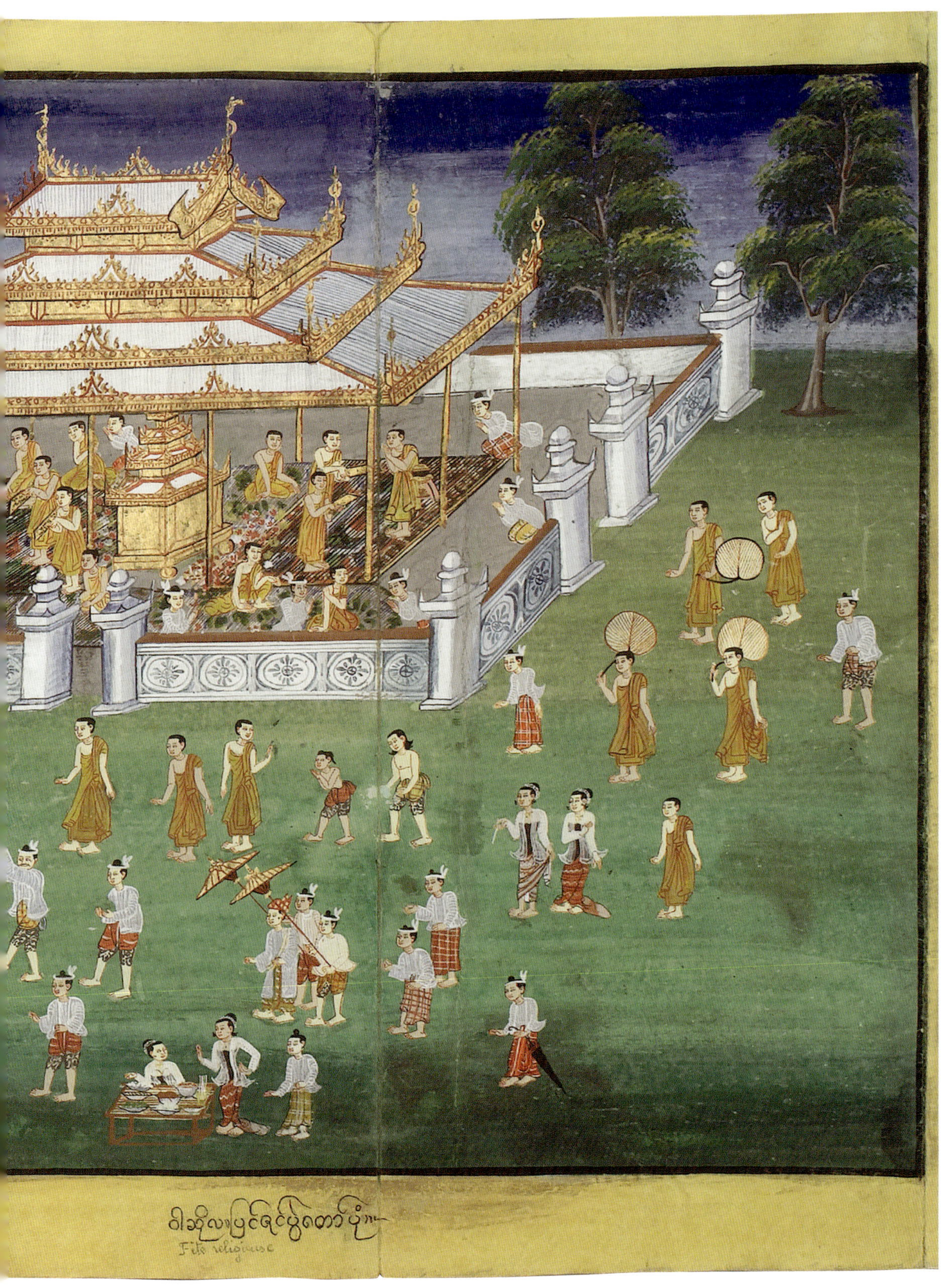
Fête religieuse

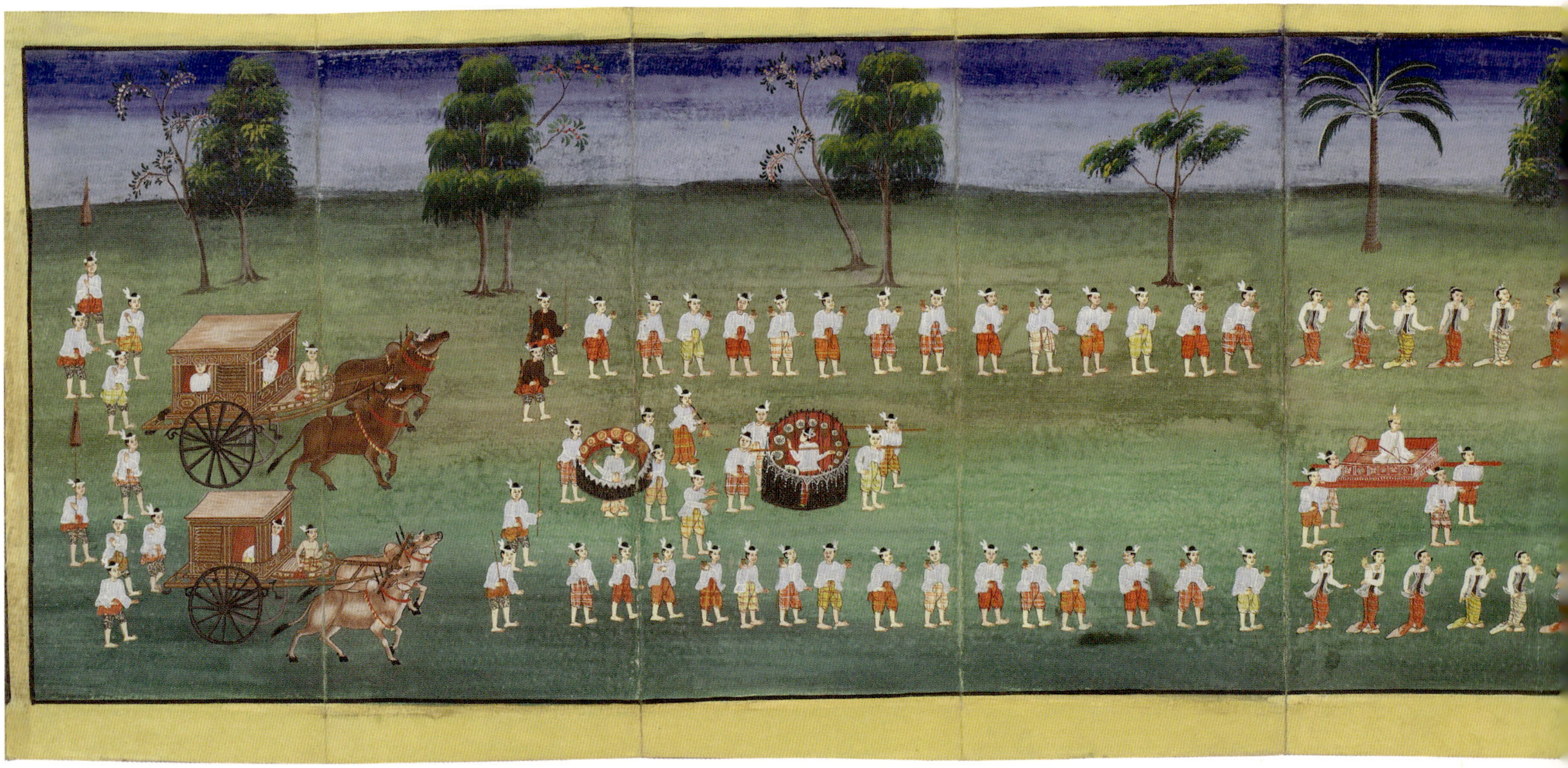

Figure 65. Nayon (May–June). Tipiṭaka festival; Waso ဝါဆို (June–July). Offering of robes (beginning of the rain's retreat).

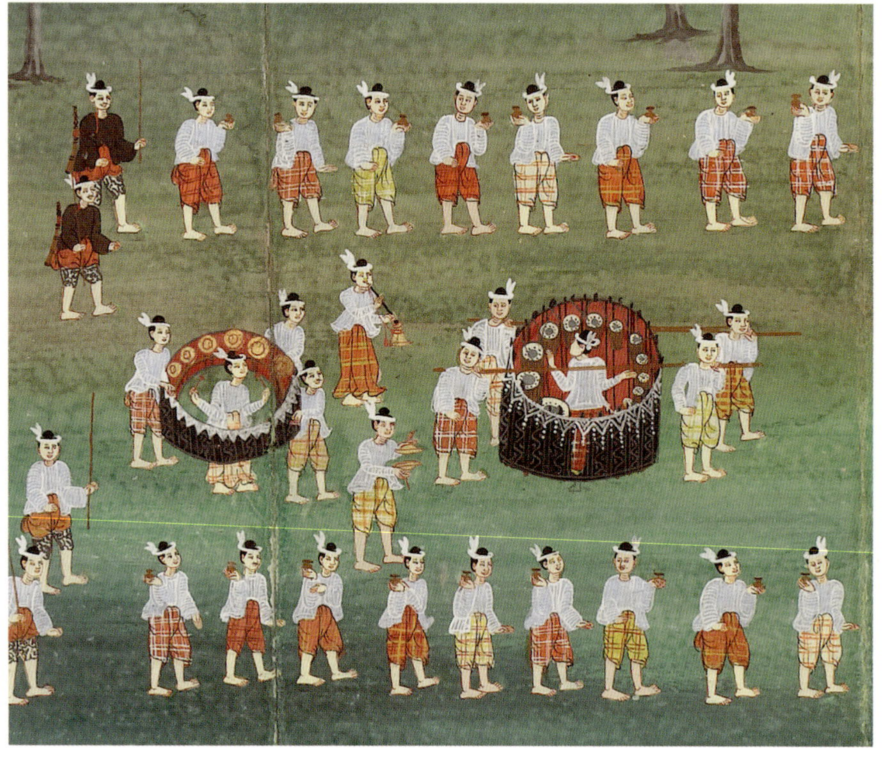

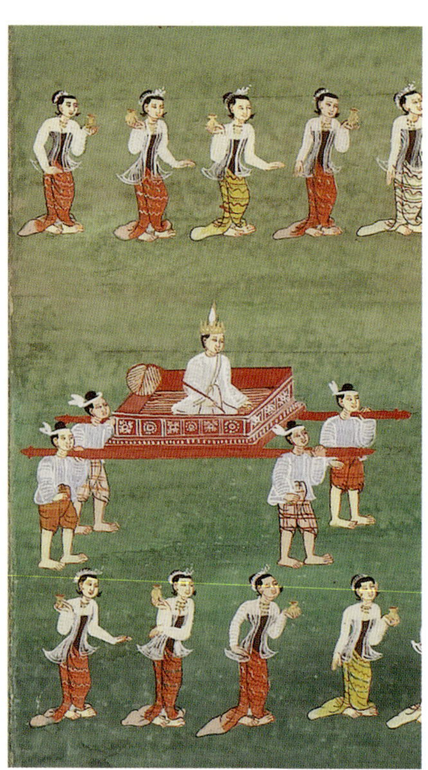

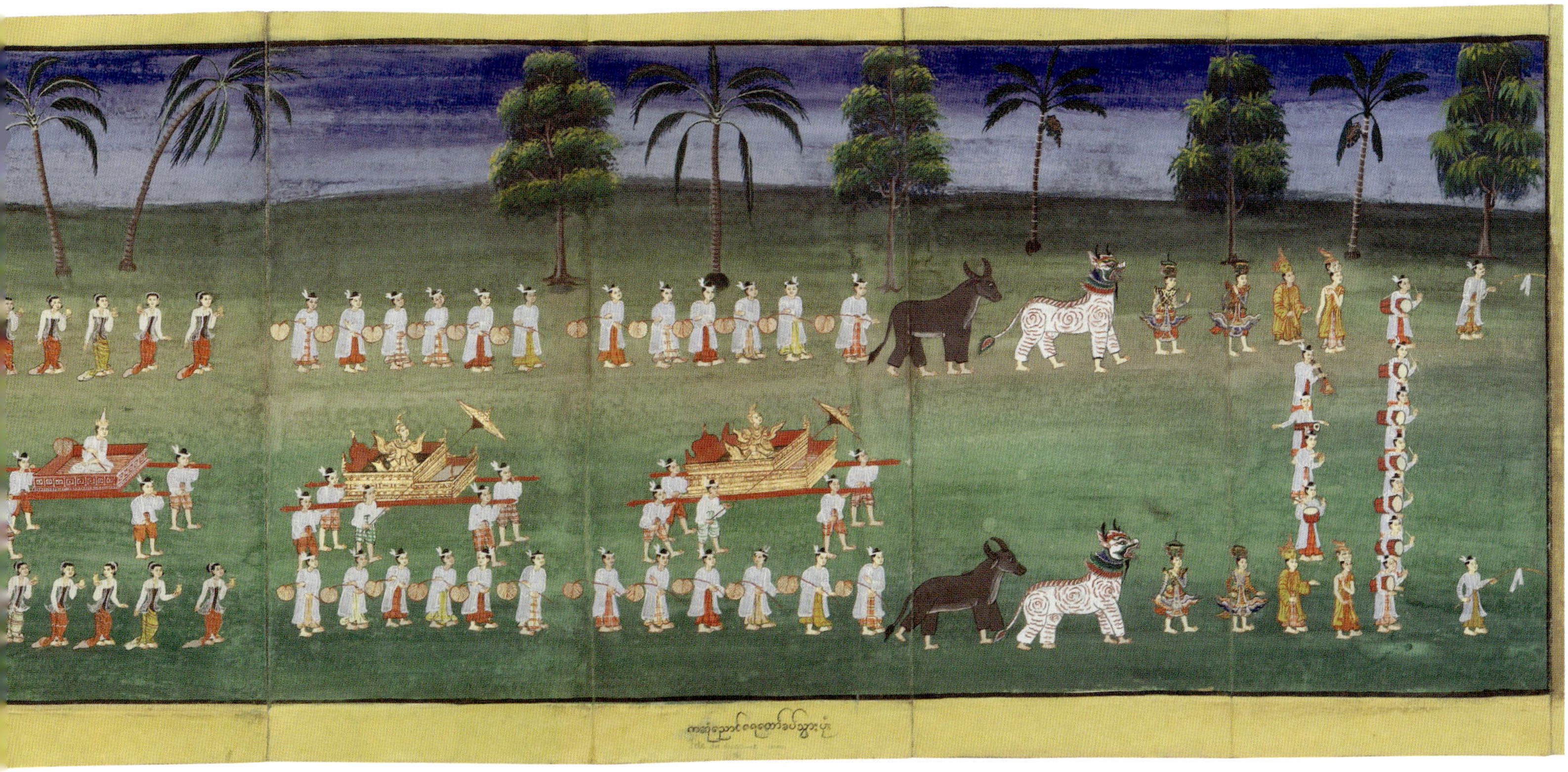

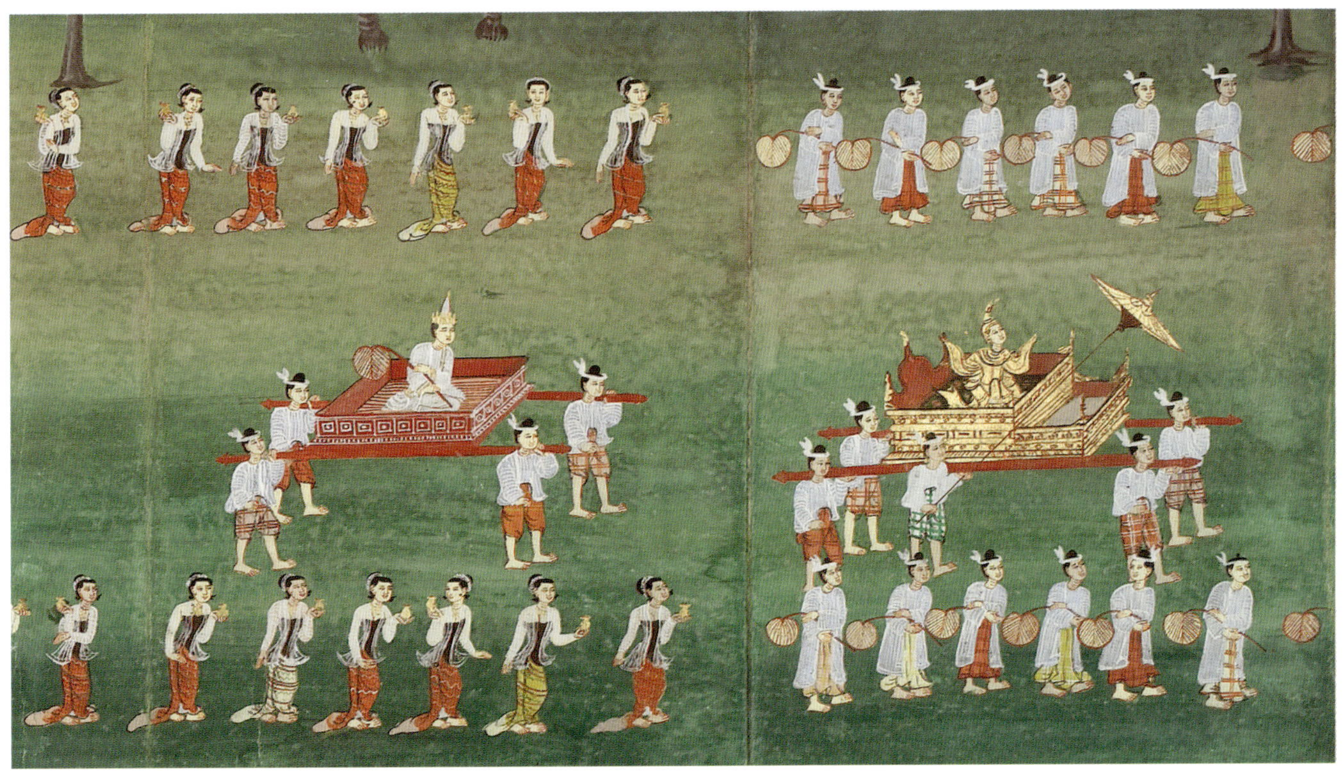

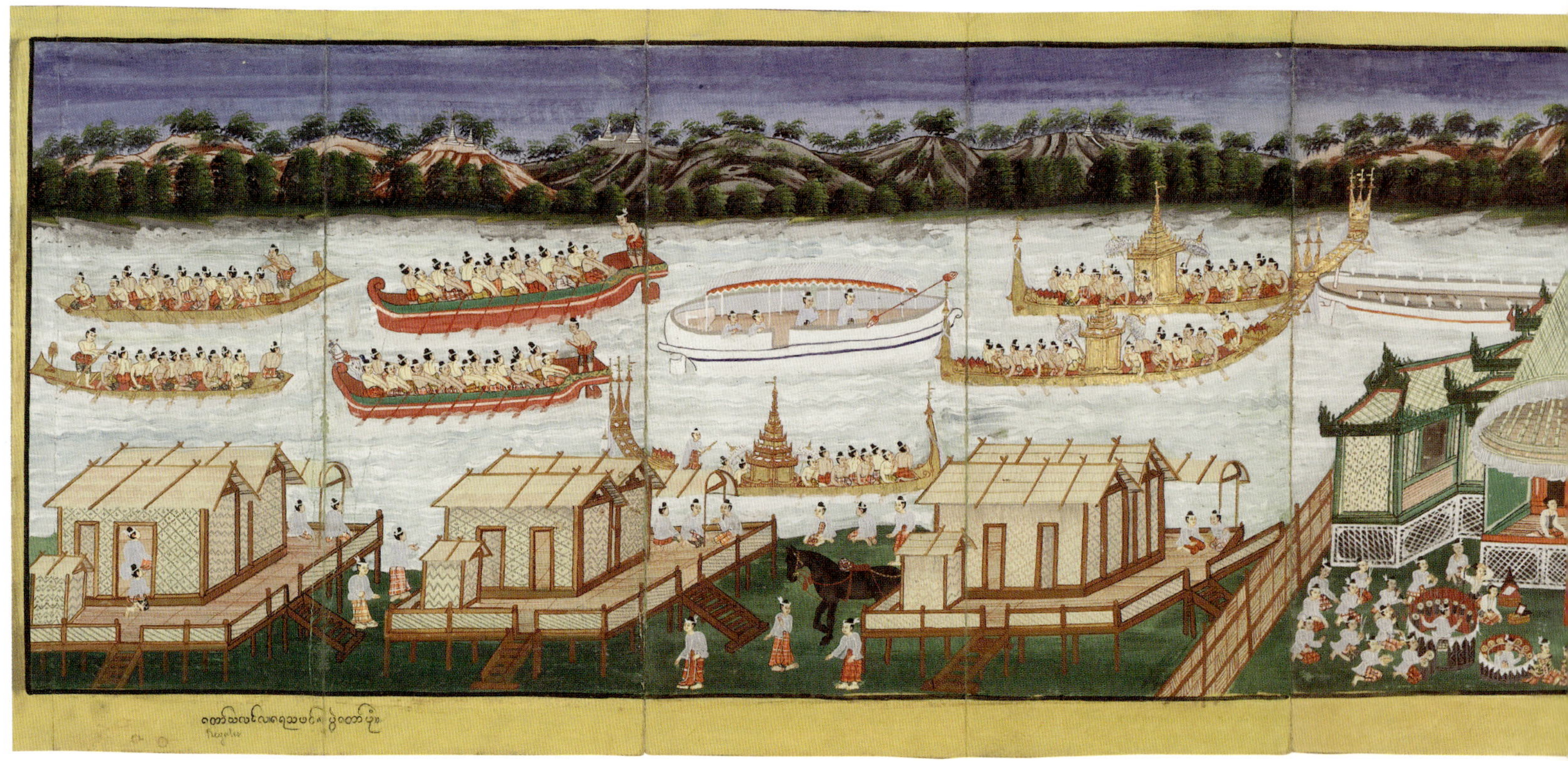

Figure 66. Tawthalin ဆော်သလင်း (August–September). Regatta Festival.

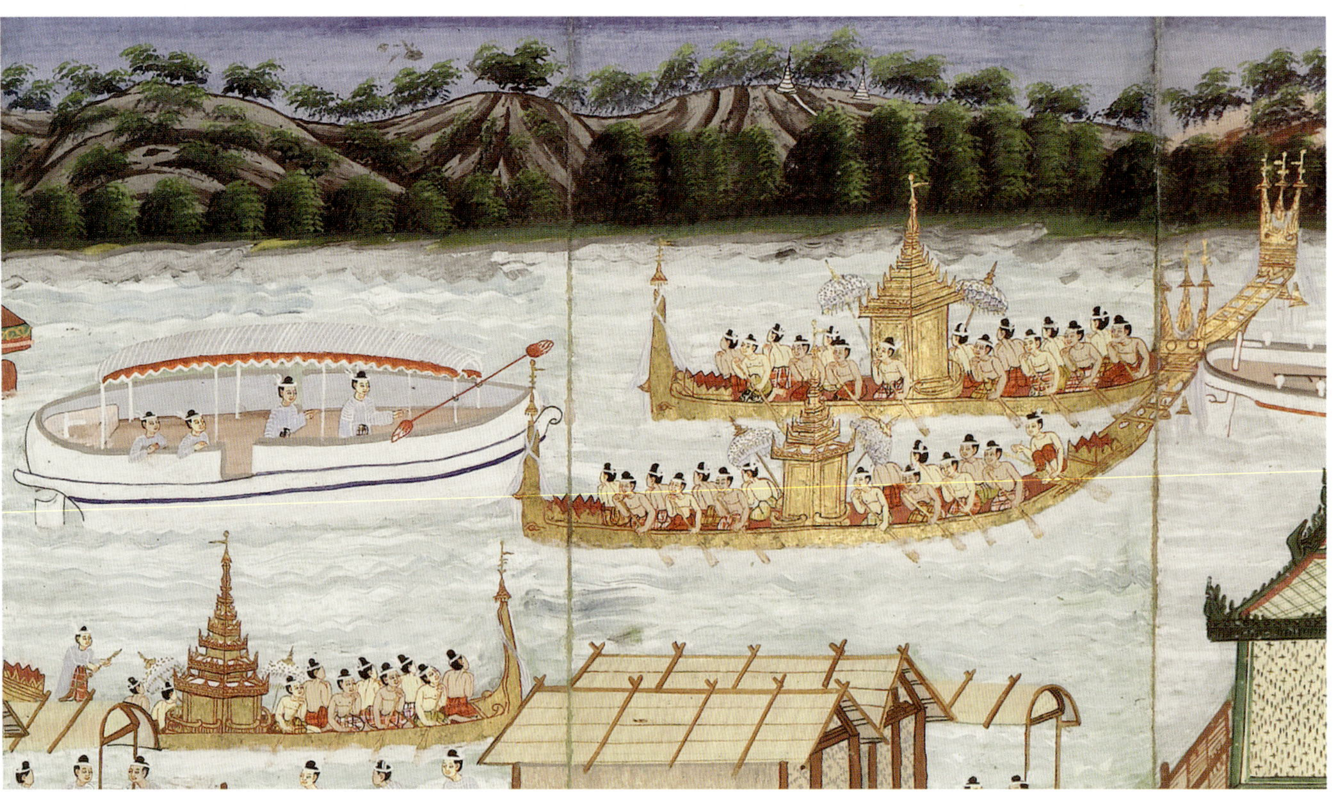

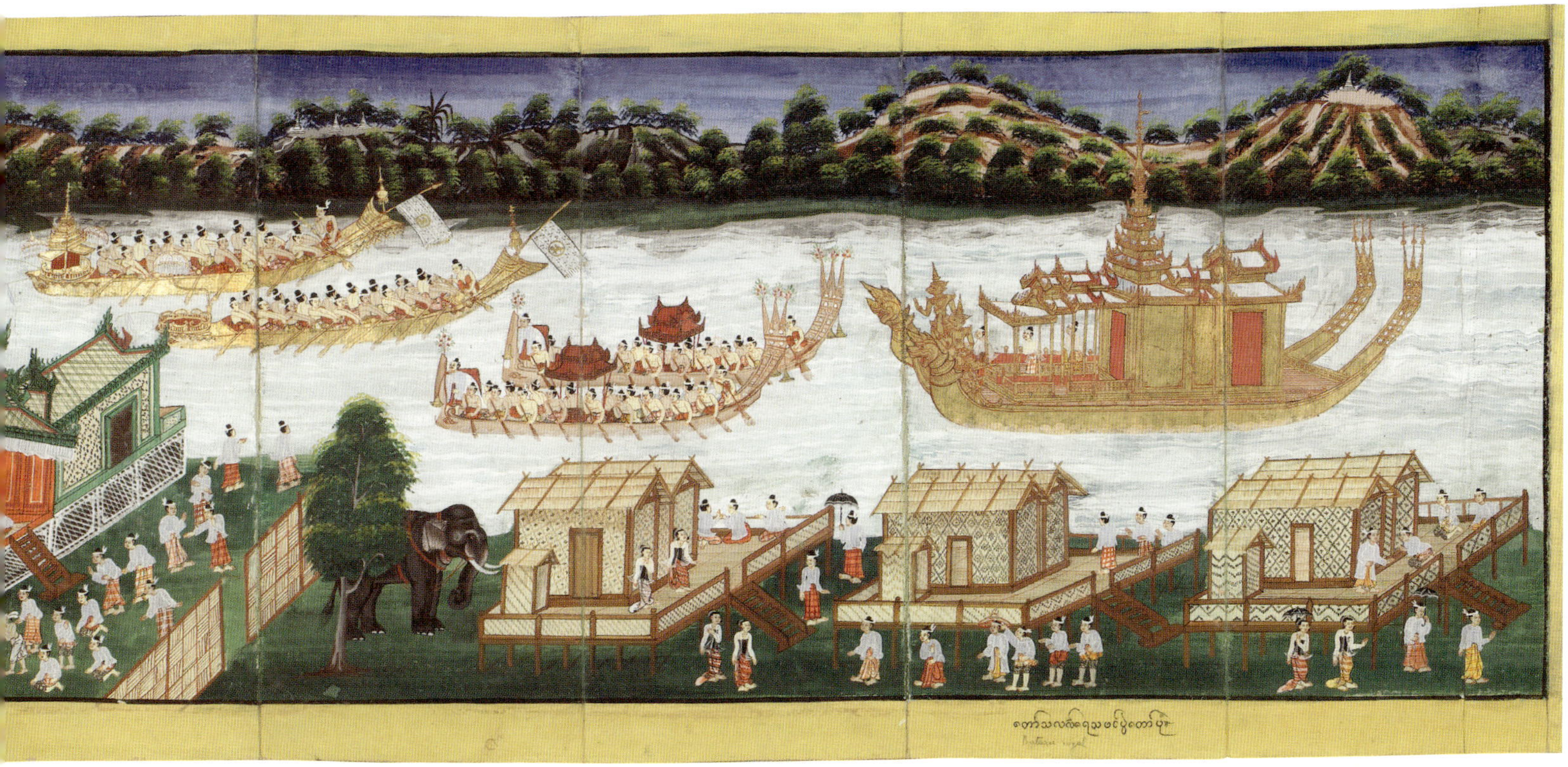

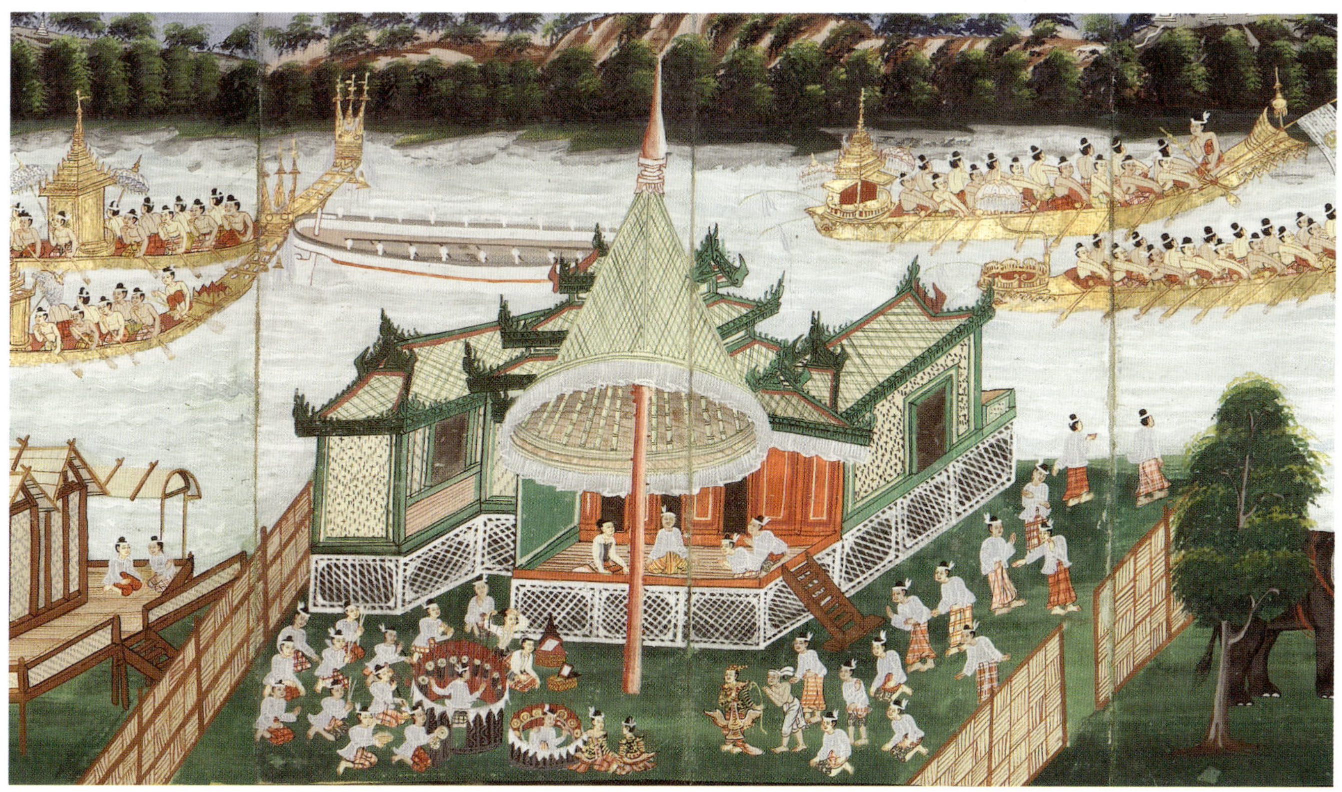

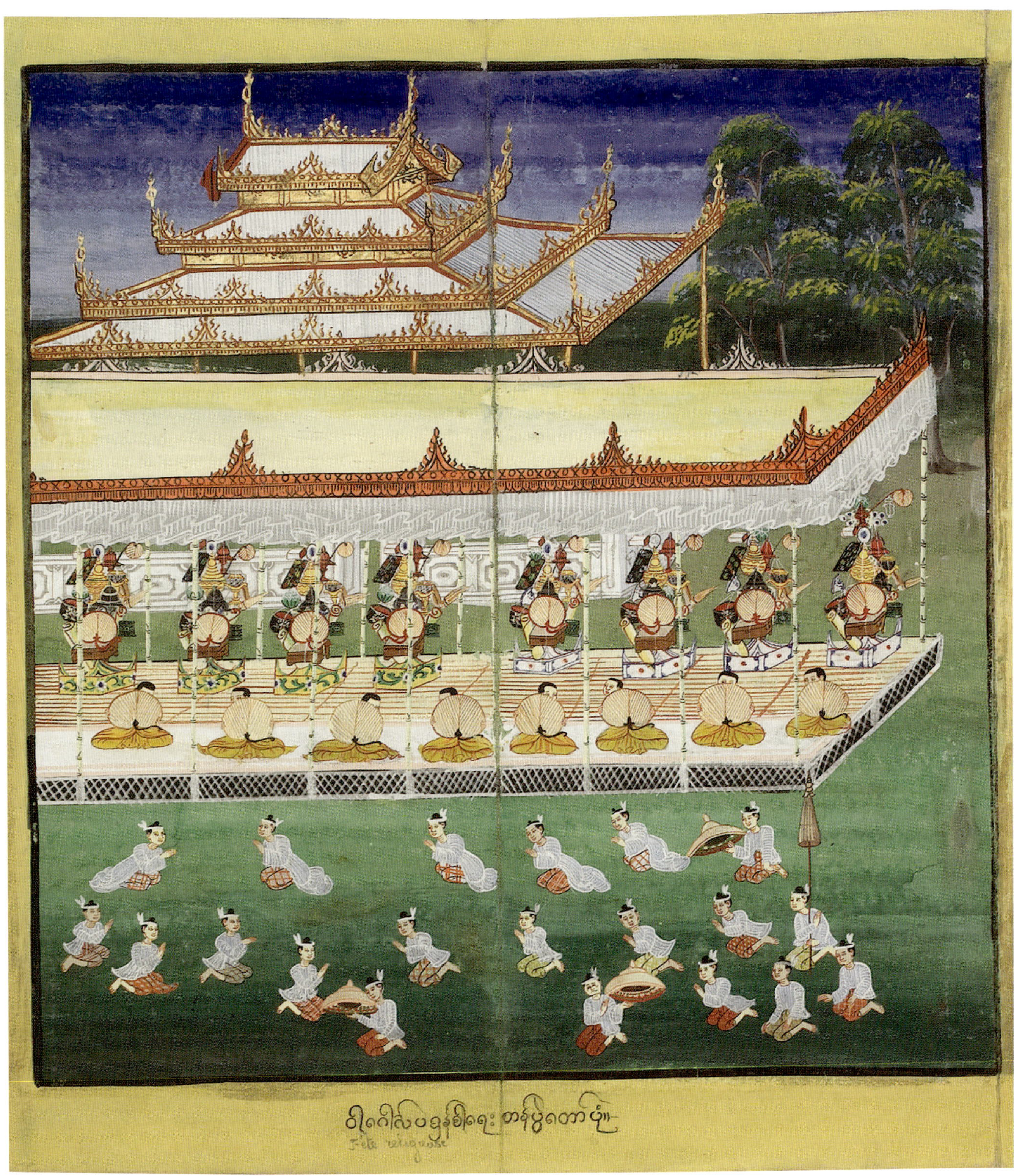

Figure 67. Wagaung ဝါခေါင် (August) Taungbyon Nat Festival.

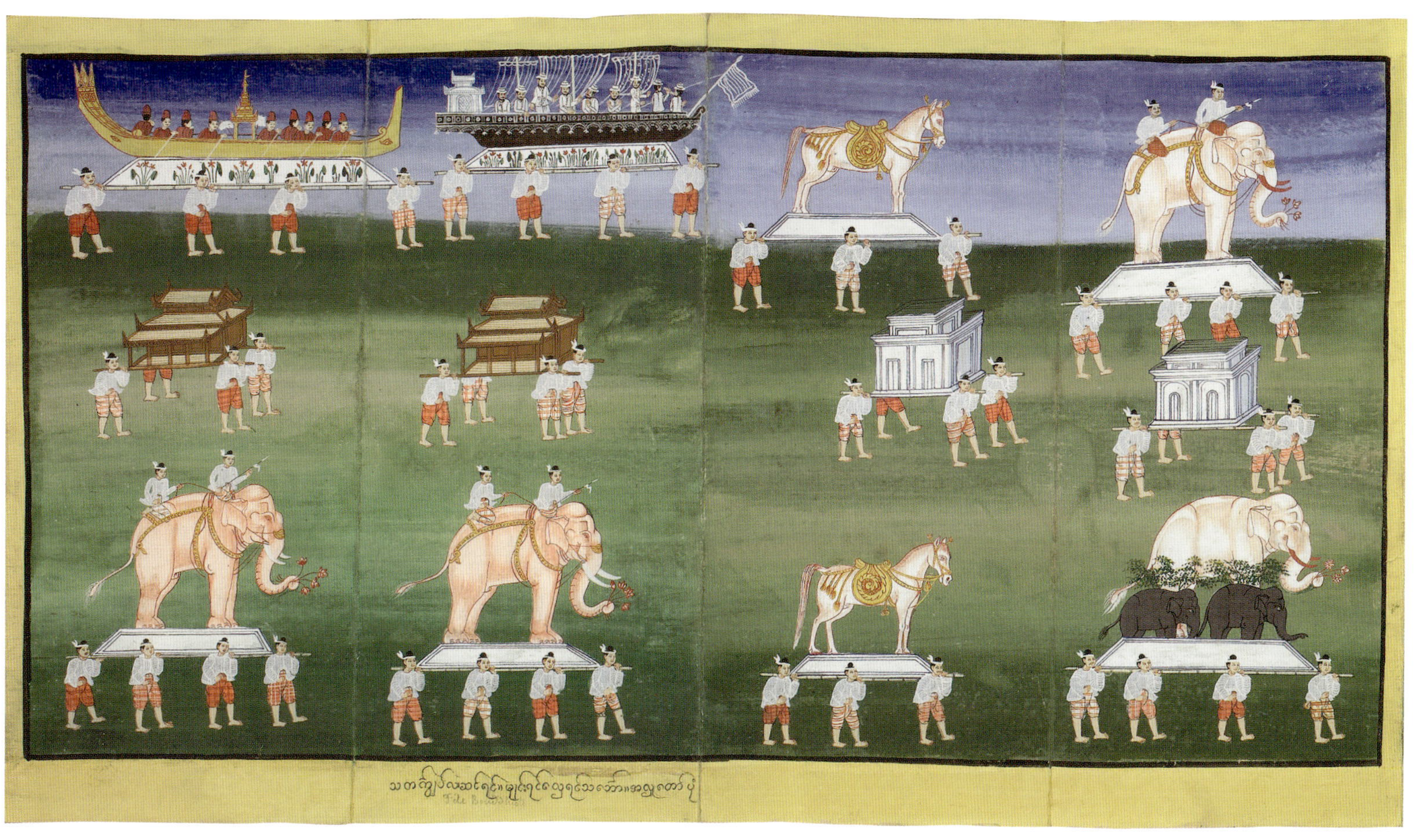

Figure 68. Thadingyut သီတင်းကျွတ် (September–October).
Parade with models celebrating the Festival of Lights

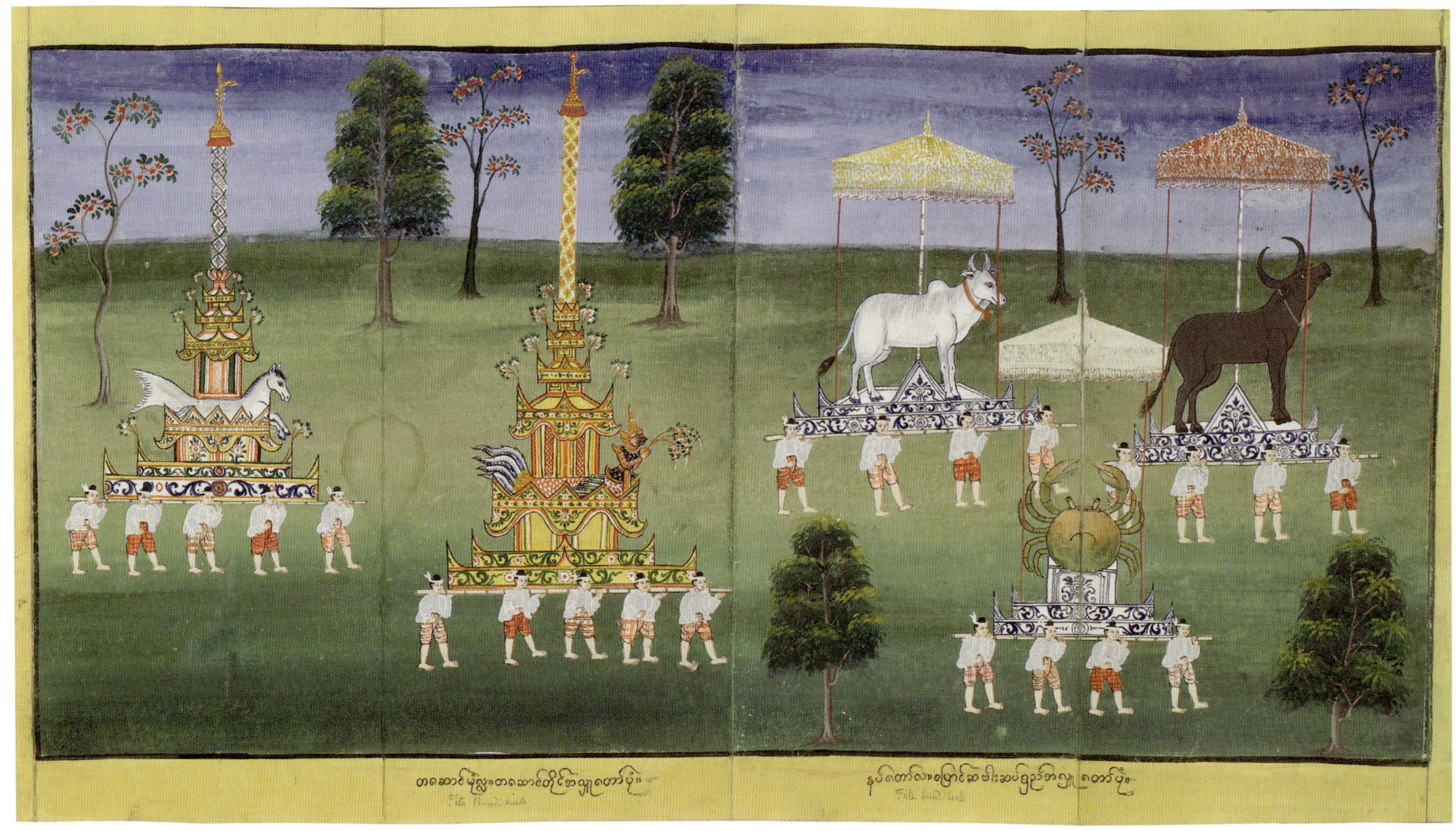

Figure 69. (*Above*) Tazaungmon တန်ဆောင်မုန်း (October–November). Religious offerings at the end of the rainy season. *Right*, Nadaw နတ်တော် (November–December). Nat festivals.
Figure 70. (*Facing page*) Pyatho ပြာသို (December–January). The festival of the elephant enclosure; here showing a mock battle.

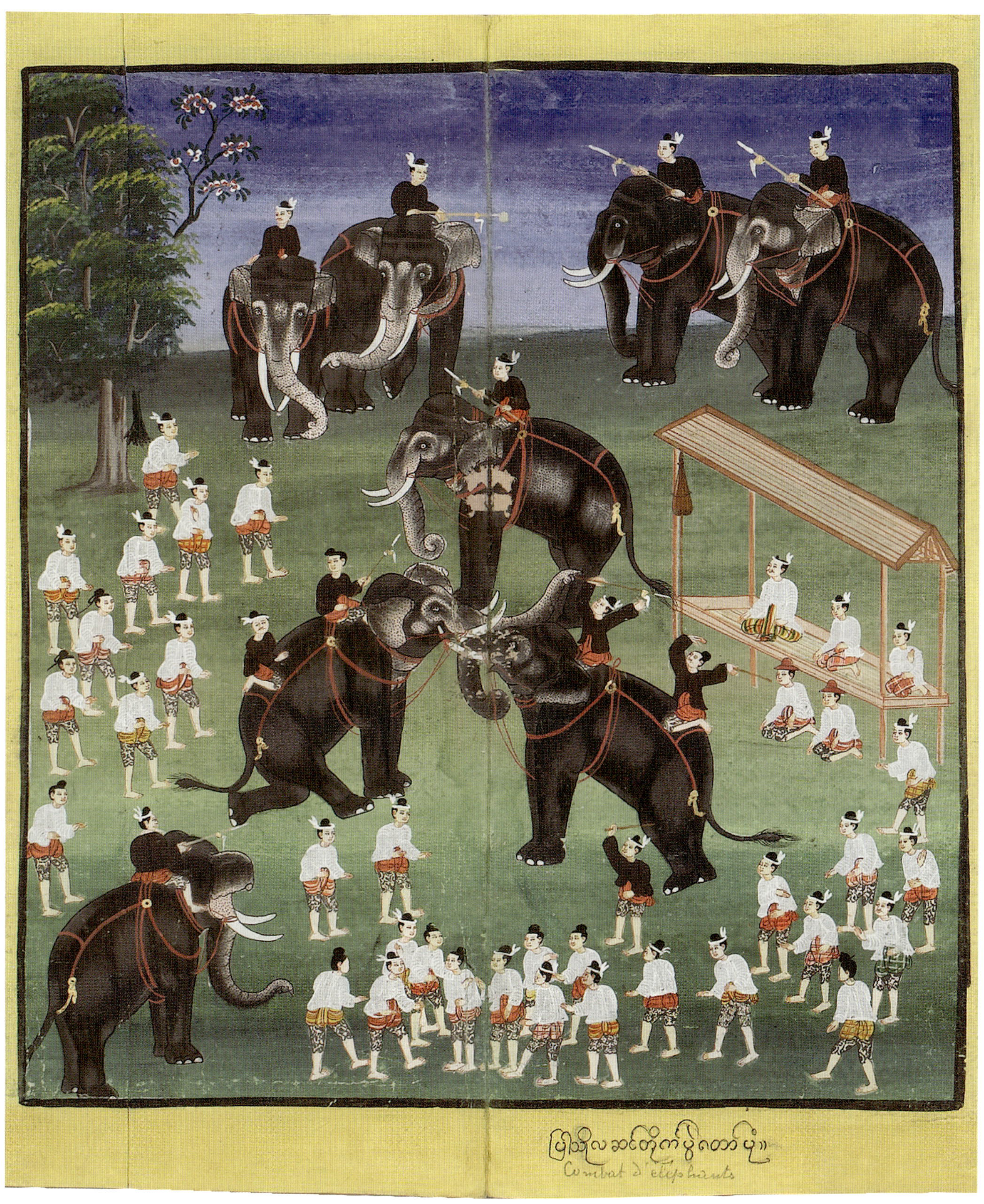
ပြာသိုလ ဆင်တိုက်ပွဲတော်ပုံ။
Combat d'elephants

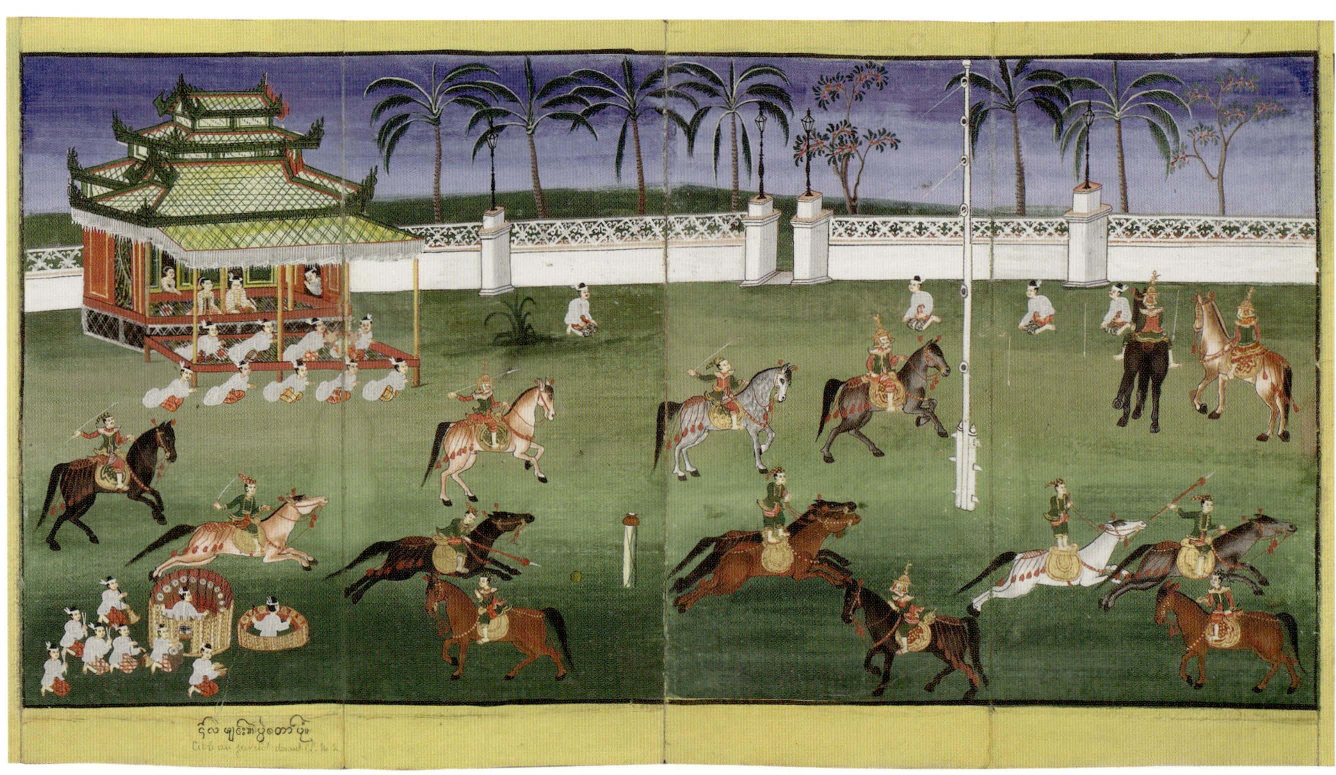

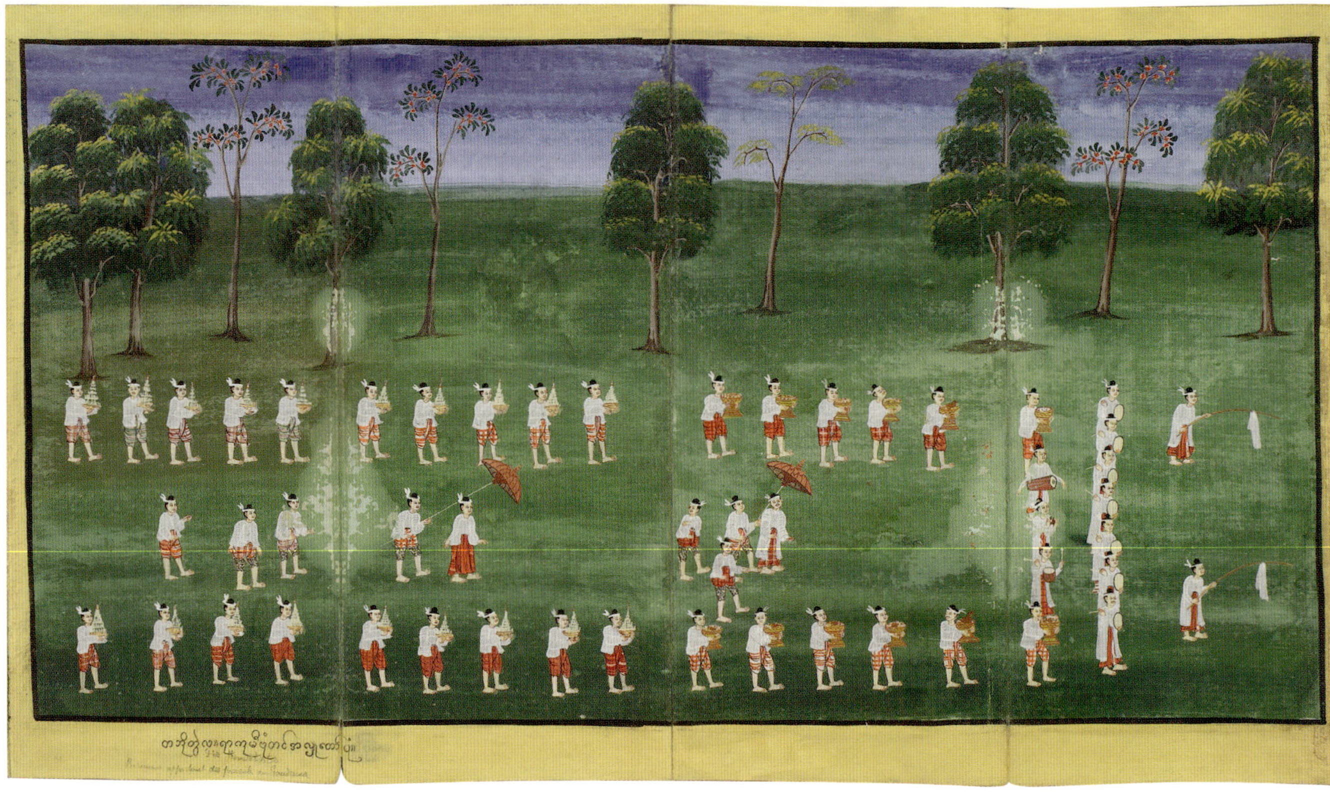

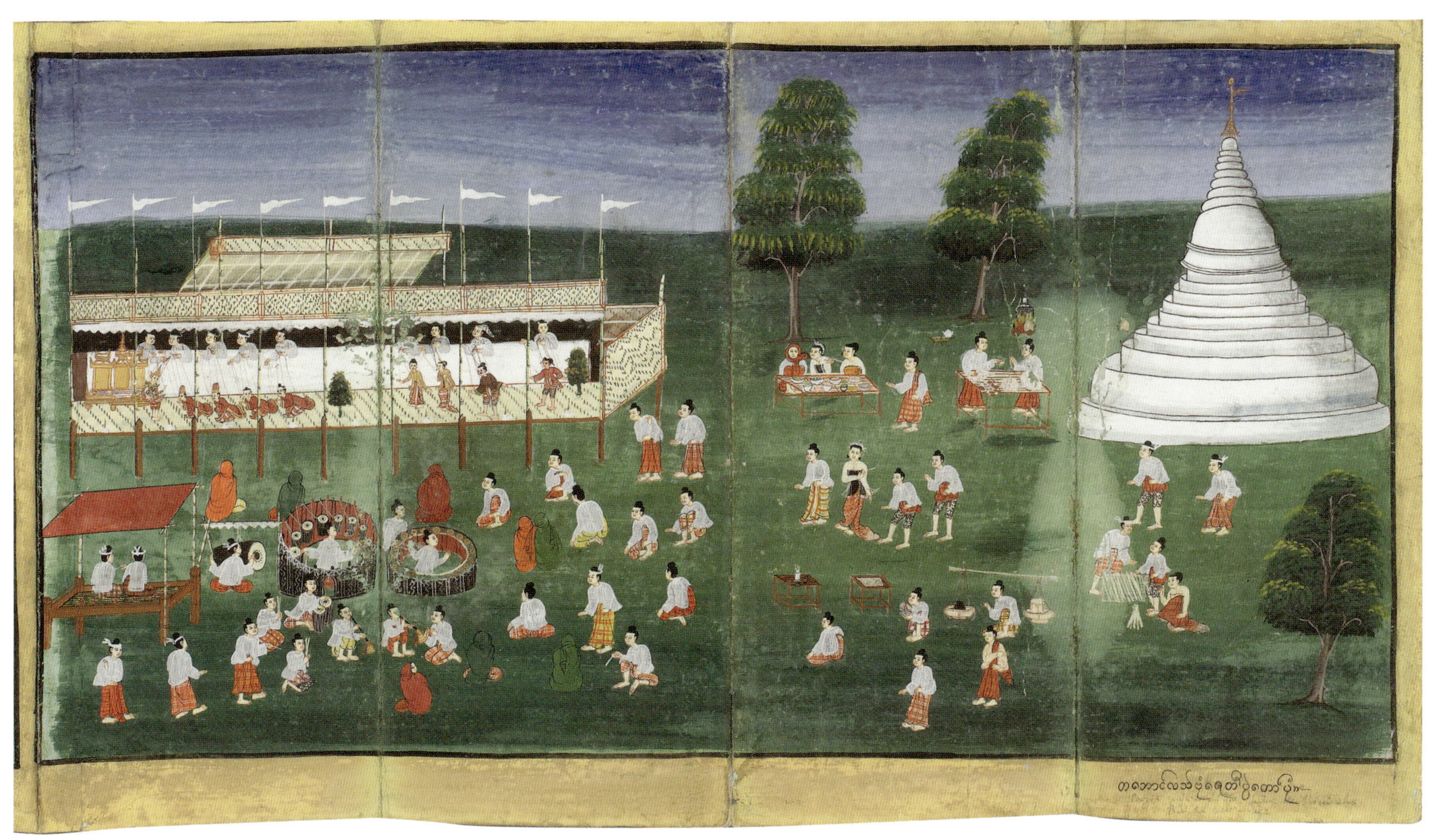

Facing page from top:
Figure 71. Pyatho ပြာသို (December–January). Javelin contest accompanied by a traditional orchestra.
Figure 72. Tabodwe တပို့တွဲ (January–February). Harvest festival; a procession with offerings for monks.

This page:
Figure 73. Tabaung တပေါင်း (February–March). Pagoda festival with puppet show, orchestra, and food stalls.

BURMESE MONASTERIES

Francis Macouin

Former General Curator Librarian, Musée Guimet

MANUSCRIPTS are largely associated with the monasteries of the *saṅgha*, the community of Buddhist monks. The monks in Burma belong to the school of the Doctrine of the Elders (Theravāda), also called the Small Vehicle (Hināyāna) by the members of the Great Vehicle (Mahāyāna). For important monasteries, their establishment consists of a number of buildings: the monastery (*kyaung*), one or more stupas, and an ordination hall as well as other buildings. During the Kongaung dynasty, monasteries were usually built of wood and elevated on posts (*pongyi kyaung*), though some were made of brick and stucco.

The connection between manuscripts and the monasteries was a strong one, for this is where the texts were studied and taught. They are moreover closely associated with the social life of the whole community, as all children were educated in the monasteries. The monastery had a library that included the canonical Buddhist texts, and a great many manuscripts were prepared for the monks and their students. In this religious and scholarly context, manuscripts were used as texts to be read, texts to be learned and shared, and texts to be preserved and copied.

Example: Shwe In Bin Monastery

The Shwe In Bin ("Gilded Wood") Monastery is named after the wood that was used in its construction, keruing (*Dipterocarpus obtusifolius*),

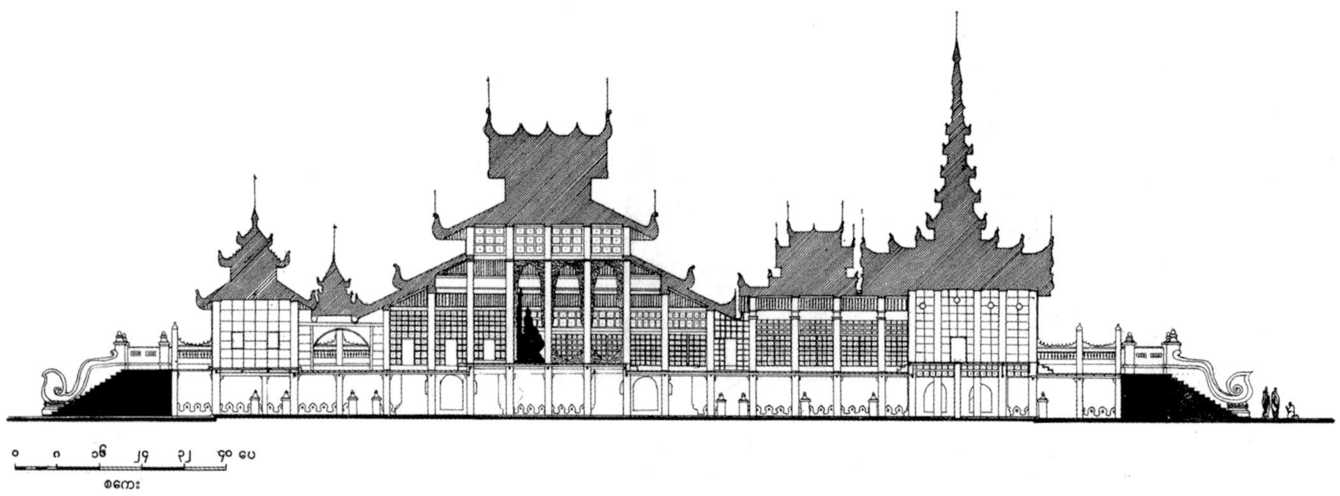

Figure 74. Representation of the Shwe In Bin monastery according to U Myo Myint, Department of Archaeology, Rangoon University, 1966.

which turns dark brown over time. It is in the southwestern section of Mandalay and was constructed through a private initiative in 1895.

The wooden building rests on 167 teak pillars that support a large platform with eight stone staircases leading up to it. It is 55 by 24 meters and has several rooms—each covered by a specific type of roof—aligned along the east–west axis (going from right to left in the illustration): (1) a small square pavilion with a spire (*pya ta shaung* [*pyathat* = spire and *saung* in the taxonomy of Pierre Pichard] which comes from Sanskrit *prāsāda*); (2) a small passage sometimes used by the head monk as a reception room or as his residence (*sanu shaung*); (3) the main building in the monastery, which is divided into two rooms by a partition (*marabin*) and which serves as a reception hall, classroom, and dormitory; and (4) a room with an archway leading to the storeroom (*bo ga shaung*). A veranda surrounds the rooms. The spire is over twenty meters high, rising above receding roofs. The main building has a central section with a Buddha statue. Various rooms are used for monastic functions, teaching, bedrooms, and to receive monks and novices. The storeroom is used for objects used in daily life, such as the monks' bowls.

Figure 75. Plan view and front.

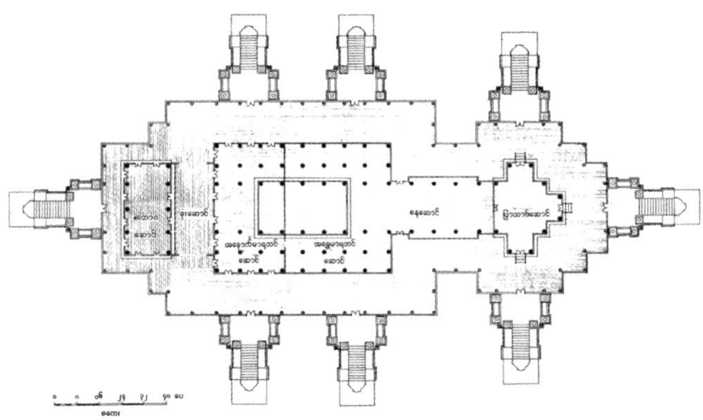

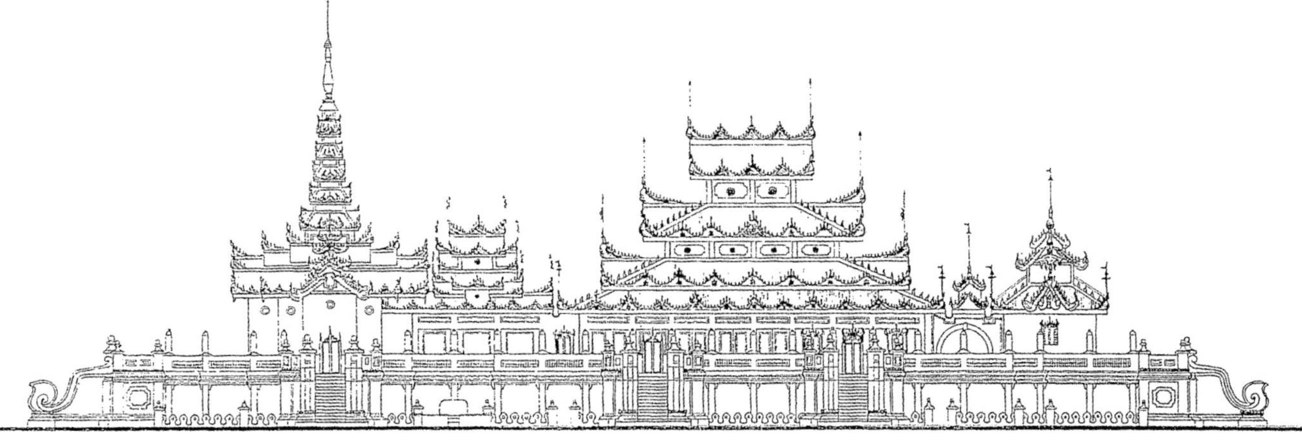

Bibliography

Fraser-Lu, Sylvia. *Splendour in Wood: The Buddhist Monasteries of Burma*. Bangkok: Orchid Press, 2001.

———. "The Preservation of Wooden Monasteries in Burma." In *Burma: Art and Archaeology*, edited by Alexandra Green and T. Richard Blurton, 107–18. London: British Museum, 2002.

Pichard, Pierre. "Ancient Burmese Monasteries." In *The Buddhist Monastery: A Cross-cultural Survey*, edited by Pierre Pichard and François Lagirarde, 59–73. Paris: École français d'Extrême-Orient, 2003.

THE BURMESE MODEL OF A MONASTERY BUILDING: *A Style of Architecture That Has Largely Vanished*

Pierre Baptiste
Senior Curator, Southeast Asian collections, Musée Guimet

IN 1894, there was the first mention of the existence in the galleries for "Indochinese religions" of the Guimet Museum of a "large reproduction in teak wood of a famous Buddhist temple in Ava." The guidebook for that year goes on to say, "This model belonged to the head priest of Mandalay (Burma)."[1] Six years later, in 1910, more information was given in the sixth edition of the same guidebook. It states that the model "was given to M. Haas, French consul, by the head monk of Mandalay when the English entered the city," that is to say, in 1885.[2]

Frédéric Haas (1846–1915) served as a diplomat in India starting in 1877, holding several posts there, notably one in Pondicherry. On February 20, 1885, he was made vice-consul of Mandalay, which was the capital of Burma at that time.[3] The post was an especially sensitive one as it entailed trying to temper the ambitions of the British in Burma. A secret treaty between France and Burma was signed in relation to this on January 18, 1885. On the first of June in the same year, Frédéric Haas managed to have King Thibaw sign a contract for a railroad to be built between Mandalay and Toungoo, a distance of more that 350 kilometers. The king also agreed to establish a state bank. But it seems that the consul

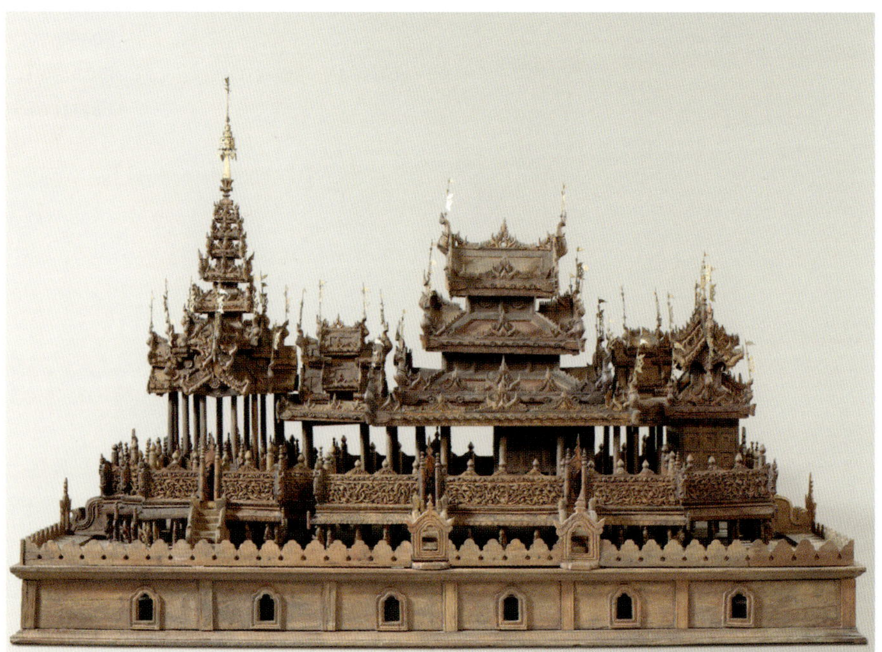

Figure 76. Model of a royal monastery. Teak wood, 1881–85 (?). Given to the museum by Frédéric Haas.

had gone beyond his orders from Paris, as he was recalled in October 1885. The following month, the English took Mandalay, deposed King Thibaw, who was exiled to India, and annexed the entire country.

It was during this brief eight-month stay in Burma that Frédéric Haas collected various objects, which he offered to the Guimet Museum when he returned to France. He had already shown an interest in Émile Guimet's museum some years before when he gave him several donations, including such important objects as Indian wooden chariots representing various Hindu deities. He had acquired these in Srirangam (Tamil Nadu) when he was posted to Pondicherry. He offered them to the museum on July 7, 1884.[4] Among the objects given when he returned from Burma were several that had belonged to "the head priest of Mandalay." The model, however, was not entered in the museum's inventory until a much later date.

One unverified account says the model is a reproduction of "a great temple in Ava," referring to a famous monastery dating from the first half of the nineteenth century, the Mahā Aungmye Bonzan. It was built of brick and stucco under the direction of Nanmadaw Me Nu, King Bagyidaw's chief queen (1819–37), to serve as a residence for the monk who was her spiritual guide. It is one of the rare monuments that did not disappear after a major earthquake in 1838 destroyed most of the city. It is more solid than the wooden buildings that preceded it, but it still imitates the traditional architecture that used teak wood. It was restored in 1873 by Sin-byu-ma-shin, the daughter of Me Nu and wife of King Mindon (r. 1853–78).[5] It must be noted, however, that few elements of this innovative monastery are found in the model in the Guimet Museum. It seems unlikely that a brick building whose design was inspired by wooden structures would then have its design retranslated into a teak-wood model.

On the other hand, it is very tempting to connect this model with the monasteries built in Mandalay during the second half of the nineteenth century, after the court was installed in the new capital in 1857 by King Mindon. The elegance of the roofs, with their elaborate ornaments, the tapered profile of receding roofs, and the decorative play of numerous birds in the sculpted foliage of the main railing are all reminiscent of various monuments dating from this period—for example, the Salin Monastery (Salin Kyaung) built in 1876 by Princess Salin, or more especially the one built by Su-hpaya-lat, the wife of King Thibaw (1878–85), the Mya Taung Kyaung. The second example was built between 1881 and 1885 to the southwest of the royal palace in Mandalay. It was better known as the "golden monastery of the queen" because of the beauty of its gilded sculptures. It follows the classic style of Konbaung architecture and was designed by the architect Hsaya Khin. There are many similar features between it and the Guimet model.[6] This meritorious work of Queen Su-hpaya-lat was financed using funds from the national lottery. It is known today through old photographs, especially those taken by Willoughby Wallace Hooper, a member of the invading British army in 1885. This masterpiece of Burmese architecture was unfortunately destroyed during the Second World War along with most of the buildings in the splendid capital, which had already suffered from its treasures being taken away during the colonial occupation and from a systematic dismantling of the city.

It would not be surprising to learn that the model in the Guimet Museum was used in connection with the construction of the Mya Taung Kyaung. The model would have made it possible for the architect to give a convincing presentation of the project to the queen. This tempting explanation would account for why such a model was made and place its manufacture a few years before the arrival of Frédéric Haas in Mandalay.

Figure 77. (*Left*) Detail of the railing.
Figure 78. Detail of one of the doors.

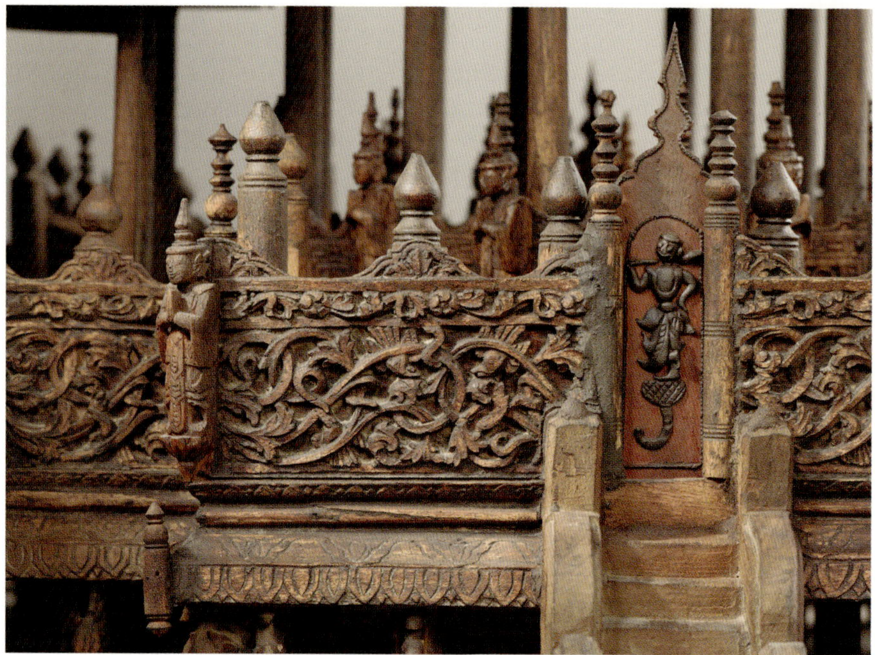

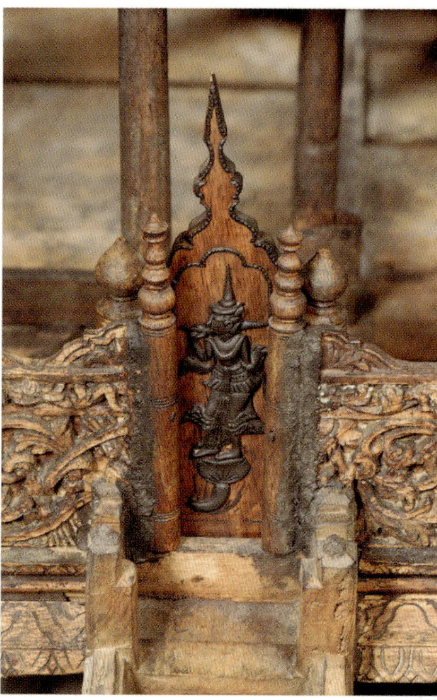

We do know that architectural models were used in processions for some pagoda festivals.[7] But those models do not seem to have been as detailed as the museum's model. It remains to be seen why in this model the whole structure rests on a large terrace surrounded by a wall decorated with many-petaled flowers and with six doors placed along the axis of the main staircase. The sides of the tall terrace have trefoiled bays spaced at regular intervals. It is true that these are similar to the ones at the base of the Ava monastery, although they are arranged more systematically in the model. Or is it simply a formal element to insure stability of the model's foundations? This cannot be determined. Whatever the case may be, the resemblance between the model and the Ava monastery ends there. Otherwise the model appears to be a perfect example of wooden monasteries of the Konbuang dynasty, both through its proportions and

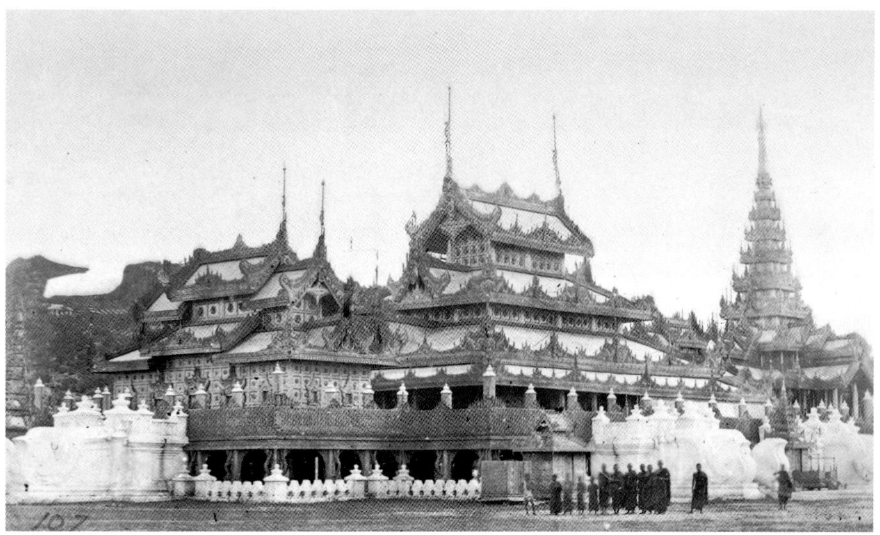

Figure 79. Picture of Mya Taung Kyaung monastery in Mandalay. Anonymous photograph, Musée Guimet.

ornamentation, as we have said, and by the very nature of the building it represents.

Indeed, many of the Mandalay buildings follow a pattern very similar to the model, with the different parts of the monastery arranged along the central axis.[8] Thus, from east to west, we have the main hall (*mayabin shaung*), which can be recognized by its central position and especially by the tapering roofs placed one above the other, reminiscent of the superimposed parasols that used to be placed above stupas and which symbolized the presence of the Buddha and of the stupas themselves. Next to this tower, there is a small secondary structure (*sanu shaung*) that was reserved for the head of the monastery. It is protected by a roof that is a reduced version of the main section of the building next to it. The main section served as the assembly hall, a study hall, and a dormitory for the monks (*shaung ma gyi*). Beyond that, the last part of the building is placed perpendicular to the main axis and seems to close off the structure. It has paneled wooden walls surrounding it and was used as a storeroom for the treasures of the monastery (*bo ga shaung*) as well as nonperishable provisions and the institution's fortune.

Erected on pillars carved in animal forms to protect it from humidity and insects, the whole structure shares a single floor spread over a large terrace. A large brick staircase leads to the floor, the brick being represented in wood but easily recognized by the large molded casing of the staircase. This served as the only direct contact with the ground and is the reason a more solid material was used for the actual monasteries.

The terrace is completely surrounded by a high banister that is richly sculpted with foliage and topped with posts in the shape of lotus buds. The banister is in harmony with the rest of the building and is punctuated by projections with small figures of deities (*devatā*) with hands raised, palms together. The doors have guardians (*dvarāpāla*) who are more or

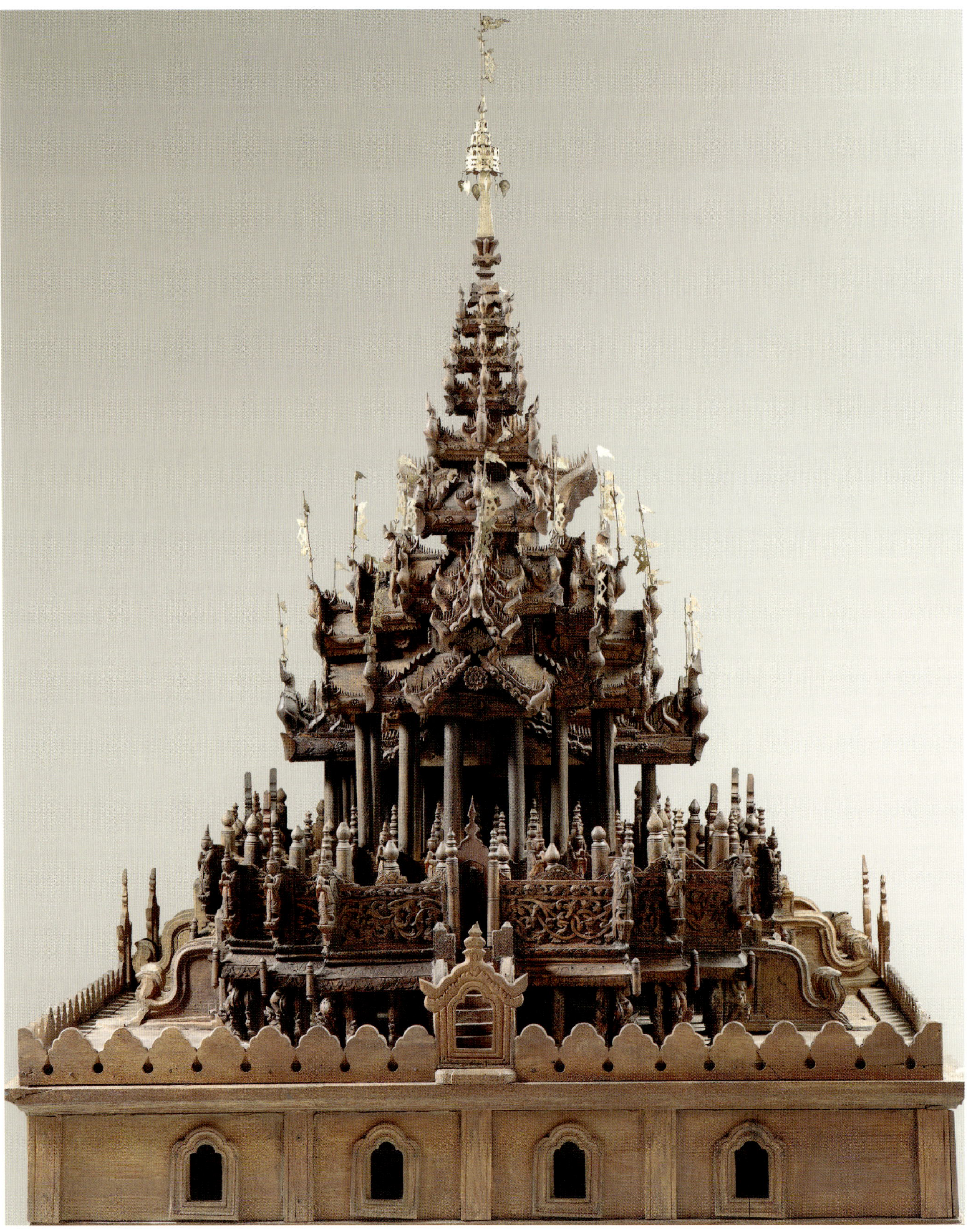

less terrifying. These are molded out of a paste of lacquer and attached to the wooden panels. Finally, a forest of gilded brass pinnacles with waving banners completes the design, giving it a surreal air. In form, the pinnacles are very similar to those that reflect the setting sun on the roofs of the monasteries built by Princess Salin and Queen Su-hpaya-lat. The model in the Guimet Museum is a modest but very moving reflection of the exquisite wooden religious architecture of the Konbaung dynasty, which saw its last flowering in Mandalay.

Notes

1. Léon de Milloué, Petit guide illustrée au musée Guimet (Paris: E. Leroux, 1894), 47.
2. Ibid., 131.
3. Ministère des affaires étrangères, chapter 6, 214–15. Frédéric Haas wrote an account of his travels in India, published as L'Art hindou: Voyage aux Indes orientales (Paris: Chr. Krüsi, 1885).
4. Le jubilé du musée Guimet (Paris: E. Leroux, 1904), 43. The date these objects were donated is mentioned in the manuscript version of the inventory of people who donated to the museum. Objects brought back from Burma are mentioned, with the notable exception of the model.
5. See Thiripyanchi (U Lu Pe Win). Historic Sites and Monuments of Mandalay and Environs. Rangoon: Buddha Sasana Council Press, n.d., 127.
6. Sylvia Fraser-Lu, "The Preservation of Wooden Monasteries in Burma," in Burma: Art and Archaeology, ed. Alexandra Green and T. Richard Blurton (London: British Museum Press, 2002), 110; and illustrated in Pierre Pichard, "Ancient Burmese Monasteries," in The Buddhist Monastery: A Cross-cultural Survey, ed. Pierre Pichard and François Lagirard (Paris: École française d'Extrême-Orient, 2003), 67.
7. Especially at the time of the festival of Thadingyut (September–October). There is an illustration in the Guimet's *parabaik* MA 1661.
8. Fraser-Lu, 108, fig. 10.1.

Bibliography

Ministère des affaires étrangères. *Annuaire diplomatique et consulaire de la République française*.

Fraser-Lu, Sylvia. "The Preservation of Wooden Monasteries in Burma." In *Burma: Art and Archaeology*. Edited by Alexandra Green and T. Richard Blurton. London: British Museum Press, 2002.

Haas, Frédéric. *L'Art hindou: Voyage aux Indes orientales*. Paris: Chr. Krüsi, 1885.

de Milloué Léon. *Petit guide illustrée au musée Guimet*. Paris: E. Leroux, 1894.

Le jubilé du musée Guimet. Paris: E. Leroux, 1904.

Pichard, Pierre. "Ancient Burmese Monasteries." In *The Buddhist Monastery: A Cross-cultural Survey*. Edited by Pierre Pichard and François Lagirard. Paris: École française d'Extrême-Orient, 2003.

Thiripyanchi (U Lu Pe Win). *Historic Sites and Monuments of Mandalay and Environs*. Rangoon: Buddha Sasana Council Press, n.d.

Figure 80. Side view of the model.

A MAP OF AVA

Cao Thi Liêu
Librarian, Southeast Asian collections, Musée Guimet

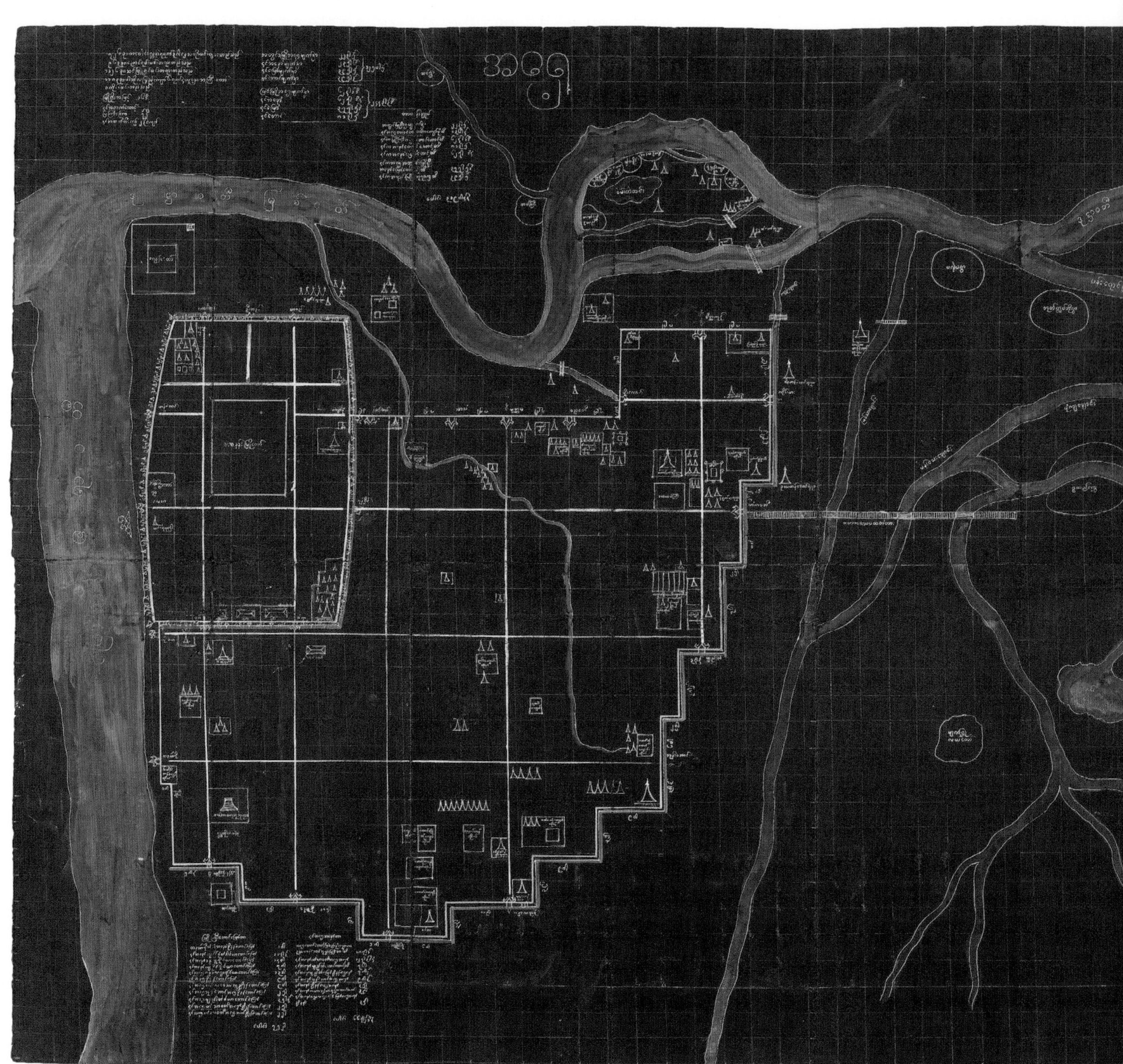

The royal city of Ava (အဝနန်းမြို့တော် *Innwa-nan-myo-to*), which was also the capital of Burma from 1364 to 1841, was situated at the confluence of two rivers: the Irrawaddy (ဧရာဝတီ) and the Myit-nge (မြစ်ငယ်, also called Dutthawati ဒုဋ္ဌာဝတီ). The city was founded on Tuesday,[1] the seventh day of the ascending moon in March (တပေါင်း *tabaung*), by King Thadominbya (သတိုးမင်းဖျား).[2] Then, after draining the swamps to settle it, he named the city Ratanapura in 726 of the Burmese Era—AD 1364.

Thereafter the city was rebuilt several times by successive kings during the seventeenth, eighteenth, and nineteenth centuries until July 9, 1840, saw the end of the city as the capital. Various reconstructions were carried out by a succession of kings: King Nyaung Yan (ညောင်ရမ်းမင်းတရား) in 963 BE (1601); King Sin Phyu Shin (ဆင်ဖြူရှင်မင်းတရား) in 1126 BE (1764); and finally, in 1183 BE (1821), on Wednesday, the sixth day of the ascending moon of July (ဝါဆိုလ *waso*), King Bagydaw (ဘကြီးတော်), also known as the sovereign of Sagain, who was dethroned by his brother, Prince Thayawaddy (ထရာဝတီ), on April 30, 1837. The prince established the city of Amarapura (အမရာပူရာ) as the new royal capital.

The map presented here shows a space surrounded by several fortifications with villages, bridges, and pagodas. The royal city is enclosed by a wall spiked with many turrets, The royal palace is in the middle, and alongside the river is the residence of the future king (ဒခိမ်ရွှေတော်ရာ *ein shwe to ra*). According to the tradition of royal dwellings, his residence was elevated and well ventilated (လေသာ *le ta*). Next is the pagoda (ယင်းရမုဋ္ဌော *yin ya mu thaw*) recalling that the completion of the building coincided with the lunar eclipse.[3] To the northeast is the Golden Pagoda of the Release (ရွှေမုဋ္ဌော). To the right of the palace, the Pagoda of the Royal Grotto (ကူတော်ဘုရား) is in line with the square dedicated to the leading figures of the country (စံရာ *son ya*) with other edifices for the elder monks of the king (သက်တော်ဘုရား *thato buya*).

To the west, along the Irrawaddy River, the city itself is spread out with religious buildings, such as the imposing pagoda *loka tarapu buya* (လောကစရာဘူဘုရား "pagoda of the world and of the crown," informally referring to Queen Victoria), and another royal construction named the "golden lotus" (ရွှေကြာမင်တိုင် *shwe ca min tai*). There are many monasteries, along with schools and libraries, as well as the enclosures of the royal white elephants (ဆင်ဖြူးတော *shin phyu to*). Beyond the fortifications, about 111 meters[4] from the turrets, there is another enclosure for the untamed elephants (ဆင်တုံး *shin chun*).

To the east, inside the walls and in the center of the royal city, is the great pagoda Mahā Myat Muni (မဟာမြတ်မုနိဘုရား), with the library of the monastery *bu chaung tai* (ဘုတ်ကျောင်းတိုက်; *bu* ဘုတ် is from the English word "book") nearby. On both sides of the stupa (ရှင်ပင်ချရာတီး *shinbin cayati*; the first term ရှင်ပင် refers to the revered Mahā Myat Muni) are found a building designated for legal proceedings of the monks

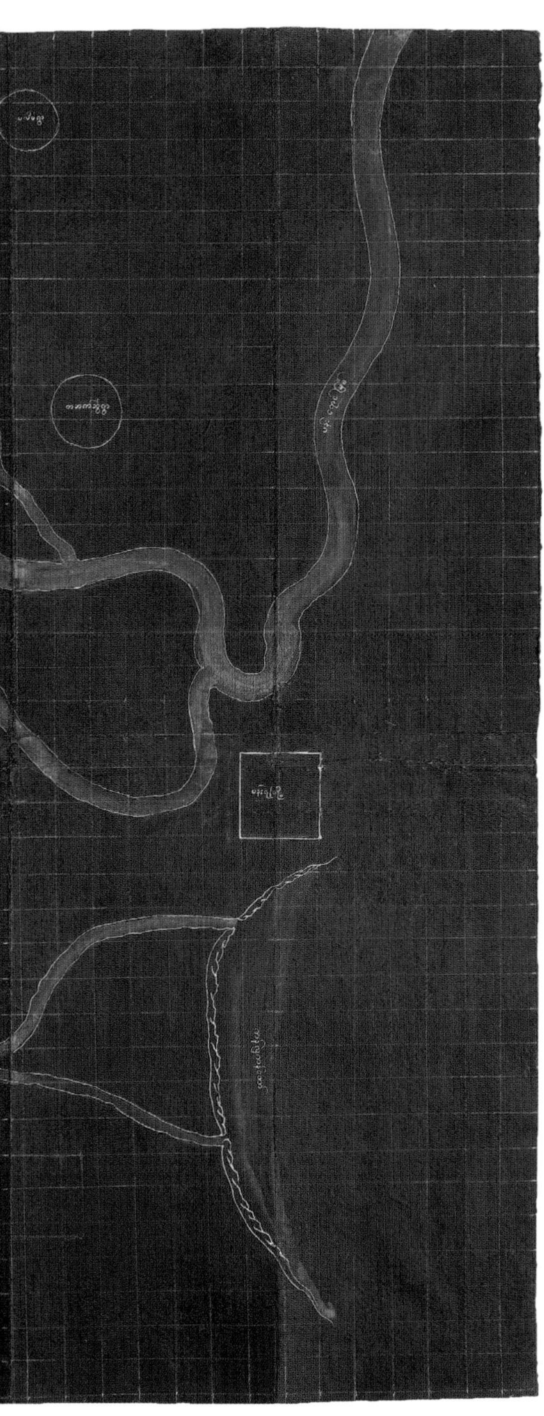

Figure 81. Map of the city of Ava.

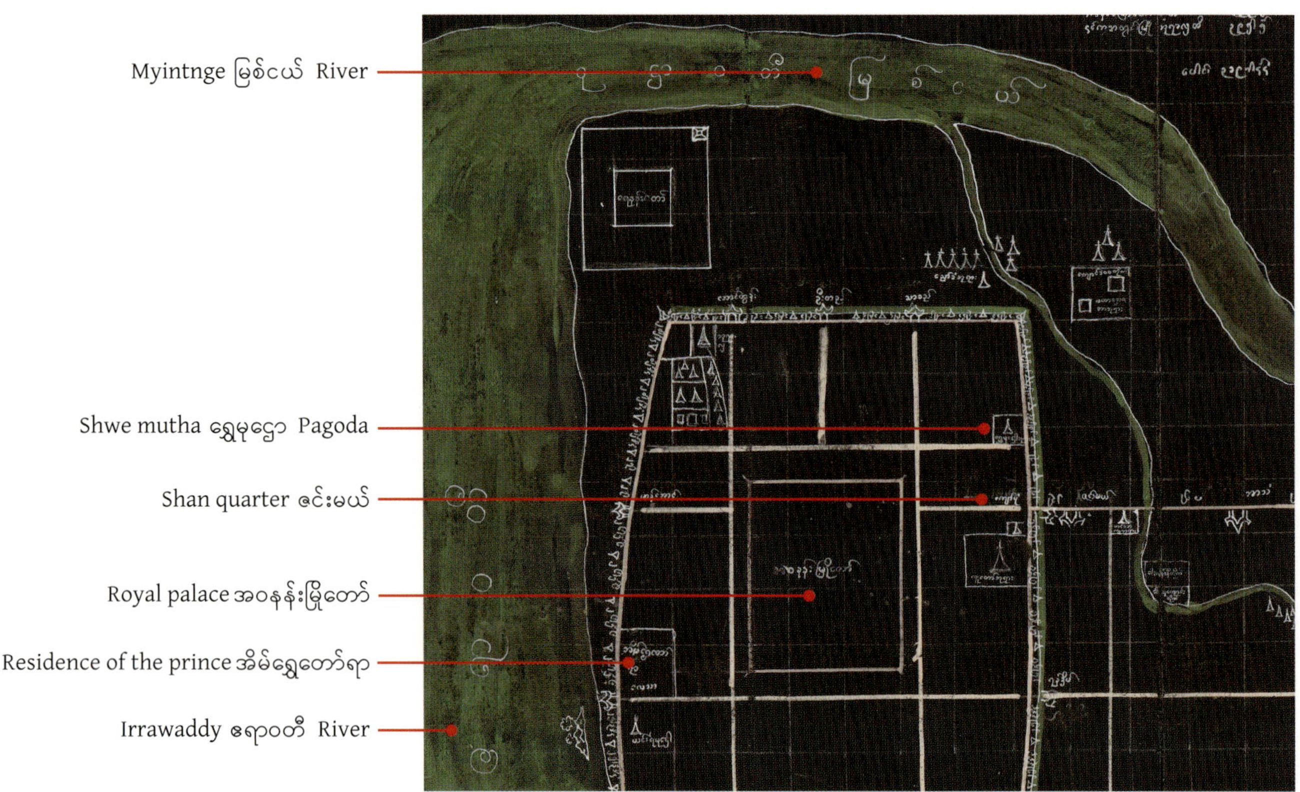

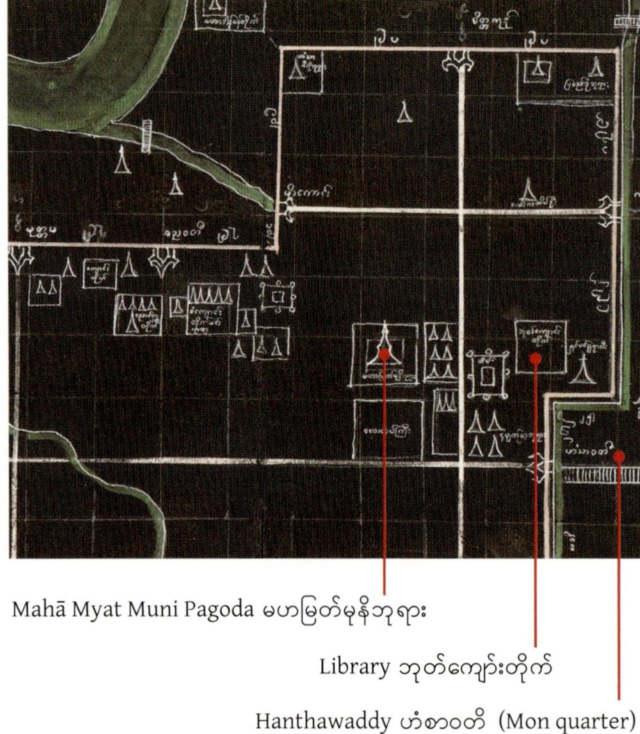

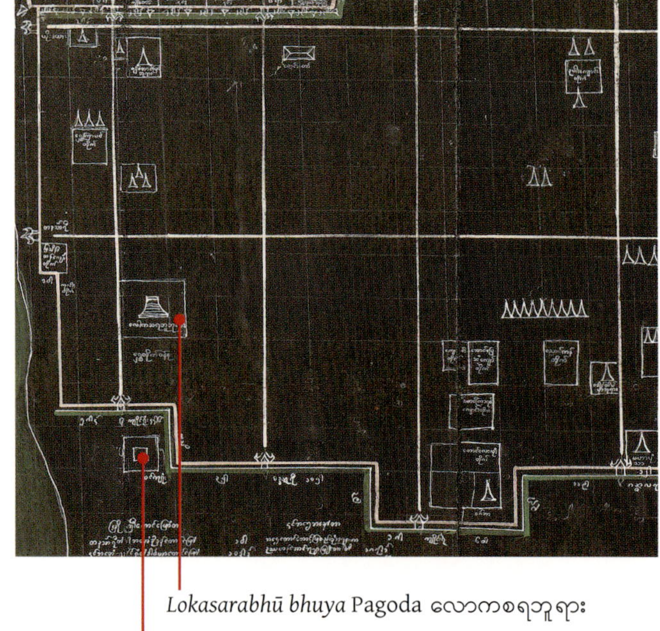

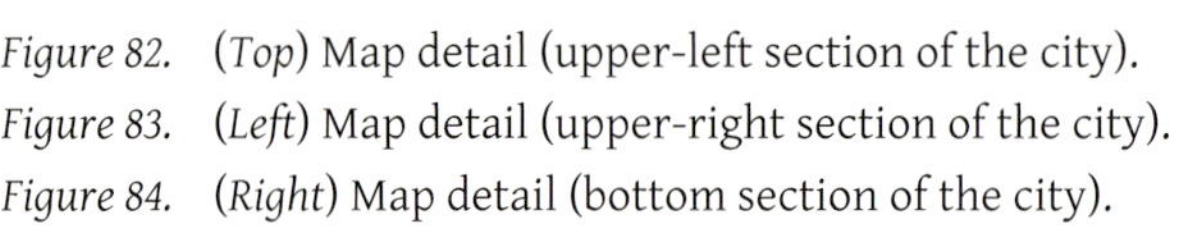

Figure 82. (*Top*) Map detail (upper-left section of the city).
Figure 83. (*Left*) Map detail (upper-right section of the city).
Figure 84. (*Right*) Map detail (bottom section of the city).

such as ordinations (*sīmā* သိမ်) and the "pagodas of the four cardinal points" (၄ မျက်နှာဘုရား *le myena buya*), while the royal monasteries (စံကျောင်းတိုက်မင်းရာဇ *son chaung tai min raja*) and a monastery named the "golden banyan" (ညောင်ရွှေတိုက် *ñaung shwe tai*) are found along the wall.

Beyond the fortifications, the Shan area (ဇင်းမယ် *zin may*) is to the east of the royal palace. On the other side of the palace, near the Manoraman garden, according to the chronicles, King Min Gaung II (ဒုတိယမင်းခေါင်) held a celebration of the dedication of the *sīmā* in AD 1480 (842 BE).

Above the royal city, on the smaller of two islands accessed by bridges, are the cemetery and the cremation grounds (သုသာန် *thou than*); in the south, near a long bridge, is the site known as the Hanthawaddy (ဟံသာဝတီ) district,[5] which was the living quarters of the Mon with an imposing pagoda (ဒုသာမာန်ဘောင်ဘုရား *douthaman baung buya*).

Looking over this map of Ava, we can appreciate the wide area it takes up at the confluence of the Irrawaddy and Myitnge Rivers. Its historic significance is marked by the presence of the Shan and Mon (or Siamese) quarters, and its cultural importance is clear, especially taking into consideration the royal and religious buildings with their monasteries, schools, and libraries.

Notes

1. Tuesday is the day of the lion in the Burmese horoscope. Timing events according to astrological calculations plays an important role in Burmese history.

2. G.E. Harvey, *Outline of Burmese History* (Calcutta: The Art Press, 1947), 61.

3. *Judson's Dictionary* says that *muṭṭho* is from Pāli and means "a pagoda with a recess in each side." He quotes Colonel Horace Browne as saying *shwe* (မုဋ္ဌော, "golden") muṭṭho (mue@a) pagodas "are said by the Burman annalists, to have been ordered to be completed, all at a certain time, when the moon would be emerging from an eclipse . . . from a Pali word signifying the release of the moon from eclipse." It is not clear that this is from Pāli, however.

4. The number 35 (၃၅) multiplied by 7 (၇) equals one *tā* (တာ /taa/; 3.5 yards), so 35 × 3.5 = 122.5 yards, or in meters, 122.5 × 0.91 = 111 meters.

5. Burmese people use the term Hanthawaddy to refer to the Mon kingdom, whose emblem is the ruddy shelduck (ဟံသာ *hamsa* = *hantha*).

Bibliography

Cornyn, William S., and John K. Musgrave. *Burmese Glossary*. Program in Oriental Languages, ser. A, no. 5. Washington: American Council of Learned Societies, 1958.

Judson's Myanmar-English Dictionary. Revised and enlarged by Robert C. Stevenson and F. H. Eveleth. Yangon: M. B. C. Publication Department, 2005.

Myanmar-English Dictionary. Yangon: Photolitho Press, 1993.

Harvey, G. E. *Outline of Burmese History*. Calcutta: Art Press, 1947.

Aung Nyein Chan (Man Takkasuil), Thutaythana Kha, and Yee Thwar Pinya. *Inwa Mhat Tam Mya*. Yangon: Sarpaybeikman Press, 2008.

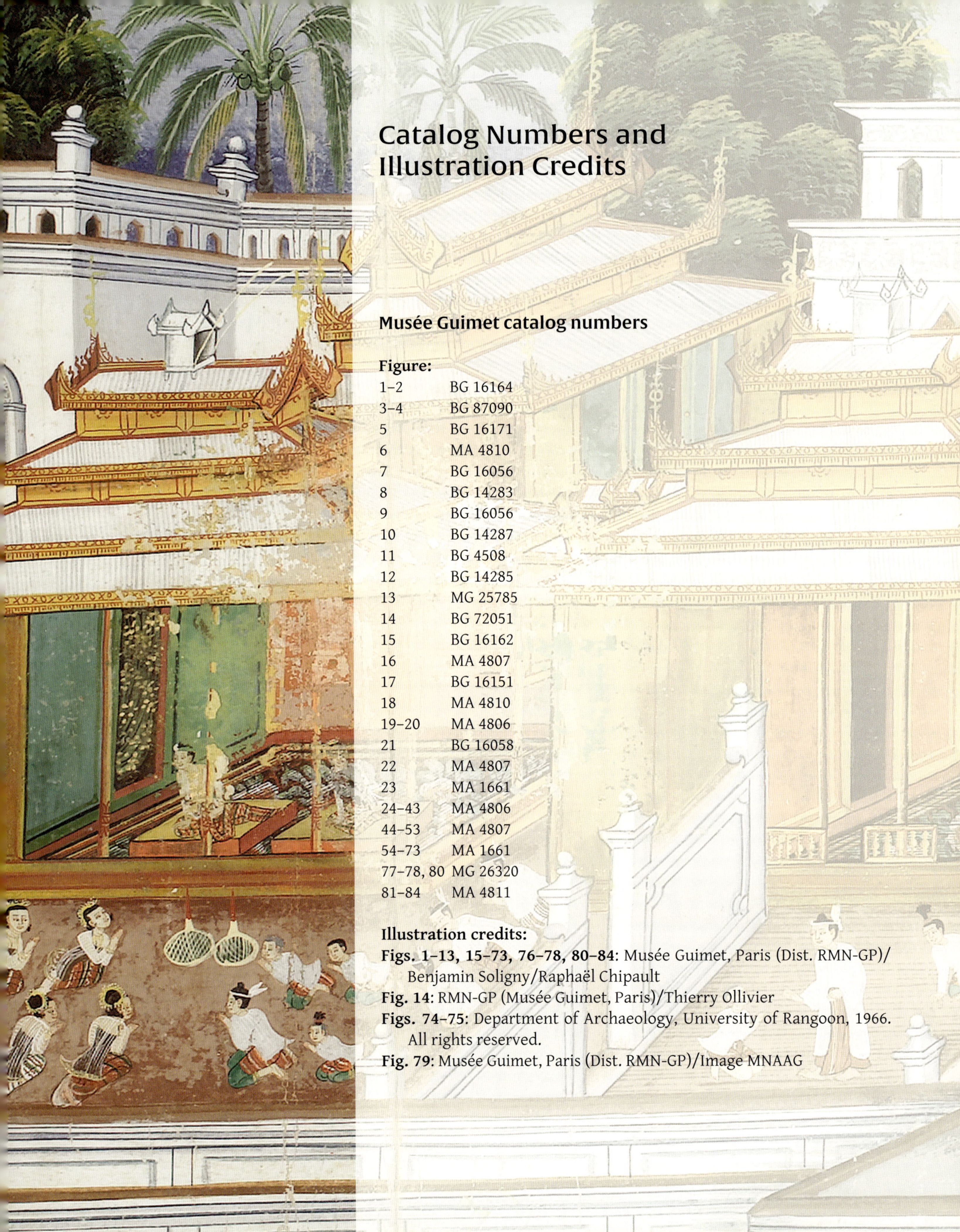

Catalog Numbers and Illustration Credits

Musée Guimet catalog numbers

Figure:

Figure	Catalog number
1–2	BG 16164
3–4	BG 87090
5	BG 16171
6	MA 4810
7	BG 16056
8	BG 14283
9	BG 16056
10	BG 14287
11	BG 4508
12	BG 14285
13	MG 25785
14	BG 72051
15	BG 16162
16	MA 4807
17	BG 16151
18	MA 4810
19–20	MA 4806
21	BG 16058
22	MA 4807
23	MA 1661
24–43	MA 4806
44–53	MA 4807
54–73	MA 1661
77–78, 80	MG 26320
81–84	MA 4811

Illustration credits:

Figs. 1–13, 15–73, 76–78, 80–84: Musée Guimet, Paris (Dist. RMN-GP)/ Benjamin Soligny/Raphaël Chipault

Fig. 14: RMN-GP (Musée Guimet, Paris)/Thierry Ollivier

Figs. 74–75: Department of Archaeology, University of Rangoon, 1966.

Fig. 79: Musée Guimet, Paris (Dist. RMN-GP)/Image MNAAG